The Education

For all students on the MA Language,
Arts and Education course University of Sussex
in appreciation of their inspiration and support

By The Same Author

Poetry

For Man and Islands
Songs of a New Taliesin
Icons of Time
Personae

On the Theory of English Teaching

English for Diversity
Root and Blossom: the Philosophy, Practice and Politics of English Teaching
English Within the Arts

Practical Guides to the Forms of Literature

The Forms of Poetry
The Forms of Narrative

On Culture, the Arts and Education

Autobiography in Education: An Introduction to the Subjective Discipline
    of Autobiography and its central place in the Education of Teachers
Proposal for a New College (with Graham Carey)
Reclamations: Essays on Culture, Mass-Culture and the Curriculum
A is for Aesthetic: Essays on Creative and Aesthetic Education

Edited Symposia on the Arts

The Black Rainbow: Essays on the Present Breakdown of Culture
Living Powers: The Arts in Education
The Symbolic Order: A Contemporary Reader on the Arts Debate

The Educational Imperative:
A Defence of Socratic and Aesthetic Learning

Peter Abbs

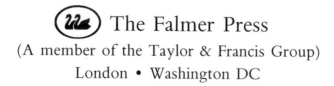 The Falmer Press
(A member of the Taylor & Francis Group)
London • Washington DC

UK   The Falmer Press, 4 John Street, London WC1N 2ET
USA   The Falmer Press, Taylor & Francis Inc., 1900 Frost Road, Suite 101, Bristol, PA 19007

First published in 1994

A catalogue record for this book is available from the British Library

Library of Congress Cataloging-in-Publication Data are available on request

ISBN 0 7507 0332 6 (cased)
ISBN 0 7507 0333 4 (paper)

Jacket design by Caroline Archer

Typeset in 11/13 Bembo and printed by Graphicraft Typesetters Ltd., Hong Kong.

Contents

Contents

List of Plates and Figures

Acknowledgments

While books are written in quiet and sometimes lonely rooms, they yet depend on an invisible community of voices and echoes. It is never possible to locate all the voices of that conversation and in a conventional preface it is only ever possible to name a few of the more salient.

The Educational Imperative is dedicated to all the Language, Arts and Education MA students who, over ten years at the University of Sussex, have helped to shape and influence my thinking. They have been both sensitive listeners and agile critics. I have learnt much from them. I must also, in the same breath, quickly thank many colleagues, fellow-writers, teachers and academics who have encouraged me to go on exploring education under the two great categories of the Socratic and the Aesthetic. I would like to thank, especially, Anne Bloomfield, Anna Carlyle, Val Denning, David Evans, Lynne Gibson, Keith Grant, Bernard Harrison, Brad Haseman, Terry Hodgson, David Holbrook, David Hornbrook, Marian Metcalfe, John Morris, Trevor Pateman, Crys Pearce, Kathleen Raine, John Richardson, Rod Taylor, Rob Watson and Edwin Webb. Their support has been, quite simply, invaluable.

My gratitude also goes to Falmer Press, who have supported a programme of work on aesthetic education which, I believe, in the prevailing mean climate no other British publisher would have had the courage and insight to take on. In particular, I must thank Malcolm Clarkson, Jacinta Evans (in the earlier stages of the work) and Alison Woodhead. They have provided a real context for intellectual work.

Finally, I must thank my two secretaries, Brenda Martin and Pat Bone, who at different stages have laboured to give my frenetic handwriting conventional form and respectability. Without their sustained labour there would, quite simply, be no book. I am deeply indebted to both of them.

Peter Abbs
University of Sussex
January 1994

She was captured by two vengeful, damaged women who beat her and shaved her head. They locked her in a cupboard. They bound her to a bed, gagged her, tortured her, left her to lie amid her excrement until logic demanded she could no longer be held in the squalid little house.

Suzanne was loaded into a car boot on 14 December last year, driven to scrubland on the outskirts of Stockport and doused with petrol . . .

McNeilly retained keys to the house. Detectives found a small library of occult and horror fiction, including a copy of *Misery*, a horror novel by Stephen King, the best selling author.

They also found a cassette which was played constantly to Miss Capper through headphones. It repeated: 'I'm Chucky. Wanna play?' The question is asked menacingly by a possessed doll in the horror film *Child's Play* . . .

The prosecution did not claim fictional influences were entirely responsible for motivating the four killers. But the imitation of art, particularly by McNeilly, alarmed police and lawyers involved in the case.

Report in The Independent, 18 December 1993

Art and conduct, science, philosophy and history, these are not modes of thought defined by rules; they exist only in personal explorations of territories only the boundaries of which are subject to definition. To have command over the languages of our civilization is, not to know the rules of their grammar, but to have the opportunity of a syntax and a vocabulary, rich in fine distinctions, in which to think for oneself. Learning, then, is acquiring the ability to feel and to think, and the pupil will never acquire these abilities unless he has learned to listen for them and to recognize them in the conduct and utterances of others.

Michael Oakeshott

Plate 1: Frontispiece: Socrates, *archetypal teacher, philosopher of dialogue and the collaborative exploration of questions.*

Introduction:
Our Present Predicament

The Educational Imperative is a defence of Socratic and aesthetic education in a period in which education is neither Socratic, nor predisposed
towards the aesthetic. Many of the chapters are attempts, in no way
definitive, to disclose the nature of educational thinking, feeling, sensing and imagining; many of the arguments relate to arguments in the
world of educational discussion and academic controversy as also to
the actual practice of teaching and learning. Yet it would be mislead-
ing to present the book as a piece of distant research. It is, essentially,
a work of advocacy, putting forward a notion of education that has
become contentious in our time, perhaps even deeply unpopular. In
this introduction, therefore, I want to come clean; I want to place the
general argument of the book in the current arena of public debate, and
to do so without apology and without equivocation. Whatever the
reader may make of this consciously polemical opening, I would
like to think that he or she would go on and, at least, consider the
somewhat more measured educational arguments put forward in the
chapters that follow.

We are living through a cultural catastrophe which is extremely
difficult to define but which concerns, most profoundly, the quality
and depth of the human spirit. At the centre of our materialist and
alarmed society there would seem to be a massive denial of spiritual
energy, of intellectual enquiry, of aesthetic beauty and public virtue.
Nearly all of these words have become shy and fugitive words in our
language, embarrassed speech, words that are uttered ironically or when
printed marked with inverted commas to indicate to the reader their
dubious nature. The denial of the intellectual, in particular, displays
itself at all levels in our society: in the various forms of postmodernist
irony; in the 'nothing but' arguments of much academic discourse
where the higher category is understood through the lower; and in the
general anti-intellectualism that runs like a contagious disease through
our entire society. Everywhere, a low, anxious, pragmatism would
seem to prevail. In fact, we live now in a puddle culture so shallow one

can hardly get one's toe in; and yet, somehow, there is no protest, no resistance. The media have become, almost in their entirety, an entertainment machine and, as the media mediate our culture, that may partially explain the astonishing intellectual silence, for criticism is *never* really a species of entertainment.

This may well define our educational problem but, alas, there is a further problem. Education itself has fallen into the hideous black hole of unmeaning. It has been taken over by instrumental powers and its programme rewritten by instrumentalists and politicians. To put it bluntly, education has lost any sense of the transcendent ends which, when it is true to its own nature, it willingly and lovingly serves. It has been converted, over the last decade, into a centralized mechanism for social control and, often, into a scapegoat to blame for our acute social ills; as I will show, these are dialectically related. You blame and then you are free to take over; you castigate then you conquer. The language of visionless control can be found in virtually every major and minor official document published over the last ten years.

At the same time, it would seem that simply everybody is ready to step forward and offer a passing (and, often, passionate) opinion on teaching or the curriculum. Education now makes the front pages and has become, at once, the hot matter of chat-shows and the cool matter of earnest editorial columns. Of itself, this is no bad thing. We all need constantly to hear and appraise a plurality of views and conceptions – that, of course, is in itself a Socratic activity that teachers have to both nurture and protect from suppression and censorship. But the public debate has had a negative side. All the easy talk has led to a journalistic debasement. Too many have felt quite free to parade their prejudices, to air their immediate opinions without any rudimentary attempt to define terms, without any significant knowledge of actual classrooms, without any understanding of recent educational research or any comprehension of the history of education in our own long European culture. Furthermore, by a most perverse logic it has been assumed by many – and by politicians, in particular – that teachers and educationists have next to nothing to contribute to the debate.

One of the controlling strategies of the Government has been *that parents and employers, in contrast to teachers, know what education really is.* As a result of this bizarre position and the general dread of ideas which informs our consumer society, much sophisticated professional thinking has never been presented to the public and much excellent teaching practice has gone largely unregistered and publicly unrecognized, especially in the arts.

All too often the 'great debate', first inaugurated by the Labour

Party in 1976 – now nearly two decades ago – has deteriorated into the 'great hype': the hype of tired slogans, of untested prejudices and a politically driven rhetoric that has had nothing to do with education as an activity of mind, as a progressive initiation into the diverse realms of intellectual and aesthetic meaning. Thus we have witnessed the diffusion and diversion of mere opinion; we have witnessed the political hijacking of education (by the Left as much as the Right). But what we have *not* witnessed, and now stand in desperate need of, is a philosophical analysis of the educational questions of our time, especially in relationship to Socratic thinking and aesthetic experience. There is a deep dread of ideas at work in British culture; and an almost instinctive revolt against the disciplines of intellectual inquiry. It is not a new phenomenon. Some of the best Victorian critics examined it: John Stuart Mill, Matthew Arnold, John Henry Newman. And they all came up with the same diagnosis: the English positively loathed 'ideas'; they invariably eschewed the formal elements of the thinking mind. The defect has been labelled 'English philistinism' but that has become an easy tag tending to terminate any further analysis. *Of course, we're philistines!* But what does this mean?

It means that the English have acquired an all but inveterate disposition to undermine the critical mind, to mock theory, to lampoon what Matthew Arnold described as 'the free play of mind over experience'. Some years ago the pseudo-satirical television programme *Spitting Image* had a fairly regular item called 'Jonathan Miller talks Bollocks'. While this was unredeemably crude and lacked wit, it yet remains extremely telling. It formulates precisely what the English feel. Jonathan Miller talks bollocks because he talks 'ideas', because he follows the unfolding logic of interlocking conceptions, and, in so doing overlooks what the English love to call the 'real world': the world of things, of manufactured goods and tabulated facts: national tests, salary increases, the *Guinness Book of Records, Master-Team, Block-Buster* and *Brain of Britain* and other fact-mania programmes.

It is depressingly pertinent that even Dame Mary Warnock recently complained that our teacher-training courses wasted too much time on 'the history and philosophy of education'.[1] In our culture even the intellectuals are anti-intellectual! Or so it would seem. Now it is a truism that teaching is a practical activity learnt by doing, but it is also true that such activity is informed by both conscious and unconscious sets of values, judgments and understandings, which require patient elucidation and scrupulous evaluation. Any activity presupposes certain assumptions about meaning and value and it is these assumptions that have to be excavated and brought up for impartial examination,

3

particularly where the activity purports to be educational. Teaching is not just a set of skills for transmitting knowledge. Yet Mary Warnock, a distinguished intellectual herself, says in typical English fashion, 'no' to philosophy, 'no' to history and 'yes' to practice, failing to perceive that the three are quite inseparable. For how could there be any practice without the context set by history and without the mediating and shaping power of human conceptions? And yet now we see in our reformulated Postgraduate Certificate in Education courses an emerging generation of teachers who know little of the past and virtually nothing of philosophy, who have an essentially *uncritical view* of what they do and a managerial language which dims intellectual perception. (A young teacher told me recently at an MA interview that he had just come from 'delivering Shakespeare'.) As the collective demand for speculation and critical thought dies, so the commercial publishing houses are rapidly closing their lists of seminal and theoretical work and publishing merely national curriculum manuals and guides. And once the great works of Plato and Rousseau, of Cardinal Newman and Michael Oakeshott are off the shelves and bibliographies it becomes progressively more difficult to locate the excluded element of critical and subversive thought. *Teachers become the technicians of subjects, not the critical guardians of a long culture; nor the midwives of the creative potentialities of living children.*

It might well appear that at least some of the terms used in the educational debate negate my argument. Consider, for example, the much vaunted world 'excellence'. It has become a buzz word. Yet most of the contexts in which this buzz word is used disclose that 'excellence' all but never denotes *intellectual* excellence or *scientific* excellence or *artistic* excellence. Most often, the word signifies little more than a gasp of excited approval. It means 'yes, yes'. 'Excellence' is, well, excellent. Who could oppose such a tautology? At the same time, the word excellence in the current hype has come to carry a certain group of assumptions. It has become a highly coded word particularly loved by the Right. The word connotes an intense competitive striving for visible results: prizes, percentages, league places, chart positions, which, by a fairly obvious transference, become the signs and portents of subsequent success, of high salaries, high positions, high offices. Mrs Rumbold, when she was the Minister of State for Education remarked: 'People who have not got the most wonderful middle-class backgrounds can climb up the ladder provided teachers and schools allow them the opportunities'.[2] Excellence in education it would seem is fundamentally a matter of climbing the ladder; the competition of all against all, for the high materialist overview of the few. This, needless to say, is *not* an educational goal but a socio-economic one. The excellence does not refer to that inward and collaborative striving for meaning first developed by Socrates – examined in the first chapters of this book – and still rooted in the best of our educational institutions; it signifies, rather, *competitive energies of a market-economy ruthlessly transposed to the nursery, the school, the college and the university.* By the strongest of paradoxes, 'excellence' could be the antithesis of all true educational practice, an enemy of the good curriculum, an enemy of collaborative education whether in the sciences, humanities or the arts. I notice as I write these words, the noble motto for today's *Daily Mirror* (28 December 1993): HONESTY, QUALITY, EXCELLENCE. Three fine concepts are reduced to three buzzes.

The Exclusion of Teachers and Educationists

If the analysis is accurate it explains why the Government has tended to exclude teachers and educationists from the debate. The political debate, in important ways, has not been about the *interior meanings of educational activity.* It has *not* been about intellectual and cultural life. The dramatic exclusion of teachers and educationists from much of the organizational process has been motivated by other forces that need to be documented and understood. As early as 1987, Peter Wilby, then the level-headed Education Editor of *The Independent*, claimed:

> Ever since she was Secretary of State for Education in the early 1970s, the Prime Minister has been convinced that the nation's 33,000 maintained schools and 500,000 teachers need a kick in the pants.[3]

That metaphoric 'kick in the pants' came, most often, in the form of virtually unqualified accusations that teachers have been directly responsible, not only for present levels of illiteracy and innumeracy, but also for much of the ethical malaise of our society. Teachers, it has been openly alleged and covertly suggested, are causal agents for the delinquency, the violence, the apathy and all the behavioural aberrations that surround us. Such a claim must be relative nonsense; it is akin to blaming doctors for cancer or dentists for tooth-decay, yet, again and again, it has been asserted. However mind-numbing, such allegations, backed by the verbal panegyrics of the tabloid press, have been politically powerful because they have enabled the Government to act *without full teacher consultation.* If teachers are the causal agents of moral degeneracy then it is only right *not* to ask them about the contents of a balanced curriculum. It is better for the Government to decide on behalf of the people. As a result many unique powers to determine the content and style of education have passed from the teachers, local authorities and universities to the Government and to the Secretary of State for Education. The effect of this is to substantially disempower the teacher, to rob him or her of that vital sense of creative agency that marks all good teaching.

So it is that teachers emerge as an unexpected proletariat in the new technocracy. They will do the labour, but will be told what and how to do it. They become the serving functionaries, not of the life of culture and the intellect, but of either the state or the free market – or a combination of both. And like the older industrial proletariat they become largely invisible, yet always at hand to blame and vilify; the desperately needed workers but, at the same moment, the powerless scapegoats of a new entrepreneurial semi-civilization. The same unenviable fate has fallen to the social worker and to the educationist, the one who has the audacity to offer counter conceptions and counter proposals. In the Government and media propaganda *educationists* are always linked to the 60s, are nearly always unnamed and consistently are seen as the villains of the piece. They have come to form the 'stinking ninth category'. The sneering allegations are hardly worthy of analysis; they are no more, and no less, than the powerful blades of propaganda to diminish the power of thought and shut down any form of Socratic thinking or cultural engagement. At another level, it involves the erasure of philosophical language and the triumph of cant and ahistorical jargon, the rise of a one dimensional language of 'total quality control', 'customer satisfaction', 'consumer-need' sprinkled with a few buzz words like 'excellence'.

The Fallacy of Catoism

What, exactly, is the fallacy informing current educational policies, policies that give so little room to the intellectual, to the creative and the aesthetic? It is the fallacy of Catoism. The elder Cato opposed the introduction of Greek ideas into Roman culture because he regarded them as *useless*. In *The Idea of a University*, Cardinal Newman formulated Cato's position as follows:

> The fit representative of a practical people, Cato estimated every-
> thing by what is produced whereas the pursuit of knowledge

promised nothing beyond knowledge itself . . . He (Cato) despised that refinement or enlargement of mind of which he had no experience.[4]

The fallacy of Catoism concerns the displacement of the notion of practicality on to every possible kind of human activity. It is the organizing principle of the entrepreneur become inflated and gone mad. It is the notion of thrift applied to a wedding or a banquet. Under Catoism the vast range of human experience and potentiality is subjected to only one question: *what use is it?* Under its tyrannical power the plurality of consciousness steadily contracts to fit the size of one small category. Catoism is common sense become intolerant. Catoism is common sense elevated to the singular principle of all acceptable human conduct. Catoism has, at least, for a practical people, a tremendous power to simplify. This confers upon it, in complex disintegrating times, a mesmerizing authority; but at the same time its effect is always to reduce, to cut down, to level. Hence its dangers, hence its threat to the intellectual, aesthetic and imaginative life of Great Britain.

Yet one has only to ask a few simple questions to expose its cardinal weakness. Ask what *use* is God? What *use* is Beauty? What *use* is virtue? What *use* is love, compassion, care, justice? And one immediately discovers the distorting narrowness of Catoism, for questions like these, metaphysical, aesthetic and ethical, cannot be comprehended through the category of practical use. If the symbols of religious worship, if the symbols of artistic creation, if action based on ethical choices were only the practical means for individual or collective advantage, they would have disappeared centuries ago as sure obstacles in the path of utility and common sense. The principle of Cato is fine in its own realm, but transposed to the imaginative and cultural life it is a degrading force. Under the tyranny of Cato, there is a marked tendency to see education as having merely a practical use and therefore of conceiving all forms of education as no more than a species of training. The attempt to make state schools useful, the desire to see them train pupils for work began way back in 1976 when James Callaghan in his (ironically titled) 'Ruskin Speech' proclaimed that 'the educational system was out of touch with the fundamental need of Britain to survive economically in a highly competitive world through the efficiency of its industry and commerce'.[5] It was followed in 1977 by Shirley Williams' Green Paper, *Education in Schools*, which reiterated the 'Ruskin Speech'; and since then, for nearly twenty years, that strong practical current has forced its way into every nook and cranny of the state educational system.

The True Values of Education

If the fallacy is that of Cato, then the answer to it must lie in the cultivation of a philosophy that recognizes, both radically and generously, *the multiplicity of meanings that reside within human experience* and the cultural inheritance. Our task is to place Cato; to let him stand as *one* figure in the pantheon of the mind and the plethora of human activity; but it must also be to reclaim the lost figures that represent other essential elements of our daily and plural experience. No civilization can stand on the single premise of the practical. A society, furthermore, based on the competition of all against all for the private advantage of a few can only usher in a materialist nightmare. We need a set of principles larger, deeper, more sustaining, more comprehensive, more public. In education we need a different figure from Cato; we need, in truth, that very figure that Cato desired to erase; we need, at the very least, the image of Socrates. As image and exemplar, Socrates remains the prototype of all good teaching and learning or so I will argue in the opening chapters of this book.

To adopt the Socratic view of education is to reaffirm that education should be primarily concerned with critical reflection, with personal development and with the sustained enquiry into the various forms of meaning. These meanings are *not* all the same; they are incorrigibly plural and cannot be reduced one to another, and many of them are not obviously practical. They involve the body, the feelings, the mind and the imagination. They can be classified in different ways: traditionally as the arts, humanities and sciences, or in the contemporary terms of Harvard research, as the kinaesthetic, the logical, the musical, the linguistic, the spatial and the personal. However they are classified, these different activities are *primary forms of understanding*; they need to be generically and equally included in the good curriculum.

To adopt the Socratic view is to conceive of education as a life-long process which has, at once, an ethical bearing and a transcendent function; it goes well beyond the enclosing pressures of the acquisitive ego, the temporary (always temporary) status quo, the ephemeral clamourings of party politics and the mundane media. To adopt the Socratic principle is to envisage the main purpose of teachers as that of promoting and continuously feeding the primary symbol-making proclivities of the mind in its quest for understanding; and, in so doing, slowly to enlarge the range of consciousness and, as a consequence, develop individual life. It would mean, furthermore, grasping one elementary insight; that much of the meaning of education can only be located in the actual educational activity itself – *this* moment of understanding now, as it takes place in reading *this* poem, making *that* dance, reading *this* theory, solving *that* equation. If these crystallizing moments of understanding are to accumulate and develop then crude utilitarian pressure has to be kept back; the vested interests of Coca-Cola manufacturers or political missionaries have to be seen as too 'recent and relevant' to be allowed. Such exploratory activity, inherently valuable, requires a formally protected place, an institutional space more like the theatre than Tesco, more like the cathedral than the Stock Exchange.

If the image of Cato is to stand at the gates into the consumer economy, then Socrates must stand at the gates of our schools, colleges and universities. Industry matters; technology matters; but so does the imagination, feeling and intellect. And it is the latter in our society that, starved of the artistic and rational means for renewal and development lead, directly and indirectly, to those various collective pathologies of withdrawal or active unconscious revenge that mark our current violent and unhappy society. The mindless violence which now surrounds us on all sides shows just how dramatically we have failed to educate, failed to extend the sensibility and intellect of the young, failed to turn their energies to the creative elaboration of their lives.

Socrates is, therefore, the presiding spirit of this book but its major theme, paradoxically, does not concern the development of critical intellect so much as that of aesthetic intelligence. The failure to establish a comprehensive arts curriculum is a further contemporary educational scandal unremarked by the educational journalists. The Socratic impulse to question and explore the nature of experience must remain at the heart of the educational enterprise, but questioning and exploring do not have to take place through concepts; they can also be developed, to even greater effect, through the organized sounds of music, through the gestures of the body, through the metaphoric language of the poet, as well as through the tonal values and vibrant textures of paint. Rembrandt and Cezanne, Martha Graham and Isadora Duncan are as much philosophers as Socrates or Plato, only *their symbolic means are different*. This, too, has not been widely understood in our philistine culture or in our philosophical tradition; and one of the aims of *The Educational Imperative* is to disclose the philosophical power of the arts, together with their power to animate and shape lives and cultures. In this aspect the argument follows in the wake of the 'Falmer Press Library on Aesthetic Education', confirming and extending the approach established there.

The book, then, will seek in its opening chapters to define a Socratic conception of education. In the middle two sections the Socratic conception of learning will be extended to the arts; the aim is to sketch the new paradigm of arts education, to disclose the principles on which it rests and to describe some of the practices it has given birth to. Finally, the work will close with three critical evaluations of writers who have influenced the main arguments of the book. *The Educational Imperative* is, I hope, in spirit, a celebration of real education in a society that has no vision of education, and that desperately needs it.

Notes

1 DAME MARY WARNOCK (1987) 'Teacher Power', *New Society*, 2 October.
2 Quoted on p. 10 of *Times Educational Supplement*, 16 October 1987.
3 PETER WILBY (1987) 'Parents Hold Key to School Privatization', *The Independent*, 5 January.
4 CARDINAL NEWMAN (1982) *The Idea of a University Defined and Illustrated*, Notre Dame, IN, University of Notre Dame Press, p. 80.
5 JAMES CALLAGHAN (1976) 'Ruskin Speech'.

Section I

On Education as Socratic Enquiry

Chapter 1

The Nature of Socratic Learning

Modern governments are not interested in education; they are concerned only to impose 'socialization' of one kind or another upon the surviving fragments of a once considerable educational engagement.

Michael Oakeshott

The workers've got it so let's give them what they want. If they want slop songs and film idols we'll give 'em that then. If they want words of one syllable, we'll give 'em that then. If they want the third-rate, BLUST! We'll give 'em THAT then. Anything's good enough for them 'cos they don't ask for no more! The whole stinkin' commercial world insults us and we won't care a damn. Well, Ronnie's right – it's our own bloody fault. We want the third-rate – we got it! We got it! We . . . (Suddenly BEATIE stops as if listening to herself. She pauses, turns with an ecstatic smile on her face) D'you hear that? D'you hear it? Did you listen to me? I'm talking, Jenny, Frankie, Mother – I'm not quoting no more.

Beatie at the end of Roots *by Arnold Wesker*

Introduction

It is perverse that in our society there has been a 'debate' about education that has never touched on the activity itself. The highly engineered debate has been about standards, about testing, about organization, about management but almost never *about the nature of education*. On this momentous issue there has remained a great and perplexing silence. Is it that we all know what education is and that, therefore, there is no need to discuss it? That seems unlikely, not only because a moment's reflection discloses that people *do* have very different views about education but, also, because the debate itself has constantly revealed an almost pathological suspicion of teachers, educationists and all those who *theorize* about education. Tellingly, John Major has declared 'aggressive theorists in education have had their day'. The tabloids, for their part, have kept up their cacophony of nonsense against intellectuals, and not only the tabloids but also most of the so-called 'quality' papers, where it has been frequently claimed that educationists have been responsible for the failures of our educational system. What we have witnessed is not an open-ended enquiry committed to the examination of evidence, of claims and counter claims, but rather an ideologically driven move to make schools more functional, more competitive and more submissive.

This 'great debate' has been little more than a piece of hypocrisy, of duplicity and bullying on a vast scale. So much dust has been churned up that it has become difficult to see anything with clarity. In such an ideological dust-storm it is essential to turn back to philosophical principles. We need to excavate the buried questions: *What is education? And why does it matter?* The real discussion on education has yet to start. I will, therefore, briefly examine in this opening chapter a crucial distinction between training and education and then move on to consider the example of Socrates and its permanent value for our understanding of teaching and learning.

An Analysis of Training and Education

To understand the nature of education we need to analyse two terms that are central to the debate, namely the terms *to train* and *to educate*. At the moment, there is an insidious attempt by politicians and bureaucrats to amalgamate these words, to make them slide into each other, to make them referentially synonymous. George Orwell warned us of this manœuvre when he wrote:

> Every concept that can ever be needed, will be expressed by exactly *one* word, with its meaning rigidly defined and all its subsidiary meanings rubbed out and forgotten . . . Every year, fewer and fewer words and the range of consciousness always a little smaller.[1]

To lose the rich connotations and some of the key denotations of the word *education* would indeed be a severe loss, and yet this is happening on an alarming scale and with alarming consequences. Education, in many minds, has become a species of training and thus, by a semantic trick, many major problems pass unnoticed.

We talk about 'potty-training', 'dog-training', 'training an army', 'training' engineers or technicians. It would seem that training invariably involves a narrowing down of the consciousness to master certain techniques or skills. These techniques (the techniques, say, of typing or driving) are known in advance and can be unambiguously imparted by the trainer and assimilated by the learner. What is transmitted is functional and predetermined, a set of skills matching a set of operations. When we use the word education, in contrast, there is a strong sense of an opening out of the mind that transcends detail and skill and whose movement cannot be predicted. Education is to do with educing, with releasing, with liberating. It is to do with the free and animated play of mind over experience. Educating Rita is *not* training her; it is essentially releasing her into the life of thought and, therefore, existential possibility. It is no accident that the word *school* derives from the Greek word *schole* meaning both leisure (freedom from necessity) and discussion: freedom, we might say, for discourse. It is pertinent that the word 'academy' derives from Akademus, the man who owned the garden or grove in which Plato and his students discussed philosophy. The metaphor of the garden – a protected place where the mind can struggle to think its own thoughts – gives an essential resonance to this cluster of key words: *education, school, academy*. Certainly, education bears within it the distinct resonance of transcendence.

This brief amplification of words demonstrates that the two sentences: 'we must train our work force' and 'we must educate our work force' possess radically different, if not antithetical, meanings. To train a work force entails the strong sense of *imparting closed skills predetermined by the status quo*, whereas to educate a work force entails *a movement outwards to ask questions, to make enquiries, to reflect and evaluate*. Training nearly always has a definite purpose generally affecting behavioural responses in the learner; education does not have a direct utilitarian purpose; it leads to a certain mode of consciousness, a delicate, sustained, reflective disposition towards experience, an openness towards potential truth and possible meaning, though it generally presupposes the internalization of various skills and techniques (as we shall see in later chapters on arts education). The confusion between the two terms and the marked tendency to reduce the larger transcendental term to the smaller pragmatic one has wrought havoc on our curriculum.

The effect of the semantic reduction of education to training now permeates our schools. It has its most obvious expression in those ubiquitous vocation lists that simply yoke intellectual and aesthetic disciplines to the market place. More than anything else these lists reveal the instrumental imperative invading the curriculum to usurp

SOCRATES

general educational purposes and meanings. For, surely, religious studies exists not to create the nurse or even the priest, but to promote personal understanding and some evaluation of the various religions created by humankind? Subjects should be in the curriculum not as preparations for defined jobs but as forms of intellectual, imaginative and aesthetic enquiry. Teachers hope to initiate their students into these enquiries *because it is valuable to do so*, because to do so is to expand and deepen consciousness itself. If teachers attempt to justify the various disciplines of investigation and expression – the disciplines of the Arts, Sciences and Humanities – in utilitarian terms, they have already begun to betray them.

A Return to Educational Sources

Considering the constrained and fiercely instrumental conditions of our schools we stand in need of a return to sources, a return to primary meanings. Pragmatic arguments drawing on facts and figures do not allow one to get to questions of meaning for, as Jean-Paul Sartre claimed, essences and facts are incommensurable. If one takes only facts one will never reach the domain of value or meaning. *A million facts do not constitute a single meaning.* The technicized language of much educational discourse is one of our greatest problems for that too blocks the necessary movement of mind, for when language congeals the human mind petrifies with it. To return to sources is, in large measure, to return to Socrates who lives both at the root of the best traditions in our educational system and at the root of the best innovations during the last few decades. We need to ponder his extraordinary ability to engender critical reflection in his students. We need also to see that education while it contributes to and vitalizes society yet, by its own nature, must transcend it. The essential dynamics of authentic education always takes the student beyond the status quo into what is not fully known, fully comprehended, fully formalized. Education is the expression and development of a primary impulse for truth, a deep epistemic instinct that we inherit as part of our biological nature. A civilization that cannot recognize the intrinsic value and beauty of education has already condemned itself either to permanent ethical and cultural stagnation or, worse, extinction.

The Principles of Socratic Education

The animating, deeply disturbing power of the Socratic tradition runs like an electric current through western civilization. Socrates envisaged the educated mind as one that had the ability to live in a state of creative ignorance, of inner perplexity and the emotional unease such perplexity created. It was the aim of his extraordinary teaching to free the mind for critical reflection and probing insight. What follows is not so much a piece of historical reconstruction as a series of reflections on a kind of engaged, dialectical thinking which in our specialized and technical age is in danger of disappearing and, with it, an essential dimension of consciousness. In the next chapter I will consider its implications for the life of universities and for the place of intellectual research.

The first principle of Socratic education is that it cannot be simply transferred. Education is not an object (a mass of knowledge or information or skills or know-how) that can be unambiguously handed from the teacher to the student. Education is, rather, an activity of mind, a particular emotional and critical orientation towards experience. The noun 'education' is here peculiarly deceptive for there is no object to correspond with the word. We would do well to employ a participle – educating or, even better, a series of participles: thinking–imagining– participating–relating–dividing–joining–anticipating etc. At least, such a stringing of hyphenated participles escapes the deceptive stasis of nouns and evokes a sense of personal drama that, for Socrates, education ineluctably is.

Socrates was one of the first to recognize the intimate and necessary relationship between education and personal commitment. His pedagogy was skilfully shaped to penetrate the protective armour of custom and opinion to release in the suddenly exposed and vulnerable individual a sense of shocked engagement. The aim of the *elenchus* – the name given to his teaching method – was to give birth to a desire for authentic learning. Intellectually the *elenchus*, as it worked on the student, moved from strongly held opinion, to floundering uncertainty, to loss, to not-knowing, that engendered the authentic quest for meaning, the desire for finding out. Emotionally, the *elenchus* began with smug ease ('I know what I think') that dissolved into unease, then into anguish, then into concern and, finally, into collaborative and reflective curiosity. The aim of the *elenchus* was to bring about self-reflection and critical enquiry. As a teaching method the *elenchus* is indirect, has little immediate prescriptive content, is individual (related to the actual people who surround the teacher) and dialectical:

> At first he falsely thought he knew and did not feel at a loss;
> whereas now, though he knows no more than he did before,
> he does at least feel at a loss and no longer thinks he knows

> ... At least it seems that we have made him more likely to find
> out the truth ... And do you think he would ever have tried
> to discover the truth if he had not fallen into puzzlement?[2]

So Socrates in the *Meno* describes the characteristic intention of the
elenchus. Things are not tidily resolved because the state of existential
perplexity in the student is intrinsically valuable, is indeed, invariably
the precondition for authentic education. The Socratic enterprise
appears, at first sight, highly negative; the *elenchus* works to clear away
the junk that clutters up the average human mind. In this respect, to
some extent, it resembles the teaching methods of Logical Positivism
during the earlier part of the century.

However, for Socrates, the *elenchus* is more than this. Its deeper
purpose is ethical: it exists primarily to engender *virtue – a thinking that
actually works through and on existence and which therefore develops the
personality*. Teaching is an ethical activity and education is, in part, the
act and art of releasing a critical–ethical process in the other, the final
outcome of which cannot be known in advance. In *The Sophist*
Socrates compares the action of the *elenchus* with that of the doctor
cleansing the system of the patient:

> For just as the physicians of the body believe that the body
> cannot benefit from the nourishment it receives until the in-
> ternal hindrances are removed, so do those who perform this
> purification believe about the psyche. She cannot profit from
> the knowledge offered to her until the *elenchus* is applied and
> the man is refuted and brought to shame, thus purifying him
> from opinions that hinder learning and causing him to think he
> knows only what he does know and no more. That is the best
> and most temperate state to be in.[3]

The moral advance is explicitly stated.

Indeed, it would seem that all education has within it an ethical
imperative for the term 'education' denotes an activity we value. An
educational encounter, by definition, is one that we morally approve
of. It denotes an increase, a human advance of some kind or other. In
this it is unlike the word 'training' that is neutral: one can train to be
a lawyer or a concentration camp guard. The irony in Socratic education is that the necessary purification of the psyche (a word to which
Socrates gave a new depth and complexity) is often experienced as loss,
as disorientation, as a painful emptying. But irony, then, is ubiquitous
in Socrates, and also serves a deeper ethical intention.

The Role of Irony

Irony permeates Socratic discourse. In part, the irony is another weapon (along with the rigorous method of interrogation) in the onslaught on those internalized opinions, internalized ideologies, internalized half-truths, around which the human ego, and all the defensive emotions of the ego, has crystallized. To shatter opinion, psychologically, is to disturb and break the ego which was, perhaps, the essence of Socrates' alleged crime against the state. Somewhere in his writings Thomas Mann has celebrated that form of irony which 'glances at both sides, which plays slyly and irresponsibly – yet not without benevolence – among opposites and in which there is no great haste to take sides and come to decisions which may prove premature'. This form of irony is Socratic. Its gadfly irresponsibility, however, is there to stir the tired horse of the Athenian state into movement, into life. The ego must not be allowed to harden around any protective system, and irony, a subtle personal play of mind over the actual, deprives any fixed system of infallible authority. Socratic irony is highly subversive and educational to the core.

At one level, even the honest confession of ignorance, so characteristic of Socrates, is duplex. It is, and is not the case. While Socrates proclaims ignorance, there is no ignorance in the way in which he engenders critical reflection in the other! When he applies the *elenchus*, he works with all the skill of a surgeon cutting out a cancerous growth in his patient. And, indeed, he knows exactly what he is after. His innocence is not Romantic. His ignorance is a classical mask, a persona, deliberately used to catch and destroy the vermin of received opinions.

The Existential Element in Socratic Dialogue

There is more to Socrates than this, however; irony, interrogation, indirection, logical exactitude, these alone do not explain the transformative powers of the teacher, his dramatic influence on, for example, Alciabides (if we can rely on *The Symposium*) and, of course, on Plato, his most brilliant disciple. The actual *existence* of Socrates, his particular presence before others, must have expressed an affirmation that simultaneously permeated, qualified and transcended the critical *elenchus*. This existential affirmation would have acted as a dialectical counterpoint to the profession of ignorance and the scepticism that so alarmed the society around him. It was, perhaps, Socrates' own particular relationship to what he was saying that was so captivating, so haunting and that constituted the deepest irony of all. Existentially, the man followed an inner imperative to teach and philosophize while in his explicit teaching he seemed to negate everything and claim to be no more than a sterile midwife. It was the energy surging between these opposites, between ontological affirmation and theoretical negation, which was, no doubt, the source of the transformative power. The same words in the mouth of a smart downtown sophist would not have possessed the same meaning. How appropriate it is that Socrates never wrote a word, for books freeze the flow of movement and shed their authors, whereas teaching is always through the medium and specifities of existence and relationship and is thus unique and essentially unrepeatable. The true moments of education, while they express common concerns and transpersonal preoccupations, cannot be duplicated or simply delivered; they are tied to a particular moment in time, a particular cluster of relationships, a particular complex of sequencing and coinciding.

It is this aspect of Socrates that Nietzsche[4] seemed to miss. Yes, to some extent (as Nietzsche contended) Socrates *is* 'the theoretical man'; yes, his emergence may mark a critical moment in the relationship between consciousness and instinct; yes, there are other modes of knowing (like the aesthetic which this book is largely devoted to defining and defending) that Socrates partly ignores. Yet at the same time, Socrates *is* the man who is rooted in existence, representing not only an intellectual enquiry but also a mode of being and is ready to assert its supreme transcendent value before the prospect of death and social condemnation. He is also the one who is able to hear and heed his own inner daimon – what we would now call the creative unconscious, that deep preconceptual source of human wisdom (not open to immediate discursive analysis). Here, again, in Socrates' reference to those moments of inner authoritative guidance we detect the limits he put round absolute scepticism and his readiness to discard, at critical moments of insight, his trickster's set of masks.

The creative tension between his affirmative existence and his negative mood of teaching (directly related to the actual individuals around him) generated the disturbing power of Socrates' teaching. It is Alcibiades in *The Symposium* who describes the turbulent war of emotion in himself caused by his teacher:

> Whenever I listen to him my heart beats faster than if I were in a religious frenzy and tears run down my face and I observe that numbers of other people have the same experience. Nothing

of this kind ever used to happen when I listened to Pericles and other good speakers; I recognized that they spoke well but my psyche was not thrown into confusion and dismay by the thought that my life was no better than a slave's.[5]

Later in the same speech, Alcibiades claims he would like to see Socrates 'vanish from the face of the earth' but, at the same time, if it happened, his sorrow would be infinitely greater than any relief he might experience. The existential ambivalence Socrates created is very clear.

It is also Alcibiades who described the contrast between the outer and the inner form of his language. Socrates, he says, is like a statue of Silenus sold in the Athenian market place. The visible statue represents an ugly bald-headed satyr seducing individuals with his flute-playing but the statue when opened has inside, hidden behind the outer façade, various miniatures of the sublime gods. Clearly, something more than 'the theoretical man' is at work. There are hidden levels of meaning, hidden levels of engagement. The *elenchus* is only the pedagogic yet essential starting point.

Conclusion

Reflecting on Socrates in his three volume study of Greek thought and civilization, the classical scholar Werner Jaeger wrote:

> This self-involvement of the student in the enquiry (that he was both subject and object of the investigation, both questioner and the thing in question) is one of the most striking aspects of Socratic thought. It is also its greatest achievement, for it made not only man but each individual human being as a whole the absolute centre of philosophical reflection. And this was the beginning of true philosophy.[6]

And, one wants to quickly add, also *the beginning of true education*, of *paideia*, of that inner process through which the individual moves from naive consciousness and ego to reflection and identity.

For Socrates any truth that may be established is always provisional, always must remain open, like a scientific hypothesis, to further testing, to modification, to rejection – if necessary. But one element that remains absolute is the critical play of consciousness over the field of one's experience; that *is* the educated mind, the act of transcendent intelligence that Socrates felt the teacher was there to exemplify and engender in the other. It is this critical play of mind that Montaigne, at the beginning of the European Renaissance, was to admire so much; it was the same spirit of free enquiry, of tentative examination, of holding premises provisionally, that in the nineteenth century Matthew Arnold was to evoke in the closing pages of *Culture and Anarchy* and which his contemporaries John Stuart Mill, Walter Pater and Cardinal Newman were to regard as the indelible characteristic of education, such that without it there could be no education. Arnold's evocation of Socrates is particularly memorable and apposite:

> Socrates has drunk his hemlock and is dead; but in his own breast does not every man carry about with him a possible Socrates, in that power of a disinterested play of consciousness upon his stock notions and habits, of which this wise and admirable man gave all through his lifetime the great example, and which was the secret of his incomparable influence? And he who leads men to call forth and exercise in themselves this power, and who busily calls it forth and exercises it in himself, is at the present moment, perhaps, as Socrates was in his time, more in concert with the vital working of men's minds, and more effectually significant, than any House of Commons orator, or practical operator in politics.[7]

In our own time, when education in the institutional and sociological sense has become little more than an instrument to serve the status quo, when the emphasis on technology has smothered our inner being, when strident opinions and ideologies parade as individual thought, we are in need of both the critical *elenchus* (to clear the junk, to liberate the mind) and that more intangible sense of *the value of being*. In western civilization we have, too often, tried to erase the thinker from the thought and ended in a landscape of dispossessed objects, systems without spirit, products without human purposes, closed questions unsupported by existential quests.

The recent so-called 'debate on education' described in the Introduction was never an *open* debate, nor was it often, if ever, about authentic education. It was about training, about industry, about skills, about organization, about management. *Yet we need to ask what kind of activity education denotes before we can talk about it.* So much of what is now easily named 'education' refers to unambiguous, one dimensional behavioural training or what Michael Oakeshott calls 'socialization'. Socrates gave one compelling answer to the question.[8] It is an answer that lies at the root of our culture, an answer that as teachers we can still existentially reclaim and struggle to adapt to our own altered and difficult circumstances. What this means in relationship to research and the life of the university will be explored in the next chapter.

Notes

1 GEORGE ORWELL (1990) *1984*, Harmondsworth Penguin, p. 55, but see particularly the Appendix, pp. 312–26.
2 PLATO, *The Meno* quoted in 'Elenchus' by RICHARD ROBINSON in GREGORY VLASTOS (ed.) (1971) The Philosophy of Socrates, Anchor Books, p. 83.
3 PLATO, *The Sophist, ibid.*, p. 81.
4 For a full account of Nietzsche's relationship to Socrates see WERNER J. DANNHAUSER (1974) *Nietzsche's View of Socrates*, Ithaca, NY, Cornell University Press.
5 PLATO (1957) *The Symposium* (translated by Walter Hamilton) Harmondsworth, Penguin, p. 101.
6 See WERNER JAEGER (1957) *Paideia: the Ideals of Greek Culture*, vol. 2, Oxford Basil Blackwell, Chapter 2 pp. 28–76.
7 MATTHEW ARNOLD (1869) *Culture and Anarchy*.
8 There are, of course, many books examining the work of Socrates. I have found the following to be of the greatest help and clarity: GREGORY VLASTOS (ed.) (1971) *The Philosophy of Socrates*, Anchor Books; GREGORY VLASTOS (1991) *Socrates*, Cambridge, Cambridge University Press; JOHN FERGUSON (1970) *Socrates*, Milton Keynes, Open University Press; ERIC HAVELOCK (1963) *Preface to Plato*, Oxford, Basil Blackwell; LASLO VERSENYI (1963) *Socratic Humanism*, New Haven, Yale University Press; WERNER JAEGER (1957) *Paideia: The Ideals of Greek Culture*, Oxford, Basil Blackwell; LEONARD NELSON (1949) *Socratic Method and Critical Philosophy*, New Haven, Yale University Press. See also Bibliography I, 'On Socrates and Socratic Thinking'.

Chapter 2

Intellectual Research as Socratic Activity

You treat me as if I professed to know the matters I ask about, and as if I might agree with you if I wished to. But that is not so. On the contrary, I inquire into the proposition along with you because I do not know. I will tell you whether I agree or not when I have examined it.

Socrates in Charmides

Nothing is my last word about anything – I am interminably supersubtle and analytic.

Henry James

The truth has to be my truth before it can become truth at all.

T.S. Eliot

Introduction

Because we live in a society where intellect and imagination are pitifully neglected, because we live in an age where the life of concepts and metaphors, the essential material of intellectual culture, go uncherished, what I am going to describe in this chapter may seem strange, even to some teachers and academics. Yet I regard the approach I will describe in this chapter as the *modus vivendi* of all true researchers, the Socratic activity without which there can be little reflective culture and no true university, college or school. Dorothy Sayers once remarked: 'Most Englishmen would rather die than think and many do'. One of the functions of the university is to stop that happening and one of its main weapons in the battle against mindless complacency is dialectical research and continuous reflection. Each piece of humanist research, however modest, should be out to test current assumptions, to extend understanding, to provoke contemplation, enquiry, further dissent. In a sense, as in the Socratic dialogue described in the last chapter, the process of engaged consciousness matters more than the results reached. It is this process that I will describe here in relationship to doing research and, beyond that, to the continuous act of creative learning. I want to enumerate some of the Socratic methods for developing and refining the habit of critical reflection. I want to describe the techniques for grasping emergent ideas and securing their progressive amplification into patterns of coherence. My direct concern here is with the university but the implications for both primary and secondary education should be obvious; the reader who is more interested in the broad argument of the book or in the aesthetic is invited to move directly on to Chapter 3.

The Art of Catching Thought

Many thinkers, like most novelists and poets, have found the practice of keeping some kind of journal essential to the art of locating and extending critical reflection. One thinks immediately of Pascal, Nietzsche, Wittgenstein. Pascal, the seventeenth-century scientist and philosopher, wrote on large sheets of paper, jotting down his insights as they occurred on a whole variety of subjects; each thought would be separated from the next by a line marked under it; sometimes these would be scrawled down the page, sometimes across it. Then, as the unwieldy fragmentary material accumulated, he would set up a number of master-categories and start cutting up the *pensées* and placing them into bundles that would be finally threaded together. The original manuscripts apparently show 'the feverish haste with which fragments were written down before the thought could slip away, the alterations and erasures, the very disposition of many of the fragments in the form of poetry rather than prose'.[1] A significant part of what Pascal wrote has never been deciphered, it remains a mass of tiny emerging fragments, intolerably cryptic or simply incoherent.

The same is true of much of Nietzsche's later work, particularly the fragments that make up *The Will to Power* (where neither the numbering, nor arrangement, nor selection are those of Nietzsche). Here again one finds sudden explosions of thought as well as schemas prefiguring their future elaboration. What we discern is intellectual work at high intensity in its early, darting, mercurial phase of articulation. His habit of documentation is equally erratic. Nietzsche used old notebooks that had not been completely filled so the ideas are scattered across a number of half-used journals; not only that, he tended to work from the back to the front, sometimes filling only the right-hand pages, sometimes only the left. The habit of Nietzsche's research captures well the chaotic process of following the intermittent advances and withdrawals of exploratory thought. The same is true of Wittgenstein who also tended to shape and define his formal thought from his own diverse and labile journal entries. A critic looking at these notebooks wrote:

> He seldom pursues the same line of thought uninterruptedly for very long. He is usually thinking about several topics at the same time, and records his ideas on all of them one after the other, constantly beginning from the beginning, as if he had never thought of the topic before. After dropping temporarily one line of thought, it may be hours, days, weeks, months or years before he takes it up again.[2]

According to the same critic, Wittgenstein's thinking was so constantly on the move that it has to be doubted whether there is anything that one could actually name as the philosophy of the late Wittgenstein. One encounters a pure fountain of thought, not a settled container; an animating and dialectical activity, not a fixed and stable object. And this, again, reminds one of the restless and questioning nature of Socratic enquiry, where all conclusions remain open to the next round of scrutiny and, in that sense, remain provisional and open to change.

In a book called *The Sociological Imagination* – it could have been named *The Socratic Imagination* – the American sociologist C. Wright Mills talked about the diverse uses of the journal, or what he called a file, in the following way:

> In such a file as I am going to describe, there is joined personal experience and professional activities, studies under way and studies planned. In this file you, as an intellectual craftsman, will try to get together what you are doing intellectually and what you are experiencing as a person. Here you will not be afraid to use your experience and relate it directly to various work in progress. By serving as a check on repetitious work, your file also enables you to conserve your energy. It also encourages you to capture 'fringe-thoughts': various ideas which may be by-products of everyday life, snatches of conversation overheard on the street, or, for that matter, dreams. Once noted, these may lead to more systematic thinking, as well as lend intellectual relevance to more directed experience.

You will have often noticed how carefully accomplished thinkers treat their own minds, how closely they observe their development and organize their experience. The reason they treasure their smallest experiences is that, in the course of a lifetime, modern man has so very little personal experience and yet experience is so important as a source of original intellectual work. To be able to trust yet to be sceptical of your own experience, I have come to believe, is one mark of the mature workman. This ambiguous confidence is indispensable to originality in any intellectual pursuit, and the file is one way by which you can develop and justify such confidence.

By keeping an adequate file and thus developing self-reflective habits, you learn how to keep your inner world awake. Whenever you feel strongly about events or ideas you must try not to let them pass from your mind, but instead to formulate them for your files and in so doing draw out their implications, show yourself either how foolish these feelings or ideas are, or how they might be articulated into productive shape. The file also helps you build up the habit of writing. You cannot 'keep your hand in' if you do not write something at least every week. In developing the file, you can experiment as a writer and thus, as they say, develop your powers of expression. To maintain a file is to engage in the controlled experience.[3]

The journal is the larder of reflexive intelligence. It is the place where conceptions, speculations, schemas, insights, bits of evidence, quotations, statistics, extreme positions, problems, frustrations are stored for later criticism, development and distillation. Wright Mills' paradoxical assertion that one must be able to trust and yet be sceptical of one's own experience is, of course, deeply Socratic.

Any such journal in the context of humanist research and enquiry might carry a record of books, monographs, articles and reviews. It might include summaries of their main arguments and a clear identification of the school of thought to which they belong. The journal might house significant quotations and, in some cases, the lines of opposition to them, counter propositions that may well later be elaborated to form critiques, reformulations, further developments. So often, one's best ideas come not *ex nihilo* but (as in the Socratic tradition) in response to other formulated ideas, either in some *critical* relationship where one feels compelled to reformulate and go beyond what is being claimed or in some *creative* relationship where one often finds oneself spontaneously extending the concepts to a different realm of activity.

A great deal of creative thinking depends upon *an unexpected transfer of categories* from area A to area B. According to Thomas Kuhn,[4] for example, Dalton's theory of chemical atomism arose when he applied to chemistry a set of questions and concepts previously confined to physics and meteorology. The result was a new orientation towards the field of study. For this reason, as a Socratic researcher, one cannot read too widely. Another subject of enquiry may provide the concepts, analogues and metaphors that are needed to illuminate one's own. The quintessential aim of the journal is *to catch the mind's activity in its emergent phases*, to find first verbal approximations, to scribble tentative imprecise lines, to scrawl jumbled sentences that will later need unjumbling and connecting to other formulations and so taken forward, often laboriously, through many tedious revisions in the quest for propositional clarity.

With regard to the critical examination of other people's arguments there are two crucial approaches that are deeply Socratic in nature; they apply a kind of *elenchus* to the work. The first relates to the *internal coherence* of the work; it concerns *sins of commission* that can be spotted in the actual performance of the argument; the second concerns *sins of omission* that are the things *not* declared, the failures which lurk in the gaps and fissures of the text. When considering the sins of commission one asks: *How good is the argument within its own explicit terms? Do the concepts unfold clearly and consistently? Does the evidence provided support the conclusions given?* Whereas with the sins of omission one asks a different set of questions in relationship to what has been, consciously or unconsciously, excluded: *What has been left out? What has not been done? What has not been declared in the utterance?* Locating the excluded and bringing it to bear on the argument can have devastating consequences. With some writing this can be a difficult task simply because any eloquence quickly seals the critical space making the argument seem beautifully replete. The aim of rhetoric is to seduce the critical faculty, while the aim of criticism is to liberate it by generating the subversive energy of questions, both in relationship to what has been verbally committed and what has been omitted from the utterance. Socratic philosophy developed as a critical response to the sophistry of the sophists; the sophists taught the art of persuasion while Socrates advocated the relentless search for truth. As any one argument suppresses another, so the excavation of the hidden is as important as the explication of the given. A notebook is the Socratic place for making a list of what one discovers as one glides like a wise serpent under sentences and below syntax to locate all the excluded propositions. Here Socratic criticism and psychoanalytical interpretation find an unexpected affinity; in structuralist mode one would say that they are both conscious of ways in which the signified can slip away from, or be obscured by, the signifier.

Stratagems for Agile Thinking

Intellectual work in the Socratic mode can often begin with a hunch, a vague notion, a sense of perplexity, a nagging problem of some kind or other to be sorted out. Generally, one has to be messy before one can be meticulous, confused before one can be concise. The essay should be precisely that: *an essaying out*. The aim is to give discursive clarity to the initial, often inchoate, pressurizing insights and doubts, but these insights and doubts can change, and change again, in the process of formulation, so that the whole endeavour becomes a continuous dialectical movement of discovery. Indeed, one may not know exactly what one thinks until the end of the argument and, even then, in the manner of Plato's early dialogues, this too may be highly *provisional* or even *negative*, in the sense that the evidence brought forward may defeat the original premises, but a negation can be positive. Closing down one line of enquiry may well indicate where later thinking must go. While one may hope for a positive resolution, research can always end on a speculative and Socratic note; it can be a clearing rather than a conclusion, an invitation rather than something finally completed.

As Socrates thought through the act of engaged conversation, so one can *think through the act of writing*; therefore, researchers' central preoccupations often become clearer as they go along and, at the same time, so do the necessary means of investigation. The method may be *empirical* (depending on the collection of contemporary data); it may be *historical* (depending on the examination of archive material and historical constructions); it may be *analytical* (depending on the theoretical elaboration of concepts) or *polemical* (arguing, with some intelligent passion, an unfashionable position) or, more likely, it will be a mixture of a number of these – though it has to be admitted that Socrates was blind to the power of the empirical and historical methods. What is important is becoming aware of the logical principle that informs each part and of seeing that it is consistent with the dominant category. From time to time, the researcher has to step back to sense the architectonic logic of the whole. This means that one moment one is consolidating, at another moment anticipating, and at another pressing on again, with *this* piece of historic or analytical or empirical or autobiographical argument more clearly positioned in relationship to the whole. In this too the researcher often follows the dynamic backwards–forwards movement of the evolving Socratic dialogue.

As for keeping the mind agile, self-critical, creative, here are some possible Socratic stratagems:

1   From time to time, it may help to reconceive whatever argument one is putting forward from an opponent's point of view. How would the critic formulate it? What evidence would he or she bring? One might even write down the oppositional view. In a similar vein, C. Wright Mills wrote: 'Let your mind become a moving prism catching light from as many different angles as possible'.[5] The purpose of these critical and imaginative shifts is not to encourage an enervating scepticism but rather to see that one is inevitably writing *from a position* that is not simply written on the parchment of the world but has to be maintained in a state of tension alongside and often against other competing perspectives. No proposition can be immune, by some authorial fiat, from scrutiny. In the Socratic tradition, all views are inherently problematic, especially at the beginning. The formulations of contemporary physics show that so-called common-sense views are, ironically, the most problematic of all. In brief, good researchers are often at odds with themselves and in this way become their own fiercest critics and their own finest collaborators.

2   The imaginative identification of the anti-thesis may valuably unsettle complacency but, more productively still, it may provide the possibility for a greater synthesis. So often an entrenched position has got hold of a partial truth and falsely elevated it to an all-encompassing absolute. It is always possible, then, that the precise identification of the anti-thesis may provide crucial elements needed in the analysis that, when imported, provide the terms necessary for a wider synthesis. Sometimes we have to struggle to appropriate opposed conceptions, painfully holding them together until they create new tense unities and more encompassing frameworks. Just as a star is a battleground of opposing forces kept in dynamic integrated play, so it often is with good theory. At its most exciting this involves a going beyond both prior positions into a new paradigm. These moments of combination and fusion are among the richest in the narrative of ideas. One thinks of the young John Stuart Mill drawing the work of Wordsworth and Coleridge into the framework of his father's Utilitarianism

with the most liberating consequences. So it is a shrewd move to examine the anti-thesis for any truth it may hold. If one can include *that* truth in one's own framework, then it may effect an internal expansion and transformation.

3   If the problem is one of blockage, of one's straying vessel getting stuck in the verbal sandbanks of abstraction and cliché, then one should try a more informal style of writing. For example, one might need to break off in mid-chapter and pen a letter, opening up one's preoccupations and problems to a real or imaginary friend or to a real or imaginary tutor. When unable to write poetry, the poet Rainer Maria Rilke would take to letter-writing largely to tap, at a different angle and at a different level, that part of his mind from which his poetry came. A letter with its different set of expectations – the assumption of a listening person, the acceptance of a more informal idiom, a generally freer dispensation – can release the writing block, generate new material and revivify the intellectual task. A conversation with a friend can serve a similar end.

4   Another stratagem to keep the mind agile involves becoming fully aware of *key words*. The Socratic *elenchus* invariably begins with the isolation and clarification of the major concepts. Every now and again, it is helpful for researchers to try and identify their essential concepts; to look up their etymologies, to excavate the historical life packed in their tiny cases, to examine different contemporary definitions, as well as to offer their own. As arguments depend on concepts, the more sensitive one is to one's own chosen terms the more subtle the analysis should be. This is the kind of work – etymologies, usages, definitions, synonyms – that could be done in the Socratic notebook and, where fitting, transferred to the main research.

5   From time to time, researchers will want to make an inventory of the main items they aim to include as well as to plot the changing schematic plan of the whole edifice. Similarly, they will move dialectically between impulsive scrawling and formal scripting, writing on one day jagged, near ungrammatical, sentences of a yet-to-be-written chapter and, on the next, refining the final paragraphs of an all-but-complete chapter. In the exacting task levity joins with gravity, play with precision, passionate engagement with deep self-criticism. Something of the Socratic cast of mind I am trying to describe is brought out well by John Ziman in his account of his own scientific research and enquiry:

> On Mondays, Wednesdays and Fridays, I construct 'normal' science, trying to solve the puzzles defined by the current paradigm: on Tuesdays, Thursdays and Saturdays, I take a 'revolutionary' stance and poke subversively into the anomalous cracks. On Sunday, perhaps, I pray for guidance in what Kuhn called the 'essential tension' between authority and rebellion, creativity and criticism.[6]

In brief, one must work dialectically, keeping the opposites of the mind in motion, moving constantly from a kind of epileptic stuttering to formal articulation and back again. Iris Murdoch brings out this dialectical notion well in her Platonic dialogues *Acastos* where Socrates says to Callistos: 'Remember, you are doing philosophy – and sometimes when you've been trying really hard to get a glimpse of an idea you can only talk about it in a kind of nonsense. So stop trying to be clear and just talk honest nonsense'[7] and yet later the same Socrates reprimands Plato for being too diffuse: 'Now, my dear splendid clever boy, try to put your thoughts in order, don't just pour them over us like a bath attendant'.[8] Truly productive thinking has to move continuously between these two poles of 'honest nonsense' and logical differentation. Perhaps more research, following the fine example set by Iris Murdoch, should take the shape of Platonic dialogues, for the genre allows both the rambling confusion and the logical ordering, as well as the possibility for dissent and qualification. Certainly this is another stratagem to keep the intellect agile; one can dramatize one's own warring thoughts by dividing them into characters who utter their partisan and competing insights. The notion of dialogical enquiry brings me, finally, to my last concern: the need for a communal context for such thinking in an age of cultural standardization where the life of consciousness is closing in and sustained critical reflection is in danger of disappearing.

The Socratic Context for Research

Socrates always claimed that he had no knowledge and that he was the sterile midwife who gave birth to the conceptions of others. His method is described well in the dialogue called the *Theaetetus* where he protests:

> You are not bearing in mind, my friend, that I have no knowledge; I cannot claim any such ideas as my own – no, I am

barren as far as they are concerned. But I am acting as your midwife, and that is why I am chanting and serving up morsels of wisdom for you to taste. This will go on until I have played my part in bringing your very own notion out into the world. Once that stage is over, I will examine the idea to see whether it turns out to be viable or still-born.[9]

The approach is indirect and critical; it is the antithesis of dogmatic authoritarianism. The method displaces hierarchy and promotes a democracy of listening and speaking. This is how it looks in action: Socrates, the agent of provocation, is speaking:

Well, now we're at the heart of what puzzles me and what I cannot satisfactorily grasp on my own – what knowledge in fact is. Are we in a position to give an account of it? What do you all think? Which of us should have a go first? If he misses the mark – and the same goes for anyone who misses the mark at any time – then he'll sit down and be the 'donkey', as children say in their ball-game. But anyone who comes through without making a mistake will be our 'king', and it'll be his turn to set us to answer any questions he likes.[10]

The Socratic community is a learning community where, in principle, the function of the teacher and guide can shift from individual to individual, for the first expectation is not a prior knowledge but a common intellectual curiosity. In the *Apologia* Socrates argues that it is the act of critical reflection that animates the psyche and keeps the whole civilization alive.

Humanist research will, at times, require scholars who are experts in their own fields, but it also needs an intellectual environment where ideas are cherished, where discussion is contagious and where there is a broad commitment to cultural and philosophical issues. So often today's researcher is a narrow specialist, moving from a lonely flat to a lonely library, a ghost of a person mechanically documenting more and more about less and less. Detailed research *is* important but details have to be related to a broader ethical and cultural matrix for their full significance to emerge, and it is here that a community of researchers can provide the necessary intellectual circumference, as well as the testing dialogue and a sense of personal belonging.

By a community of researchers I mean a group who meet regularly to share ideas and hunches, who give papers based on work in progress, who discuss common concerns, who keep up with intellectual developments, who challenge and confirm and care for each other. The community constitutes a learning group, testing arguments, testing evidence, moving from certainty into uncertainty, back to certainty and into uncertainty, again and again, in the Socratic rhythm of authentic exploration. Intellectual research needs such a context to flourish and it is one of the chief responsibilities of universities to offer such seminal learning environments. At the moment, when much research is being determined by those indifferent to intellectual culture, when much of it is conceived in a narrow pragmatic spirit and is little more than a form of problem solving, we are in need of such centres – centres for radical speculation and radical enquiry into all aspects of human life.

In the *Apologia* Socrates defended himself thus:

> So long as I draw breath and have my faculties, I shall never stop practising philosophy and exhorting you and elucidating the truth for everyone that I meet. I shall go on saying, in my usual way, 'My very good friend, you are an Athenian and belong to a city which is the greatest and most famous in the world for its wisdom and strength. Are you not ashamed that you give your attention to acquiring as much money as possible, and similarly with reputation and honour, and give no attention or thought to truth and understanding and the perfection of your psyche?'[11]

His question has not dated. It is as pertinent as ever. A concern for truth, wisdom and life, problematic and paradoxical as Socrates demonstrated it to be, must remain the animating concern of the true university, of the researcher and the scholar. We owe that, at least, to the materialist society we seek to serve through the power of the intellect and the imagination – like Socrates. Yet Socrates, it has to be roundly admitted, for all his transformative educational power, severely neglected the power of the aesthetic to conceive and explore the world. It is to the object of this extraordinary neglect that we must now turn.

Notes

1 A.J. KRAILSHEIMER (1966) 'Introduction' in *Pascal: Pensées*, Harmondsworth, Penguin Books, p. 18.
2 JAAKKO HINTIKKA (1990) 'Obstacles to Understanding', *Times Literary Supplement*, 28 September.

3 C. WRIGHT MILLS (1959) *The Sociological Imagination*, Oxford, Oxford University Press, pp. 196–7.

4 See THOMAS KUHN (1962) *The Structure of Scientific Revolutions*, Chicago, University of Chicago Press.

5 MILLS (1959) p. 235

6 JOHN ZIMAN (1992) 'Subversive Scholar', *Times Higher Education Supplement*, 27 November.

7 IRIS MURDOCH (1986) *Acastos: Two Platonic Dialogues*, Harmondsworth, Penguin, p. 25.

8 *Ibid.*, p. 52.

9 PLATO (1987) *Theaetetus* (translated by Robin Waterfield) Harmondsworth, Penguin, p. 41.

10 *Ibid.*, p. 20.

11 PLATO (1954) 'The Apologia' in *The Last Days of Socrates* (translated by Hugh Tredennick) Harmondsworth, Penguin, p. 61. I have taken the liberty of using the Greek work psyche rather than soul in the last sentence. The word 'soul' has become so saturated with Christian metaphysics it somewhat distorts the Greek meaning of the word.

Section II

On the Philosophy of Arts Education

Chapter 3

The Arts in the Public Realm: New Foundations for Aesthetic Education

To be a poet is to have a soul in which knowledge passes instantly into feeling and feeling flashes back as a new organ of knowledge.

George Eliot

Art brings us to the very same point that we are brought to by religion, to an experience saturated by meaning whose value overwhelms us with the force of law.

Roger Scruton

Socrates' Last Dream

Socrates was committed to radical enquiry, the critical examination of all facets of experience. His methods were, for the most part, rational and analytic; they concerned the definition of concepts and their coherent elaboration in demanding argument. The outcome of his singular pursuit was the elevation of reason. Reason, in western culture, became the highest instrument in the search for truth. The rise of the theoretical man, Nietzsche argued, led to the death of tragedy (for reason tends towards abstraction and utopia) and the diminution of the aesthetic. This may be true but in the *Phaedo* Plato tells us how Socrates, as he waits to take the fatal hemlock, informs his intellectual disciples of his last dream. In his dream he is commanded to make music. It is as if the philosopher is being invited to confront not what he has achieved in his life, but what he has neglected, even suppressed.

The speech is so pertinent to the second and major part of this book that it must be quoted at some length. Cebes has asked Socrates why, when he has never written a line of poetry in his life, he is spending his last hours turning one of Aesop's fables into verse and composing a hymn to Apollo. Socrates replies:

> In the course of my life I have often had intimations in dreams 'that I should make music'. The same dream came to me some-times in one form, and sometimes in another, but always saying the same or nearly the same words: 'Set to work and make music', said the dream. And hitherto I had imagined that this was only intended to exhort and encourage me in the study of philosophy, which has been the pursuit of my life, and is the noblest and best of music. The dream was bidding me do what I was already doing, in the same way that the competitor in a race is bidden by the spectators to run when he is already run-ning. But I was not certain of this; for the dream might have meant music in the popular sense of the word, and being under sentence of death, and the festival giving me a respite, I thought that it would be safer for me to satisfy the scruple, and, in obedience to the dream, to compose a few verses before I departed.[1]

True, it does not sound exactly like a conversion; but *some* recognition is there. Yet Socrates' earlier interpretation of the dream's meaning smacks of rationalization defending the ego's interests. Is it that his unconscious is pointing emphatically to what had been neglected and what, for human completeness, now needed cultivating?

If that is so, it is as true of our age as the age of Socrates. In our age it is not, of course, critical philosophy that needs complementing but, more, the exclusive emphasis on technique, skill and managerial organization. We need a return to music and poetry (to stay with the arts specified in Socrates' last dream) because such a return would re-connect us to the life of our feelings and unconscious, but also because the arts *are* vehicles of compelling cognition necessary for life's under-standing. The latter point is crucial to this book. If we glance, for one moment, at Rembrandt's *Self-Portrait* (1669) (see Plate 2) or Van Gogh's *1889 Self-Portrait* (see Plate 3) one can see at once that these paintings through the gestures, textures and tones of paint are profoundly en-gaged with the question of meaning. There is an urgency and gravity of preoccupation that can only be called Socratic: *what does my existence mean in the face of life, in the face of death?* This insight – this deep connection between Socratic philosophy and Socratic art (once it has transcended the tribal demand for ritual and repetition) – calls for a broader epistemology and a more comprehensive paradigm for teach-ing the arts. To establish this we must first establish the reasons for the current pervasive neglect of the arts and then move towards the new ground of aesthetic education.

The Neglect of the Arts

In British society we have failed to develop any adequate public conception of the true significance of the arts. They exist not necessarily on the margins but always in an uncertain state, constantly distorted by extraneous demands, curious expectations and fundamental misunderstandings. At the present moment under the controlling conception of a market economy, the arts are invariably placed under the banner of tourism and leisure. They are seen as commodities competing with other commodities in the hustle and bustle of the market place. Likewise, there has never been in Britain a comprehensive arts policy for our schools. The different art disciplines have been introduced at different times, under different conditions, different ideologies and different pedagogies. Their histories are highly disparate and testify to little awareness of any common web. At the moment, two arts disciplines (music and art) have been selected by the government as 'foundation subjects' (but absurdly only to the age of 14, thus at once marginalizing them); one (literature) remains invisibly tucked under language; while three more (drama, dance and film) stand in danger, not of extinction, but from remaining henceforth in a state of permanent mutilation. Much of whatever artistic activity survives may well be subject to the narrowing influences of the consumer imperative and a market-oriented instrumentalism. Presented even so schematically, the divided and partial arts curriculum tells its own story. It discloses the failure to conceptualize formally the role of the arts in civilization. Add to the schematic account the fact that for, at least, the last three decades one of the key words in nearly all arts education has been the word 'self-expression' and the picture of some overwhelming distortion may be clearer still. The emphasis on 'self-expression' (often linked to 'therapy' and various notions of 'release') eclipsed the broader conception of the arts as symbolic orders, committed to the apprehension of human significance, embodying, at their best, a kind of life-wisdom, with a vast field of achieved work and a repertoire of conventions and techniques, public and tested procedures available for emulation and development.

The notions of 'self-expression' and 'therapy' in education and the notions of 'leisure', 'relaxation', 'lifestyle' and 'pastime' in society at large belong to the same narcissistic semantic. They all suggest a similar kind of activity, often passive, severed from any wider current, taking place outside any public context, devoid of social or historic or political significance. They convey a kind of socially approved autism.

In spite of various radical rebellions in philosophy and criticism there still remains a deep mental schizophrenia about the arts and sciences. The schizophrenia lies at the heart of our technological civilization and goes back a number of centuries. It is still widely assumed that the arts are *simply* a matter of feeling and affect and that the sciences are a matter of thinking and cognition. As a result, the sciences are connected with 'tough' acts of knowledge while the arts are linked to 'soft' affects of various kinds. Science decides on the objective in a public arena; the arts play with the subjective in a private space. The sciences denote; the arts emote. This schizophrenia has, in large measure, been responsible for the uncertain and distorted condition of the arts in our civilization and helps to illuminate the hedonistic and private language of 'pastimes' and 'lifestyles' and 'therapies' so often used to discuss their nature.

In the opening paragraph of *The Intelligence of Feeling*, a once highly influential volume in arts education, Robert Witkin claimed:

> Everywhere the child turns he encounters the brute facts of history, chemistry, mathematics, and so forth. There is another world, however, a world that exists only because the individual exists. It is the world of his own sensations and feelings. He shares the former world with others. He moves around it with them, for it is a world of facts, of public space and 'objects'. *He shares the second world with no one. It is the world of private space and of the solitary subject.* (My emphasis)[2]

In this divided universe, the arts became inevitably and formally identified with the private space and the solitary subject, an emoting self in a world of brute and alien facts. A not dissimilar vision – if vision can be used for so dire and devastating a picture – can be found at the end of Walter Pater's *The Renaissance* where, in the closing chapter, the author urges the reader 'dwarfed in the narrow chambers of the individual mind' to get 'as many pulsations as possible into the given time'.[3]

Where did this mental schizophrenia come from? It derived from the dominant tradition of epistemology that can be traced back to, at least, Descartes, if not to Socrates. It demanded, as its central aim, absolute certainty. 'While there can be but one true', wrote Descartes in his *Discourse on Method*, 'I recognized as well nigh false all that was only probable'. Driven by a passion for infallibility, knowledge became narrowed to *verbal propositions that could be either developed logically or that could be submitted to empirical testing*. The mind became identified with analytical reason; truth with logic and/or verification. With regards to the arts and to aesthetic judgment the verdict was, at least in the pure version of the tradition, unambiguous; they could carry no cognitive significance. At the beginning it is expressed in Descartes, who linked poetry with 'ravishing graces and delights' and with 'the most agreeable fancies', and at the clapped out end of the tradition it is expressed in A.J. Ayer *Language, Truth and Logic* generously devoted to the whole realm of aesthetics ten dismissive sentences of which these are the most significant formulations:

> Aesthetic words . . . express certain feelings and evoke a certain response . . . There is no sense in attributing objective validity to aesthetic judgements, and no possibility of arguing about questions of values . . . The purpose of aesthetic criticism is not so much to give knowledge as to communicate emotion . . . We conclude, therefore, that there is nothing in aesthetics, any more than there is in ethics, to justify the view that it embodies a unique type of knowledge.[4]

That aesthetic response *does* embody a unique kind of knowledge is one of the essential tenets of this volume. But what is so startling is the way in which A.J. Ayer's utterly reductive views about the status of aesthetic judgments have been actively at work in the progressive tradition of education which has had such a formative influence on the teaching of the arts across the entire span of the twentieth century. There, too, it was assumed that there could be no kind of objectivity in judgment; there could be no cumulative development; there could be no evaluation of work; no knowledge, no tradition within which to work, no public face for the 'private' expressions of 'unique' individuals. In the Progressive canon there was no redeeming concept of a common and collaborative culture in which as a person one participated and to which one belonged. Dominant positivism and dissident progressivism turn out to be mirror images, two halves of the same circle, the fanatic light and the engulfing shadow of the same philosophical matrix.

The Revolution in Arts Education

The dialectically related movements of positivism and progressivism – now utterly exhausted – have been unable to provide an adequate or comprehensive aesthetic. The task now, in *creative response*, is to draw the *public* face of art, and we must try and render it without losing the better insights of the progressivists, for experimentation in art and the individuality and spontaneity of each child must still be cherished. What is needed is not so much a reactive denial, but a broader framework. That framework is now in the making and involves, at root, a broader epistemology and a deeper recognition of the significance of historic culture. To understand its nature it is necessary to return to the philosophical argument against the positivists and to the long tyranny of propositional knowledge in western civilization. For what was being virtually rejected and always epistemologically demoted was the whole variety of inherited means, both biological and cultural, through which we constantly make provisional and working metaphors of our lives and the world in which we live. Our remarkable abilities – to sequence narratives, to construe analogically, to conceive figuratively, to consider tonally, to think musically, to construct maps and diagrams, to make signs and symbols with our bodies – all of these were relegated to secondary levels, as if possessing no serious intellectual import. Yet it is precisely these excluded forms of symbolic cognition and elaboration that are now being claimed as primary sources of meaning, alongside propositional statements. The late Louis Arnaud Reid formulated one version of the epistemological revolution when he wrote:

> So instead of making knowledge a function of the truth of propositional statements, I think we should turn it on its head and say that truth is a function or attribute or quality of the mind's living cognitive apprehension of the world.[5]

Such an adroit movement undercuts the monopoly of propositional claims and reopens the way to conceive the arts as vehicles for the exploration and elaboration of consciousness-in-the-world. The nouns 'intelligence' and 'knowledge', although singular by verbal convention, have to be read as incorrigibly plural. In the house of the mind there are many mansions – and the aim of education must be to occupy and furnish all of them. If this is the emerging intellectual paradigm then it is inevitable that the philosophical significance of the arts will be again reclaimed, that their aesthetic means of operating will be recognized and that their distinctive bodies of collective practices (inside and across cultures) will be established. This may sound utopian. Yet once the concepts and apprehensions are there, the possibilities for action become at once real and pressing. And much can be done *within* the national curriculum until we have the political and cultural will to reconstruct education in the terms of the new philosophy and the emergent recognition of the full nature of aesthetic experience and the complex cultural continuum in which it operates.

To suggest, provocatively, some of the changes in arts education and to provide a terse overview I would like to conclude with ten major related propositions that together form a unified manifesto. As these propositions are highly condensed, it will be the aim of the remaining chapters to elaborate their significance in relation to the teaching of the arts.

The Ten Propositions of Arts Education

Proposition One

The first proposition concerns the *ordinary nature of the aesthetic*. It is a broad category and a definitive one. We are born aesthetic animals: *Homo aestheticus*. Long before we learn from reason or propositions we understand through our senses and sensibilities. We need to forget some of the recent limiting associations of the word aesthetic and return it to its fundamental Greek meaning: *of or pertaining to aestheta, things perceptible by the senses*. Contrary to the exclusive claims of various cultural coteries, we are all by immediate biological disposition active aesthetes. This will be developed more fully in the next chapter.

Proposition Two

The arts work in and through the aesthetic. Together they comprise the differentiated symbolic forms of aesthetic response. They are the cultural vehicles for elaborating, deepening and refining the senses and of apprehending significance and value through them. This is to say that the arts are inherently cognitive, often ethical, and educational to the core. In the nineteenth century Ruskin talked of 'the sensual pleasures . . . rendered theoretic'. In our own time the American feminist, Adrienne Rich, talks of the poet as 'translating pulsations into images, for the relief of the body and the reconstruction of the mind'. Both Ruskin and Rich, in radically different contexts, are defining the nature of aesthetic experience as it is shaped by the mediating powers of art.

Proposition Three

The six great arts – visual art (including architecture and photography), drama (including theatre), dance, music, film, and literature – form a family of related practices, all working through aesthetic engagement, all concerned with the sensory expression of non-discursive meaning. *Together they form the generic community of the arts.* Therefore, it is logically right to insist that in any coherent aesthetic curriculum the tribe of six must be equally considered and each substantially included. (This is the theme of Chapter 5.)

Proposition Four

At the same time, while they share certain fundamental characteristics, it is also obvious that *each discipline has its own distinctive and public set of practices*: its own repertoire of conventions, its own lexicon of critical and technical terms, its own masterpieces, touchstones, exemplars. The latter is as true of the twentieth-century art, film, as it is for the other five ancient arts. No expressive act is possible in the arts without being somewhere, somehow, implicated in something symbolically larger than the self. 'I discovered', wrote Umberto Eco considering the composition of *The Name of the Rose*, 'what writers have always known (and have told us again and again): books always speak of other books, and every story tells a story that has already been told'. So much for the solitary emoting subject of progressive education! One of the primary aims of arts teachers is to activate the field of their own arts discipline. Chapters 7, 8 and 9 will examine the implications of this proposition for the teaching of drama and literature.

Proposition Five

The activation of the aesthetic field in arts education has to be dynamic and in intimate relationship with the imaginative and emotional life of the student. The aim is to engender a continuous interaction between the expressive and aesthetic energies of the student and the multiform energies embodied in the tradition. In this way, students move out to engage with the forms of the culture, while the forms of the culture, in turn, come to occupy their imagination and to inform their expressive acts. It is precisely this prolonged encounter between the self and the culture, often demanding, sometimes exhilarating, sometimes exhausting, that makes possible the growth, and development of sensibility, that indirect but specific achievement of aesthetic education.

Proposition Six

One aspect of this encounter *concerns the use of models and exemplars*. The practice of emulation and imitation (once based in the case of literature on a received rhetoric and poetics) was disowned by most progressive arts educators. Yet the argument for the initiation of the child into a distinctive set of symbolic practices calls for both a concept of arts learning as apprenticeship (the trying out of various genres, techniques and devices) and an exploratory playing with the seminal narratives of our long culture.

Proposition Seven

A deep historic and parodic imagination needs to be cultivated; an imagination that is not only able to attend carefully to works of art, but also to subvert and recast them: to tell the story, for example, of Robinson Crusoe through the character of Man Friday; the story of Noah from the point of view of a woodworm; to paint the image of Icarus, not as sublime protagonist, but as an insignificant splash in an ocean over which a trading ship passes undisturbed. Myths are stories that can be eternally retold to give other resonances, other meanings. In brief, the romantic anxiety about influence should now concede to a tougher, imaginative plagiarism. This is central to the new aesthetic.

Proposition Eight

A living awareness of the culture of each arts discipline comes with a tested apprenticeship in making, presenting, responding and evaluating – the four crucial phases in the art-making process (see Chapter 6). This process requires the imparting of critical terms, of practical techniques and a growing sense of the whole symbolic continuum – the jostling procession of major and minor names and works, the endless vivifying dialectic of movements and countermovements. So far in arts teaching we have been poor in offering such historic and technical guidance, particularly so in drama, dance and film.

Proposition Nine

Yet, at root, the arts must be taught through the aesthetic mode. The aim is to foster the kind of knowing that befits a work of art, the apprehension of meaning through sensuous engagement. The introduction of terms, of techniques, even of maps exist primarily to make *the senses more precise in their sensing of art, to guide the imagination into the formal aesthetic demands of the work*, to *focus the aesthetic intelligence*. In an age of excessive criticism, it is urgent that faith is kept with the sensuous apprehension of meaning; not to do so is to forego the condition necessary for the experience of art, and thus to deny the very foundations of aesthetic education.

Proposition Ten

But why does the experience of art matter so much? The question brings me to my last proposition. Fundamentally, the arts matter because they are able to render visible or audible profound transpersonal meanings. Wittgenstein wrote in the *Tractatus*: 'We feel that when all possible scientific questions have been answered the problems of life remain completely untouched'. It is these 'problems of life' that scientific enquiry cannot touch that the arts have the power and the symbolic means to address. The arts offer us metaphors illuminating the human condition. They provoke and nurture an understanding of ourselves. They subvert our habitual expectations to usher in new apprehensions of reality. They can break open our dull congealing minds to make them more perceptive. As both Matthew Arnold and Nietzsche predicted, the arts in our century have continued to take on the office once assigned to religion and philosophy. This, at one level, may make their position strained and problematic but, at another level, it defines their supreme educational position in our limited enterprise culture, our spiritually restricted consumer civilization. For the arts, more than any other disciplines of the questing mind, can offer, both in their creation and reception, redemptive experiences.

Conclusion

If the arts are essentially concerned with the life of consciousness – with its refinement, its elaboration, its deepening – then they must be central to the curriculum and must lie at the heart of any democratic civilization. Properly conceived, they are neither luxuries nor entertainments, but philosophical necessities and spiritual forces, nothing less. As Hegel wrote in his *Introductory Lectures on Aesthetics*:

> Fine art is not real art till it is in this sense free, and only achieves its highest task when it has taken its place in the same sphere with religion and philosophy, and has become simply a

mode of revealing to consciousness and bringing to utterance the Divine Nature, the deepest interests of humanity, and the most comprehensive truths of the mind.[6]

In this chapter I have sketched the philosophical and historical background for a revolution in our understanding of the arts in education. To understand the nature of this radical shift in paradigm, we need a better grasp of the aesthetic. We need a more developed sense of the nature of *the aesthetic field*, and of the arts as a *generic community* (two key concepts in the arts revolution). We need also a finer understanding of creativity in relationship to aesthetic experience and the aesthetic field. The following three chapters will further elaborate these major concepts.

Notes

1 PLATO (1871) *The Phaedo* (translated by B. Jowett) in *The Dialogues of Plato*, vol. 1, Oxford, Oxford at the Clarendon Press, p. 410.
2 ROBERT WITKIN (1974) *The Intelligence of Feeling*, London, Heinemann Educational Books, p. 1.
3 WALTER PATER (1873) *The Renaissance: Studies in Art and Poetry*, London, Macmillan, p. 235.
4 A.J. AYER (1946) *Language, Truth and Logic*, London, Gollancz, p. 113.
5 LOUIS ARNAUD REID (1989) 'The Arts within a Plural Concept of Knowledge', in PETER ABBS (ed.) *The Symbolic Order*, London, Falmer Press, p. 13.
6 G.W.F. HEGEL (1993) MICHAEL INWOOD (ed.) *Introductory Lectures on Aesthetics*, Harmondsworth, Penguin Books, p. 9. Hegel goes on to subordinate the arts to philosophy and also to state that the arts, as living forces, are largely over. These do not logically follow from the main assertion and there is no reason for us to follow in his steps in these matters.

Chapter 4

The Primacy of the Aesthetic: On the Nature of Aesthetic Response and the Meaning of the Aesthetic Field

By an aesthetic idea I mean the representation of the imagination which induces much thought, yet without the possibility of any definite thought whatever, i.e. concept, being adequate to it, and which language, consequently, can never get quite on level terms with or render completely intelligible.

Kant

Ideology, ideology, ideology, nowhere an aesthetic concept; the whole thing is like the description of a dish in which nothing is said about the taste. The first thing we have to do is institute exhibitions and courses, i.e. for the enjoyment of life.

Bertolt Brecht

The novel is Europe's creation; its discoveries, though made in various languages, belong to the whole of Europe. The sequence of discoveries (not the sum of what was written) is what constitutes the history of the European novel. It is only in such a supranational context that the value of a work (that is to say, the import of its discovery) can be fully seen and understood.

Milan Kundera

Introduction

There has been a powerful tendency in western culture to elevate the concept over metaphor and theory over art. This means that, often, in the mediation of the arts there has been a strong pressure to talk *about* art, to believe that we are only doing something educationally worth-while when we are converting aesthetic response into propositional meaning and critical argument. Yet the intrinsic meaning of a piece of music or a sculpture or a dance can never be fully converted into language and too much prior critical theory can blunt and constrain aesthetic response. We need, therefore, to understand the nature of aesthetic experience. What are its inherent characteristics? If we can begin to answer this question we will be in a better position to locate its intrinsic value and have reasons to resist some of the premature pressures to articulate theoretical and historical interpretations (which, at a later stage, have their fitting place).

I will begin with an analysis of aesthetic experience and then go on to explore the aesthetic field. What is meant by aesthetic field? It is one of the key concepts in the changing paradigm of arts education and refers to the whole complex artistic matrix in which individual works of art are both made and responded to. The teacher has the task of both inviting *immediate aesthetic response to works of art* and, also, of pro-gressively inviting the student *into the whole field of the art form*. This is not a progressive view, nor a traditional view, but one that characterizes the emerging arts paradigm presented in the last chapter.

An Experiment to Understand Aesthetic Response

Would the case for the arts become more compelling if we could dis-close their value through a presentation of moments of aesthetic experi-ence, of memorable encounters with art, as remembered and defined by those who have deeply experienced them? Very little work has been done in the field. We have had a number of educational philosophers and many fine practitioners but few phenomologists, collecting and revealing the moments of profound aesthetic engagement. There are, of course, as with any method, problems about doing such work: problems about prior selection, problems about the veracity of the subject's own accounts, problems about collation and interpretation. Yet it would seem self-defeating not to embark on the project simply because of the obvious difficulties especially when two authors in par-ticular have given us some conception of the positive results such work can yield. The two researchers are Professor David Hargreaves and Rod Taylor. One of the sources of their work is William James' *The Varieties of Religious Experience*. They are claiming that what we need is not so much abstract philosophical analysis as the phenomenological investigation of the varieties of aesthetic experience or what they call 'the illuminating experience'.

We will return to the work of David Hargreaves and Rod Taylor later. What I want to do first is to outline a limited experiment in the examination of aesthetic experience. I wanted to see if in the analysis of ten accounts of aesthetic experience by arts teachers (all of them Arts MA students, all given one week to write a short direct account of a memorable aesthetic experience in relationship to any work of art) I could discern a common structure and common value. What is offered here is the briefest excursion into a vast territory, but it is significant that the results largely confirm those of Professor Hargreaves and Rod Taylor. I asked a group of arts teachers doing the Language, Arts and Education MA at the University of Sussex to describe briefly and directly any memorable aesthetic moment in relationship to the arts.[1] As I collated and examined these 'moments' I began to see a clear and remarkable pattern emerging. In the following analysis I am not concerned with any one specific account but with the underlying structure *for there is a remarkable consistency in structure across the accounts*; and it is *this* structure that may give a very strong clue to their deep and abiding educational value.

Objects Chosen for the Analysis

I simply asked the arts teachers to write about any aesthetic experience they had had in relationship with a work of art – nothing more. The demand was that the account should describe the experience chosen as honestly as possible.

Here is a list of the ten events or objects the students wrote about:

John Constable's *The Hay Wain* (seen at the Tate Gallery),
Waterhouse's *The Lady of Shallot* (seen at the Tate Gallery),
Brenda Lenaghan's *Two Lovers and a Canary* (a contemporary painting),
A visit to Monet's garden at Giverny,
The mandala image on the cover of Carl Jung's *Man and his Symbols*,
Some sculpture seen in the sculptor's studio,
A solo Indian dancer,
Richard Strauss's *The Four Last Songs*,
A performance of *Coriolanus*,
A performance of *As You Like It*.

The Analysis of Aesthetic Response

The first close analysis of the ten responses led me to the following formulation:

> Aesthetic experience is *overwhelming*;
> it engages *powerful sensations*;
> it involves *feeling*;
> it brings a *heightened sense of significance*;
> but it *cannot be communicated adequately in words*; and
> it leaves one with *a desire for others to share it.*

Aesthetic Experience is Overwhelming

Nearly all of the accounts described an experience that was intense and utterly absorbing. Seven of the nine are entirely explicit on the point and use what could be termed the language of excited and tranced consciousness. Here are some typical sentences and phrases:

> I stood *mesmerized, enthralled.* I was *oblivious* to the gentle jostlings of the other visitors [in the Tate Gallery]. I was *transfixed* to the spot. (Jayne)

> I was *stunned* by the clarity of intention, *transfixed* and *inspired.* (Mary)

> *I was lost* . . . nothing was important but I was seeing and touching and feeling. (Jean)

> The beauty of it all *overwhelmed* me with emotion. (Pamela)

> *Total absorption.* (Liz)

> *Totally absorbed.* (Candace)

> *Drug-like.* Transcending. (Jon)

Louise wrote:

> From being a passive disinterested observer, I had become so involved that my breathing had changed rhythm, my mind had expanded and my imagination was on full alert.

Some of the accounts gave details of the effects of this trance-like state; Jayne mentioned how the voices in the Tate Gallery became 'faint, distant'. Liz in the theatre noticed 'the woman next to me whose huge body laps over my seat with her stertorous breathing is somehow *not present*'. Candace used the word 'spell' to describe the state and claimed that time dissolved. Liz similarly claimed 'time changes its pace. My desire is that it will never be concluded'. The participants in strong aesthetic experience would seem to enter the timeless moment.

Aesthetic Experience Engages Powerful Sensations

Jayne, gazing at *The Hay Wain*, confessed she wanted to touch the painting:

> tentatively raised a hand towards the painting. I dare not touch it. Would alarm bells sound?

Jean confronting a sculptured body similarly wrote:

> I just had to touch it. The smooth curves took my hands away from me and all I could think of was beauty.

Candace, looking at *The Lady of Shallot*, had the same kind of experience, the same need to touch:

> moved so much by this power of paint, I had a sudden urge to touch the rich drapes that covered her slender figure, examine the intricacy of the woven threads that formed the series of medieval pictures on the tapestry that hung from the side of the boat

Louise wrote: 'my senses were alive'.

Three of the accounts testified to a desire to cry. Watching the Indian dance Pamela wrote: 'I had to swallow hard to stop the tears coming'. Similarly Jon listening to Strauss's *The Four Last Songs* claimed to experience a 'physical tightening of the chest. Tears but not of pathos'. Similarly Jayne before Constable's *Hay Wain* wrote: 'I could feel the tears filling my eyes and a choking sensation in my throat as I tried in vain to suppress them'.

Two writers suggested that their sensation was strangely like that of *déjà-vu*. Phil wrote in relationship to the mandala on the cover of

Man and his Symbols: 'the nearest label I can come up with to hint at this strange sensation is *déjà-vu*'. Similarly Candace wrote of the figure in *The Lady of Shallot*: 'I experienced a strange feeling of *déjà-vu* – as if she was known to me, I *knew* her, knew the countryside that surrounded her – could hear the silence she inhabited, broken only by the swishing of water moving.'

Aesthetic Experience Involves Feeling

The encounter also involved deep feeling in as much as feeling can be differentiated from sensation and the general experience of being overwhelmed. 'Various emotions bombarded me', wrote Jayne, 'I felt humble, honoured, fortunate, ecstatic, exhilarated'. Likewise, Jean described her feelings as those of elation and ecstasy. In contrast, Candace's relationship to *The Lady of Shallot* was marked by a pervasive feeling of sadness. 'Yet over all', she wrote, 'this feeling of acute sadness prevailed. She touched qualities and emotions that leapt the centuries'. While Phil, moved by some kind of metaphysical insight before the mandala image, insisted: 'But it really wasn't a cold experience. It wasn't just ideas in my head, it involved feelings too.' Similarly, Louise maintained: 'I became almost as passionate in my emotions as the young people [depicted in the painting]'. All the accounts while not necessarily tabulating the nature of the feeling gave strong evidence of its existence.

Aesthetic Experience Brings a Heightened Sense of Significance

Novalis in one of his aphorisms asserted: 'All absolute sensation is religious'. Initially, this might strike one as a rather perverse and dogmatic notion. Yet reading the ten accounts of aesthetic experience by the MA students I was constantly reminded of it, for the sensation described seemed to be *saturated with meaning* and the meaning outlined seemed to include the person as a spell-bound *participant* in something immeasurably larger. The sense of the mind being engaged is strongly present in most of the accounts. 'My mind had expanded . . . the painting excited me mentally and physically', wrote Louise. 'My head was so full of questions but only after I had taken the time to breathe what I was seeing and touching and feeling', wrote Jean. Pamela, responding to a solo Indian dance, formulated the sudden sense of heightened significance as a question:

Is it the revelation of the spiritual element in us, touching some universal collective nerve of experience which the act transcends; goes beyond simply the movement of limbs or vocal chords; reaches higher?

In a similar manner Mary, responding to Monet's garden, wrote 'the eternity of vision lives on, and I am in it'. The essence of a mysterious participation, an encounter, is brought out well in Candace's report: 'I felt like a child who had a secret possession hidden away in a small pocket, felt myself uplifted [this is in relationship to an experience where sadness has been the predominant feeling] by the secret mysterious experience of the encounter within the painting'.

The sense of the significance of the elation is brought out well in David's account of his experience of a particular production of Coriolanus:

It was, I believe, because the space between the stage and myself had vanished: the play, the production and the audience had achieved a scintillating and extraordinary harmony – this ephemeral theatrical moment had become a unique part of my permanent experience by placing me both standing on the stage looking out and seated with the audience looking in; because we were all of us in those moments, a living part of this thrilling whole.

The feeling of being tribally grounded in some universal is almost inescapable. It involves a kind of shedding of normal mundane consciousness and the willing participation in something infinitely larger in which one feels truly and absolutely alive, a form of transcendence. 'Such beauty', exclaimed Jean, 'Such universality of work. Such authority. And I was part of it. I was *there*, what else can I say?'

The sense of witnessing a universal is strongly present in Phil's account of his response to a book-jacket in a quiet library when he was a teenager:

It was complete unto itself and self-contained. Although the colours were quite subdued, the whole design glowed. A very striking feature was its minute organization and articulation. I didn't study the details of the design then, I simply took in the whole image at a glance.

I was sort of startled by it. The most startling thing behind all the experience was that I seemed to recognize it, and that it seemed to have a definite meaning. It seemed to be very, very significant.

It was as if this image positively radiated meaning. Although I could not, and still cannot, articulate the significance which this image conveyed to me, it WAS a specific meaning.

This reaction to the mandala might tempt one to go into all kinds of speculation and theorizing. Now I feel strongly that all that just takes you away from it. Whatever profundity or meaning there is, is simply *in* this image. The 'depth' is on the surface.

The last observation brings us to a further characteristic of aesthetic experience, at least as testified by the ten teachers. It cannot be adequately conceptualized. It seems to defy translation; yet, at the same time, one who has had such an experience often longs to share it, to find a language to convey the meaning of the sensation.

Aesthetic Experience Cannot Be Communicated Adequately in Words

Four of the accounts were explicit on this matter. Jon, responding to Richard Strauss's *The Four Last Songs* wrote 'the nub of this state is impossible and elusive to point, language here only operates in peripheral terms'. Phil makes the same kind of point with regard to the mandala image: 'It was a direct intuition. All this is very mysterious. Words can't be used. Even more, thoughts don't seem to be able to contain the meaning which this sign had for me'. Pamela for her part, watching the Indian dance, asserted her conviction that: 'Such moments are in a sense beyond words, difficult to analyse: a connection, a feeling, elation' and went on to refer to Nietzsche's 'will to power as Art' and 'the enhancement of life.' Jayne, before *The Hay Wain*, reiterated the point: 'words are inadequate – that I had seen this canvas – in the flesh'.

Aesthetic Experience Can Include a Desire for Others to Share It

'There is a sense of well-being', wrote Liz recalling her feelings at the end of the production of *As You Like It*, 'and a strong desire to smile and speak to other members of the audience – to celebrate our remarkable good fortune in having been present here'. Candace looking at the painting *The Lady of Shallot* 'felt sure that others looking at her would experience the same emotion, indeed, I *hope* that they would do so'. She also claimed that, while she had no desire whatsoever to 'verbalize' her 'excitement' while looking at the painting, she felt the need to later: 'it was only later on reflection that I wanted (or indeed felt able) to talk about it and share it in its truest form'. Likewise, while recognizing that no language could capture the significance of his appreciation of Strauss's music, Jon was emphatic about his desire to communicate his experience. He wrote, simply: 'wanted to share'.

The Illuminating Experience: The Work of David Hargreaves and Rod Taylor

Having made the above analysis of the structural elements that seemed to inhere in the aesthetic moments or, at least, in most of them, I returned to the work of David Hargreaves and Rod Taylor. Here the characteristics of the aesthetic moment or what, in the context of *first* important responses to works of art, Professor Hargreaves prefers to call 'the conversive trauma' of liberating response, are seen to divide into four key stages, namely: *the powerful concentration of attention, a sense of revelation, inarticulateness, the arousal of appetite.*

In *The Visual Arts in Education* (1992) Rod Taylor elaborated on each of these four stages in terms of his own research. He wrote:

> The pupils and students I interviewed substantiated Hargreaves' research through testimonies which provided further evidence of key characteristics and outcomes of the illuminating experience. In the most marked examples there was reference to what Hargreaves calls *concentration of attention*. One can literally lose a sense of time and place as one is drawn into the orbit of the art work: 'It just flew past . . . it didn't seem like an hour and a half – more like ten minutes'; 'It almost seemed to be in the whole of your view . . . your attention was drawn to it.' The second element is *sense of revelation*: 'It seemed a totally different form of Art'; 'It was a complete eye-opener.' It is not just the art form, or a new and unexpected dimension of it, which is being opened up, but it is 'as if some already existing core of the self is suddenly being touched and brought to life for the first time, and yet inevitably so.' The third element is *inarticulateness*. I have described this as the art educator's nightmare for, whereas pupils often have no inhibitions about informing

the teacher that 'it was boring', those positively affected do not necessarily formulate the experience into words for their own sake, let alone to communicate with others. Some people will keep the experience to themselves for years . . . Another key element is *arousal of appetite*. 'One simply wants the experience to continue or be repeated, and this can be felt with considerable urgency.' Arousal of appetite can be highly motivating, meaning that commitment and the desire for further exploration are two important outcomes of the illuminating experience. (My emphasis)[2]

The reader will notice that Hargreaves' 'powerful concentration of attention' largely corresponds with my first three categories, namely that 'aesthetic experience is overwhelming', 'engages powerful sensations' and 'involves feeling'. Both accounts draw attention to the reported state of timelessness through being 'totally absorbed'. Hargreaves' 'sense of revelation' is akin to my fourth category 'a heightened sense of significance' while his 'state of inarticulateness' is all but synonymous with my fifth category 'cannot be communicated adequately in words'. Our final categories, though, point in different directions; Hargreaves' arousal of appetite points towards a desire to repeat the experience (implicit, no doubt, in many of my teachers' accounts) and to discursively understand more about it; while my category 'aesthetic experience can include a desire for others to share it' may point to a universality of meaning in the artwork. If they are true, both are extremely valuable for the first has profound implications for the teaching of the arts (given detailed practical formulation in the work of Rod Taylor) and the second confirms the view that the arts are about transpersonal acts of knowing that are valued because they reveal the lineaments of a common world through the power of imagination. That would explain why we desire so much to share these moments with others.

This degree of agreement between the two accounts suggests that we are close to discerning the state of consciousness in relationship to art that holds its own educational justification. We are on the trail leading to *a defence of aesthetic response as primary and primordial engagement, as acts of revelation, as the tranced states of virtually inexplicable understanding, of modes of cognition 'free from concepts' to use Kant's formulation.*

But have we come, at this point, too far from the teaching of the arts in the classroom? Well, yes and no. Yes, in the sense that no arts teacher can possibly hope to engender these aesthetic moments of apprehension in every lesson. But no, in the sense that these experiences must remain crucial in the teaching of the arts, so that one could say categorically that if one's students had never had such experience, they wouldn't and *couldn't* know what the true nature of art is.

Here is an account of an aesthetic moment in the teaching of music to a third-year class in a comprehensive school. It is a lucid description by the music teacher, Marian Metcalfe, of a moment of collective participation in an immensely moving musical experience:

We began. 'Food deserves to go to Ethiopia' they sang. They weren't taking it very seriously, but they were giving it a go. The Gs sounded all right, the Ds having the 'tune' were secure, the Bs, trapped in the middle, were wavering. But it was there – just.

Then something happened. You could feel it. The room went intense. As they sang their faces changed. They stopped looking at each other and became still. Fingers firmly clamped in one ear, their eyes took on that far-away expression you sometimes see at revival meetings or rock concerts. A few even had their eyes closed. The sound changed, became charged, began to be active in the room. Two girls began to improvise on the three notes, singing above the general sound level, turning it into a hypnotic background. Gradually, the intensity gripped us all. Time took on a different quality. We seemed to be sinking down to the prehistory beginnings, the tribe at the sacred place invoking the Powers, calling up the Spirits, bridging the gap between man and elements and deity, all caught up together in the mystery of existence.

Gradually, slowly, as if awakening from a sleep, it came to an end. Perhaps, it had lasted a minute or an hour. I turned off the tape recorder unobtrusively. There was nothing to say. We all felt that. I looked at them, and they looked at me, and there was silence between us.

The bell rang and they went away quietly. I watched them go. They didn't appear to be saying much to each other at all. I felt shaken by what had happened.

That was really what I learnt from my third years in my comprehensive school that day. That there is a way back. Or forward, depending on your interpretation. My problem as a teacher is, do I take it? Should I take it? There are many issues here, many questions to ask and answers to be found before proceeding at all. For make no mistake about it. What happened was a fundamental thing, not to be approached lightly or without responsibility. And it couldn't be 'used' without affecting these kids in ways whose outcomes could not be predicted.[3]

What is the answer to the unease that Marian Metcalfe expresses? Certainly it should not lie in playing down or wanting to explain away the experience. While in no way wishing to deny that there can be many other less intense moments of attention to be recognized and appreciated, this moment of aesthetic transcendence must lie at the heart of the value of artistic activity. But one of the responsibilities of the art teacher is to be able to place such moments in a broader matrix; he or she is there to provide a frame in which such moments can be generated and a bed of culture in which they can be further developed and extended.

It is a matter partly of providing an awareness of technique, of providing a knowledge of the cultural continuum of the particular art form (a living awareness of the whole symbolic field in which it operates), and also of providing a language, *not* to explain the aesthetic moment, *not* to fully formulate and translate it, but to narrate and explore and relate it; at times this will be a technical language; at times it will be an interpretative language; at other times, a broad philosophical language. In this way the aesthetic moment is brought into the culture, and the culture, in turn, is animated by the raw power of the experience. Indeed, it is this interaction that arts teachers exist to promote, keeping in motion a reciprocal play between moments of *personal revelation* and the *collective revelation* implicit in the tradition of the art form (and all the techniques and formal possibilities that have been developed in relationship to that urge for meaning and disclosure).

In David Hargreaves' account of the aesthetic moment, the final stage of the experience, the arousal of appetite, leads naturally to this concern for judgment, context and knowledge:

> Then *commitment leads to exploration*. Initially one might, of course, simply seek a repetition of the original traumatising experience where this is possible – think how during an exhibition one often returns to look at pictures which have moved one very deeply, or perhaps one buys a gramophone record of a work which has been overwhelming during a concert performance – but normally one is soon led to explore other works by the same *artist*. This then leads to a more general exploration of the art form, often in a rather tentative and experimental way, by selecting works which are similar to the original traumatising

work. Thus one buys a book of other expressionist's string quartets to those of Schubert. All this is accompanied by a sense of increasing discovery and exploration and a concomitant gain in motivation. Then *exploration leads to discrimination.*[4]

This discrimination leads, in Hargreaves' interpretation, to the search for background knowledge, to the search for a biography of the artist, critical evaluations of the art form, studies of the artist's techniques and so forth. In other words, an important and unfolding element in the aesthetic moment would move towards the very work that I am claiming it is the responsibility of the arts teacher to develop. In that case, handled with care, the chances of success are very high, for then the curriculum and the students' motivating desire are running together – and that is the best and perhaps only condition for authentic learning.

The first concern in arts teaching is to establish a frame in which genuine aesthetic engagement can be released; the second is with the rooting of aesthetic response into the field of the relevant art form. Aesthetic field is a key concept in the new arts paradigm. So what is meant by it?

The Aesthetic Field

The aesthetic field refers to *the whole symbolic system in which individual work is made.* Here, for example, is how Helene Cixous in an article significantly entitled 'Listening to the Truth' described the process of composition when writing fiction:

> I don't begin with a phrase, the phrases come, joining themselves musically in the service of my theme. I use language rather as I imagine a painter uses colour. I must paint with accuracy. My singing must be in key. And language helps me to achieve this. It has its own song, own system of signifiers and phonic associations, its own cultural and poetic memory, it brings its own treasures, its own patterns and harmonies, which work together as I write.[5]

She shows how in writing her own 'original' work she is, inevitably, caught up in the field of language and its entire living history. This is not radically different from the notion of the simultaneous order first put forward by T.S. Eliot in 1917. Eliot claimed:

The historical sense compels a man to write not merely with his own generation in his bones, but with a feeling that the whole of the literature of Europe from Homer and within it the whole of the literature of his own country has a simultaneous existence and composes a simultaneous order. The historical sense, which is a sense of the timeless as well as of the temporal and of the timeless and of the temporal together, is what makes a writer traditional. And it is at the same time what makes a writer most acutely conscious of his place in time, of his own contemporaneity.[6]

The aesthetic field, then, refers to that complex interactive system of allusion, reference and structure in which individual expressions of art are necessarily constituted, from Sappho to Anne Stevenson, from the cave paintings of horses in Lascaux to Elizabeth Frink, from Balinese music to Benjamin Britten and John Adams. One of the most dramatic examples of the aesthetic field in dynamic action is that of the composition of Coleridge's poem *Kubla Khan*. Coleridge before he fell asleep had been reading a travel book *Purchas his Pilgrimage*. There he read the following sentence:

In Xanadu did Cublai Can build a stately Palace, encompassing sixteene miles of plaineground with a wall, wherein are fertile Meddowes, pleasant Springs, delightful streames, and all sorts of beasts of chase and game, and in the middest thereof a sumptuous house of pleasure.[8]

In his dream, Coleridge wrote that 'the images rose up before him as *things*, with a parallel production of the correspondent expressions, without any sensation or consciousness of effort'. Yet the key magical words, images and rhythms can all be found in the travel book he had been perusing. The poem, in part, derives most tangibly from the style and content of another book. These are the opening lines of Coleridge's unfinished poem:

> In Xanadu did Kubla Khan
> A stately pleasure-dome decree:
> Where Alph, the sacred river, ran
> Through caverns measureless to man
> > Down to a sunless sea.

Similarly, David Lodge in writing his novel *Small World* confessed to the creativity of converging influences, of pressurizing exemplars.

In his notebook, preparing for the novel and reflecting Socratically on the process of composition, he wrote:

'What could provide the basis for a story?' and just below that: 'Could some myth serve, as in *Ulysses*?' (I was thinking of the way Joyce used the story of Odysseus to give shape to one day in the lives of several modern Dubliners.) And just below that: 'E.g. the Grail legend – involves a lot of different characters and long journeys.'

What made me think of the Grail legend? Well, I had just been to see the somewhat preposterous but very enjoyable film, *Excalibur*, and been reminded of what a wonderfully gripping narrative it was, the story of King Arthur and the knights of the Round Table. But I was thinking also of T.S. Eliot's use of the Grail legend in *The Waste Land* as a structural device comparable to Joyce's use of the Odyssey – the Grail legend as reinterpreted by Jessie Weston in her book *From Ritual to Romance*. And the more I thought, and read, about romance as a genre, extending far beyond the medieval tales of King Arthur and his knights, from the Greek romances of antiquity, to the Renaissance epic romances of Ariosto and Spenser, and the romantic comedies and tragicomedies of Shakespeare, the more convinced I became that I had found the structural principle for *Small World*.[9]

David Lodge's account of the genesis of *Small World* demonstrates the power of the literary matrix – and his account only points to a few of the conscious influences, not to the web of unconscious forces that also guide the writer's hand, shaping the very rhythm and syntax of much of the thought and sentiment. In the visual arts, too, one can trace similar creative derivations. Goya's *Majas* derives from Velasquez's *The Toilet of Venus*, Matisse's dance figures derive from Mantegna's *Parnassus* and Ingres' *L'Age d'Or*, while all of Picasso's work can be viewed as a febrile ransacking of the entire visual history of western culture as well as primitive art. From the perspective of the aesthetic field, nearly all culture is an urgent affair of revision and re-visioning. Our long European culture is, in very large measure, an endless protean reworking of classical myths and Biblical narratives.

There is nothing inherently fixed about the concept of the aesthetic field, however. Just as in quantum physics the field creates a variety of forms that it sustains, then takes back, then creates again in new patterns, so in the aesthetic field the complex relationships between the parts are changing all the time, recast at different times by the driving power of different ideological movements, critical theories and artistic schools. Thus, to take one example, Donald Davie reviewing the work of the until recently obscure English poet Ivor Gurney (1890–1937) wrote:

> in Gurney we have to reckon no longer with a wistful and appealing figure in the margin but with a poet whose achievement, now that we can measure the full scope of it, demands a rewriting of the accepted accounts of English poetry this century.[10]

It is a critical claim that, if accepted, has the power to change the prevailing pattern of literary mapping. *Any major and widely accepted re-evaluation alters the relationships between other works in the field.* This is now happening on a grand scale across all the arts with the challenging of modernism by the contending forces of postmodernism. In our own century feminism has profoundly altered the simultaneous order of the arts. It is a vital process activated by the contending claims of critical and artistic movements and the counter claims to which they in turn give birth. The model is not a static one of fixed canons, yet certain figures in any of the symbolic fields are likely to remain constant (Homer, George Eliot, Picasso, Kurosawa, Mozart, Martha Graham), although the ways in which we interpret them will change constantly and, at times, quite radically.

The implications of such a conception for the teaching of the arts are enormous. Above all, it suggests that one of the primary tasks of arts teachers is to initiate their pupils into the vast, interactive symbolic system of their disciplines, and to do so in the manner of engaging aesthetic experience (as described earlier), not inert knowledge. One of the more positive elements of the national curriculum in England has been the insistence on the aesthetic field (though its application is narrower than the one defined above). This book has already been critical of the reorganization of the curriculum and will be again in the next chapter when the collective condition of the arts are examined, but *here* there is some common ground. For example, in the *Order for Music in the National Curriculum* (1992) it is stated that (at the end of stage 3 under 'Listening and Appraising') students should 'show a knowledge of the historical development of music, and an understanding of a range of musical traditions from different periods and cultures'. In the illustrative examples it is suggested that the pupils listen to:

. . . examples of Gregorian chant, orchestral music such as Handel's *Music for the Royal Fireworks*, an opera such as Verdi's *Il Trovatore*, Savoy opera by Gilbert and Sullivan such as *The Mikado*, music for ballet such as Prokofiev's *Romeo and Juliet*, a musical such as Bernstein's *West Side Story*.

Recognise and talk about traditions such as Scottish fiddle music, Indian raga or Indonesian gamelan.

Listen to and discuss music by composers such as Tallis, Monteverdi, Bach, Mozart, Beethoven, Schubert, Wagner, Verdi, Tchaikovsky, Debussy, Mahler, Stravinsky, Elgar, Sibelius and Tippett.[11]

The catalogue of names and works across various cultures suggest the aesthetic field of music, the simultaneous order, in which the individual work must, sympathetically or dialectically, take its place.

Similarly, in the *Order for Art in the National Curriculum* (1992), the aesthetic field of visual art is suggested in a range of examples. Here are those listed for attainment target 2 of '*Knowledge and Understanding at Key Stage 1*':

Consider how themes, such as 'Mother and Child', are expressed in different kinds of art; e.g. icons, sculptures of Henry Moore, the paintings of Leonardo da Vinci and Mary Cassatt, and in African tribal art.

Compare the different ways that animals and plants are represented in different times and cultures, in medieval carvings and in the work of Rousseau, Stubbs and Elizabeth Frink.

Draw children playing in the local park or school playground after talking about L.S. Lowry's paintings.

Compare the way they use colour in their own drawings and paintings of flowers with the work of other artists, e.g. William Morris and Vincent Van Gogh.[12]

How far this is from Herbert Read's *Education through Art* (analysed in Chapter 10), and how much more challenging! At the top of the page outlining the above suggestions it is clearly stated that the understanding of artistic traditions must relate to the student's own work and that creative and practical connections must be made between the two. This is essential because, if the argument in this chapter is sound, it is not *knowledge about* that is crucial in the teaching of the arts but *aesthetic participation in*, where the understanding gained is primarily through the aesthetic modality and not through the factual memory or discursive

knowledge. The orders for music, art and dance sufficiently allow for
the interaction between the individual and the culture and recognize, to
a considerable extent, the unique and irreducible value of aesthetic
response. Here there is a modicum of hope – although the amount of
time given for the new arts agenda is far too limited and the fact that
they stop as foundation subjects at the age of 14 is symptomatic, dis-
closing once again a deep lack of understanding of the aesthetic and a
dramatic failure to give it equality with other kinds of understanding.
If the battle for the recognition of the aesthetic field has partly been
won (at least for dance, music and art), the broader struggle for aesthetic intelligence and aesthetic understanding has still to be fought.
The insight of Kant that the imagination is 'a productive faculty of
cognition', claimed in 1790, has still to find a fitting educational
context, as has the concept of the generic community of the arts to
which we must now turn.

Notes

1 This first limited experiment in charting aesthetic experience in relationship to works of art has resulted in a more formal organization of questions. The reader may be interested in the 'experiential' questionnaire
which reads as follows:
Exploring the Nature of Aesthetic Response. Take any major aesthetic experience you have had in relationship to any work of art.
   A. *Details*
      1 What was the work of art?
      2 Where did you encounter it?
      3 What age were you?
   B. *The Experience*
      Try and describe as directly and fully as you can the nature of the
      experience.
   C. *Reflections on the Experience*
      1 Looking, again, at your account have you any further reflections
         on the nature or structure of the experience to add?
      2 Had anything prepared you for this experience?
      3 What subsequent effects, if any, did the experience have on you
         in relationship to the art and in relationship to your life as a
         whole?
      4 Can you say what qualities it was in the work of art that released
         your response? Could it have been induced by *any* work of art or
         any other object?
2 ROD TAYLOR (1992) *The Visual Arts in Education*, London, Falmer Press,
p. 7.

3 MARIAN METCALFE (1986) 'A Letter from Marian', *Music Teacher*, May, p. 27.
4 DAVID HARGREAVES (1983) MALCOLM ROSS (ed.) *The Arts: A Way of Knowing*, Oxford, Pergamon Press, p. 133.
5 HELENE CIXOUS (1989) 'Listening to the Truth', in SUSAN SELTERS (ed.) *Delighting the Heart: A Notebook by Womens Writers*, The Womens Press, p. 69.
6 T.S. ELIOT (1975) FRANK KERMODE (ed.) *Selected Prose of T.S. Eliot*, London, Faber and Faber, p. 38.
7 For an excellent account of the creative composition of *Kubla Khan* see KATHLEEN RAINE (1985) 'Traditional Symbolism in *Kubla Khan*', in *Defending Ancient Springs*, Ipswich, Golgonooza Press.
8 *Ibid.*, p. 89.
9 DAVID LODGE (1986) *Write On*, London, Secker and Warburg, pp. 72–3.
10 DONALD DAVIE (1990) in *The Independent*, 25 August.
11 See (1992) *Order for Music in the National Curriculum*, London, April, DES/WO, p. 9.
12 See (1992) *Order for Art in the National Curriculum*, London, April, DES/WO, p. 4.

Chapter 5

The Generic Community of the Arts: Its Historical Development and Educational Value

If we no longer believe in our own civilisation the forces of vulgarity and barbarism will surely triumph.

Ernst Gombrich

The different arts disciplines have a number of common characteristics and should be planned for together as a generic part of the school curriculum. This idea has been gathering force in education over a number of years. It has been articulated in different ways by various influential writers, researchers and practitioners in arts education including Malcolm Ross, David Aspin, Peter Abbs, Robert Witkin and David Best

Arts 5–16 Curriculum Framework

Introduction

'The six great arts . . . form a family of related practices. Together they form the generic community of the arts.' So it was stated in the manifesto at the end of Chapter 3. It is central to the new arts paradigm yet it is not, by any means, a new idea. In the heat of recent controversy engendered by the narrow limitations of the national curriculum we have overlooked how old and tested a conception it is.

Aristotle was one of the first to propose in his *Poetics* that the arts belong structurally together (though the idea would seem to be implicit in Plato's *Republic*). In his account, Aristotle lists dance, drama, music, literature and art, the five arts that with the exception of film (arriving as a dramatic addition to the arts in our own century) have remained the art forms central to western culture, the fine arts, as they have often been called. Aristotle's work could be justly deemed the first structuralist account of the arts. While mostly concentrating on the nature of dramatic art, Aristotle argues that all of the arts can be described in general terms (notice the word *general* related to *genus* and *generic*) as 'imitations or representations of life', and that then they can be differentiated according to either their media, the objects represented or the manner in which they are represented. Furthermore, in the opening general reflections Aristotle locates the source of mankind's various artistic activities in our natural aptitudes, in our biology, in an innate desire to imitate and an innate disposition towards rhythm (another idea that one can also find powerfully present in Plato's aesthetics). In brief, what we discover in Aristotle's *Poetics* is a very early formulation of the arts as a generic community. The dialectical method used by Aristotle makes clear, first, the general characteristics (all art is concerned with representation, with *mimesis*) and then proceeds to isolate some of the differences while rooting the whole phenomenon in the universal dispositions of human nature.

In our own century the idea that the arts (in this case with the addition of film) formed a generic community in need of a coherent philosophy was put forward over four decades ago by Susanne Langer in *Feeling and Form*. The title alone gives a strong indication of the book's major thesis. Following the work of Ernst Cassirer and, more broadly, the tradition of Kant she argued that all art involved 'the creation of forms symbolic of human feeling'. She went on:

> The making of this expressive form is the creative process that enlists a man's utmost technical skill in the service of his utmost conceptual power, imagination . . .
>
> To expound that principle, and develop it in each autonomous realm of art, is the only way to justify the definition.[1]

The concerns are identical with Aristotle's: to name the general principle that unites all the arts and, then, to differentiate according to each of the distinctive types; a kind of genus and species methodology or taxonomy. For Susanne Langer, as for Aristotle, the arts belong together as a logical group made up of autonomous members. These examples provide a frame for the discussion of generic thinking about the arts in education. Certainly the idea cannot be dismissed lightly as an 'expedient myth' or a kind of fad dreamt up by educationists in response to current pressures.

In the educational context there has not been, it is true, such systematic thinking as that provided by Langer, but there has been considerable reflection on the nature of the aesthetic and the value of the arts, in, for example, the work of Louis Arnaud Reid, Paul Hirst and

R.S. Peters and in the US, the work of Philip Phenix and Howard Gardner. Much of the thinking about the arts in education, as we have seen in earlier chapters, has had to struggle against the grain of the pre-selections and pre-locations of subjects, and, beyond that, against the profound apathy of the English towards all sensuous cultural manifestations, all eruptions or revolutions of compelling thought and feeling, whether foreign or indigenous. These initiatives have been badly hampered by a lack of a philosophical tradition in both educational thinking and in aesthetics. They have been overdependent on psychology and sociology. In particular, they have worked alone in a kind of hermeneutic isolation, sometimes forging an uncongenial language, often unwittingly repeating what had been done in some other pocket of isolation before them. It is becoming increasingly clear at the end of the twentieth century that they were also too deeply influenced by the most questionable assumptions of modernism and progressivism (and, one must add, Marxism), all of which turned mindlessly away from the past, thus seriously neglecting the vital cultural continuum transmitted down the generations. These major ideologies led to either an elevation of contemporary and ideologically relevant work or of the self-expressing, self-emoting solitary individual.

At the same time, the formidable attempt to draw the arts together, to conceive them holistically, to bring them into productive self-consciouness and relationship, has been, without a doubt, a positive force; and it is to the slow and spasmodic evolution of this transformative idea, still struggling to find its best conceptual form and practice, that I first wish to turn.

The Arts in the English Curriculum: An Historical Sketch

To narrate the story of the arts in the English curriculum is to tell a story of division and dislocation, a story of different traditions, different goals, different concepts, different pedagogies, different budgets, different placements and priorities. There has always been a remarkable gap between rhetorical claims and actual realities. All the main educational reports from Hadow[2] (1926) to Newson[3] (1963) affirm the educational significance of the arts and decry their neglect and their insecure status in the curriculum. The Spens Report[4] (1938) for example urged that 'a more prominent and established place in the ordinary curriculum of schools should be assigned to the aesthetic subjects'. In similar vein, The Norwood Report[5] (1943) pointed out that the arts

73

were 'too often regarded as 'special' when the one thing required is that they should be regarded as normal subjects'. It offered a brief historical explanation for their eccentric position:

> When they were adopted into the curriculum they occupied an uneasy position, lying apart from the rest of it; there seemed uncertainty – less perhaps as regards art – how they were related to other subjects, and they *themselves* did not always justify their inclusion on grounds which carried conviction.[6]

The Newsom Report pointed similarly to the neglect of the arts claiming that only half the schools examined by the committee had proper accommodation for the visual arts and less than a quarter had a proper music room and went on to affirm that non-academic children could gain 'intense creative satisfaction in making and doing', in this way giving what they called necessary constructive expression to the common life of human feeling.

The affirmation of the arts in these official reports is as morally earnest as it is conceptually confused. It is not at all clear which subjects taken together collectively constitute the arts nor quite why they matter educationally except that they relate in some unspecified way to the life of feeling and contribute in some vague way to the life of civilization. The rhetoric is magnanimous but the arguments are minimal and the structures advocated are muddled. There is nothing like an epistemological grounding of the arts, nor any common conception of good practice. The arts are invariably grouped under different educational categories and in some cases not listed at all – drama, dance and film being most prone to exclusion or, if not exclusion, severe marginalization. This has, of course, continued right into the national curriculum and remains one of the educational scandals of our century. To examine the way in which the major educational reports structure and allocate the arts disciplines is to quickly make visible and explicit their fundamental disunity and division in the curriculum. Take, for example, some of the key reports in chronological order starting with The Hadow Report of 1927 and ending with The Newsom Report of 1963.

The Hadow Report in 1927 states that the school is an ordered society in which children are disciplined into forms of activity that have permanent significance. It divides these activities into two kinds, 'the moral and physical activities'. The former comprise 'moral and religious instruction', general physical training, dancing and corporate games (to foster the spirit of team work). So here in 1927 we find dance – referring in this context to folk-dancing – and PE yoked together and separated from intellectual activities.

The intellectual activities are seen as being necessary for an understanding of the body of human civilization and for an active participation in its process. They divide into six categories as follows:

1 Language, including literature and the arts of writing and reading. Under this heading may be included both the study of English in its various aspects, and that of a foreign language.
2 Geography and history, of which the former on its physical side has connections with natural science, and the latter is closely related to the study of literature.
3 Mathematics, including the elementary study of number and space.
4 Elementary science.
5 Handwork, including drawing and applied art, and the various branches of practical instruction.
6 Music.[7]

From the perspective of a unified arts community, one needs to notice the fragmentation of the arts. Dance (in a minimal form) is annexed to PE and RE; literature is linked to a foreign language and history; art is seen as being applied and related to handwork and 'the various branches of practical instruction', while music alone is given autonomy. Drama is not included, nor, for obvious reasons, is film (Eisenstein completed his film masterpiece *The Battleship Potemkin* in 1925, two years before the publication of the report).

This fractured pattern, essentially *ad hoc* in nature, essentially mindless in typology, was to be typical of the reports and the curricular organization that followed. The Spens Report in 1938 eloquently affirmed the value of the aesthetic and all but identified it as a great modality of understanding to be distinguished from the discursive. It claimed with an almost visionary directness:

We take first Music and the Arts for their value in awakening and developing that aesthetic sensibility which is one of the most valuable of human gifts, and which, although its possibilities vary greatly from one child to another, is wholly denied to none. In the past, particularly in boys' schools, these subjects have often received too little attention, but we believe that their importance is now more generally recognised. We still, however, feel it necessary to reaffirm the recommendation which we made in our report on Differentiation of Curricula between the Sexes in Secondary Schools (1923, p. 138): 'That a more prominent and established place in ordinary curricula of schools for both boys and girls should be assigned to aesthetic subjects, including Music, Art and other forms of aesthetic training, and that spatial attention should be paid to developing the capacity for artistic appreciation as distinct from executive skill.' We feel this training to be as important as the training of the intellect through Languages, Sciences and Mathematics, and should like to see a larger proportion of the school hours available to subjects of this nature.[8]

Even so, when it offered its own grouping of subjects the report obscured and betrayed its own best insights. Its emphasis on developing the capacity for 'artistic appreciation as distinct from executive skill' did not prevent the coupling of music and art with handicraft and domestic science; nor did it offer any formal place to dance and drama; furthermore, it kept literature bracketed with English, religious knowledge, history and geography. The Spens Report laid the foundation for the grammar schools and those schools, while genuinely committed to the life of culture, never provided a thorough practical education in all the arts or transmitted any living (or dead) sense of their multifarious interconnections.

The grouping provided by The Spens Report of 'Music, Art, Handicraft, Domestic Science', was to be taken up and endorsed in subsequent reports. The 1943 Norwood Report, for example, declared 'Art, Music and Handicraft have certain affinities which entitle them to be discussed together'. In the 1947 publication *The New Secondary Education* they become entitled 'the practical subjects'. In that report it is claimed that 'the practical subjects that will be taken include physical education, art, music, handicraft, housecraft and various kinds of craft work and, wherever possible, gardening and animal husbandary'. What is at work here is a reorganizing of the Hadow Report's bifurcation of 'moral and physical activities' and 'intellectual activities'. The moral (taking with it religious education) has been housed with the intellectual and the physical has been expanded to take in any activity where the hand might be a constructive and fashioning agent – for it is very hard to see what, apart from that, could unite music with animal husbandry. It is, in truth, a rag-bag category, the outcome of facile thinking and the inertia of inherited and unexamined practice. It testifies to an English tradition that has left the vast majority of its pupils culturally illiterate and aesthetically maladjusted.

The notion of 'the practical subjects' is taken up and further applied in The Newsom Report of 1963 where the arts become absurdly divided into two isolated camps. What *is* positive about The Newsom Report is that most of the arts, particularly film and television, *are* generously recognized. When considering the necessary activities of the curriculum, the report recommends that 'attention to imaginative experience through the arts and the promotion of personal and social development are essential'. The report divides school activities into three categories: the practical subjects, science and mathematics and the humanities. Some of the arts are placed under practical subjects, others under the humanities. Thus under practical subjects we discover arts and studio craft, handicrafts, rural studies, housecraft, needlework, PE and music; while under the humanities, we discover drama, film and literature all, significantly, grouped under English (a kind of grouping that was to be perpetuated under the national curriculum and the Education Act of 1988) and placed alongside a second Language and history, geography and religious education. In brief, the report offers a structure that divides the arts into two epistemological groups. In spite of its recognition of the expressive element, there are similar discrepancies in its judgments and omissions. Film, for example, *is* recognized, with some passion, as 'a unique and potentially valuable art form in its own right' to be placed alongside literature, music and painting. This, indeed, was forward-looking. But against that dance is only mentioned *once* as a discipline valuable in its own right. It is not listed in the appendix and in the section on PE is merely listed with other athletic and recreational activities, such as swimming, squash and archery. That dance is a great art form comparable to literature and music is nobly mentioned and never returned to again, an insight that must have been smothered the moment after it was born, a good example of that high rhetoric without action, which marks the story of arts education in England.

In the report, then, we encounter much support for the expressive and imaginative dimension of human existence but in the curriculum proposed there is a most confused bifurcation of the arts under two separate categories. There is no sense of a coherent group of disciplines. In the humanities, drama and film are placed under the sovereignty of English; in the practical subjects, art and music (described as 'frequently the worst equipped and accommodated subject in the curriculum' and described as 'unduly narrow' in its range) are given their autonomy, but dance is conspicuous by its absence.

The exacting search for philosophical principles in arts education was to emerge, not in official reports, but in a number of publications and projects, both personal and collective, coming most often from the departments of education in the universities. It is in this formal context that the effort to create a more logical system, a more comprehensive curricular structure for the arts, began. It is to these intellectual initiatives made against the sullen indifference of the English towards their own art makers and their own paradoxically profound culture, that we must now turn.

The Intellectual Challenge

One of the first books to propose a concept of a common arts community in an *educational context* was the volume *The Arts in Education* edited by James Britton (first published in 1963). In the spring of 1962 James Britton brought together a number of arts teachers and lecturers to give a programme of lectures across the arts (in the Institute of Education, London) which were then published in the following year. With the exception of film, all the main art forms were fully represented.

Britton himself in his own chapter on literature revealed briefly the kind of educational advance that can come from an active comparison across the arts. Britton wrote:

> Last week we had music, tonight literature, next week painting. Three of the arts which play a major part in general education: three arts therefore in which you might expect to find boys and girls taking special courses in the sixth form, with their future professions in mind. Pursue those sixth formers, and I think you will come across a very odd thing. The chances are that those with a special interest in painting will, when they go on to full-time further education, paint. If it is music they have chosen, the chances are they will at least learn an instrument, or learn to sing music – and they will also, increasingly, I believe, be expected to compose music. You already see what I mean by a 'a very odd thing': full-time further education for those interested in literature will have nothing to do with writing it, nor even performing it (which for poetry and drama would be conceivable). This means that as far as institutions of further education are concerned, painting and music are things you do, but literature is something that other people have done.[9]

Such comparative analysis across the arts can be, as this example demonstrates, extremely productive, but unfortunately such comparisons were rare in this volume. For the most part the essays, shot through with the dated assumptions of modernism and progressivism, show little collective coherence and offer no sustained comparative analysis. The editor may have had some vague idea of unity but most of his contributors disclosed a stubborn enclosure within their own subjects. If there was any common theme, it lay in the spurious concepts of 'self-expression' and 'self-discovery'. Had James Britton written a long afterword analysing the various unities and differences, with an eye to creating philosophical coherence, he might have created a book of historic significance. As it was, the book failed to delineate the terms necessary for any synoptic understanding of the arts.

The first project in Britain which *was* to have a serious go at formulating the nature of the common ground was called *Arts and the Adolescent*; it was set up in 1968 for four years, was directed by Malcolm Ross and Robert Witkin, and resulted in two publications *The Intelligence of Feeling* (1974) and the Schools Council monograph *Arts and the Adolescent* (1975). Here too the notions of 'self-expression' and 'self-discovery' were to be given further formulation and made, alas, all but axiomatic in the teaching of the arts. Indeed, it would seem that it was around this time, let us say between 1963 and 1974, that the idea of any reference to a cultural tradition that stretched back through the ages became badly disrupted. From this period children were to express themselves in a growing vacuum, without the means, often, of adequate articulation, without exemplars, without predecessors and without the challenge of great art.

These exemplars and predecessors were to be linked with the emotive word 'élitism' and largely discarded as the products of alienation and ideological deception. Sometimes the attack was to be explicit; more often it was implicit and revealed itself obliquely only in a number of silences and omissions. Here in this near conspiracy the major movements of Marxism, modernism and progressivism exerted their influence and all to the same tune: western civilization was not good for one. The tag 'high culture' became a pejorative term. If it was to be referred to, then it needed the tag of a cultural health warning: *Beware, élitism lurks here.* The more explicit message was, as we shall see, either *stick to the contemporary forms of culture* or (quite often) *stick to the child's act of 'self-expression'*. Hermann Goering may have said 'When I hear the word culture I reach for my revolver' but many arts teachers have surreptitiously thought it. As a result most of the children in Britain's democracy have grown up in cultural exile. On the other hand, the arts (however emaciated) *were* brought together with an informing notion of a common epistemology.

The project based at the University of Exeter had set itself three main aims:

> What materials and methods in the field of the arts are most likely to elicit a lively response among young people? The arts for this purpose are taken to include visual art, music, dance, literature, film and photography.
>
> How do young people view their own involvement in the arts in school and out of school; how much connection is there between these two forms of often disparate activity?
>
> How much connection can be made, and how much transfer of interest is possible, between one art and another, and between the arts and other subjects in the curriculum?[10]

Out of these holistic questions came the first major attempt in education to formulate a common philosophy and common practice of arts education for state secondary schools.

In their various discussions with teachers of the arts Malcolm Ross and Robert Witkin found what they saw as a lamentable lack of intellectual clarity. There was, they claimed, a fund of enthusiasm but a paucity of reasoning:

> When asked about their aims and their general understanding of their own educational function most of the arts teachers I spoke to were either struck totally dumb or rapidly collapsed into incoherence. It was not that they had no sense of where they were going or of what they were doing – rather that their own best work seemed to derive more from intuition than deliberation and, although they insisted that in some respects they were concerned with areas of experience not easily expressed in words, they none the less remained uneasy about their inarticulateness and felt that somehow it should be possible to say what arts education was about and why it was important.[11]

What was needed and what Robert Witkin felt he could provide was a conceptual framework both for the empirical study of the arts and as an ideal model for their systematic reconstruction. Early in 1969 Ross took the reformulated programme to the Schools Council:

> When I met the Schools Council to discuss the proposal I was able to offer them the prospect of a language which would enable arts teachers better to understand and control their work:

a language that would have to be equally applicable to all the arts. This language would emerge as part of a more far-reaching study of the educational function *of the arts based upon original work in the psychology of affect,* on which Robert Witkin was already engaged.[12]

Here one sees both the attempt to formulate a common language for the arts (an aim we will return to examine in the next section) and the curious assumption that the language would derive from 'the psychology of affect', not aesthetics.

In *The Intelligence of Feeling* Witkin struggled to forge a common language for the arts in the context of the secondary curriculum. His basic argument was that the arts were primarily concerned with subjectivity and its conversion into symbolic form through a continuous and developing interaction between the expressive impulse of the art maker and the expressive medium of the art form. All the arts were concerned with the reflexive understanding of feeling within itself.

Moving outwards from his own psychological commitment to the study of affects, Witkin proposed five common categories for the collective examination of the arts; they were as follows: 'self-expression and individuality', 'control of the medium', 'the use of realized form', 'personal development' and 'examinations and assessment'. Then in Chapter 8 he offered an account of the creative act common to all the arts moving from the release of impulse or what he termed 'the setting of the sensate problem', to 'the making of a holding form', to 'a movement through successive approximations to a resolution'. According to Witkin an understanding of the creative process in the arts allows the teacher to structurally enter, as a kind of guiding co-artist, the pupil's expressive act.

Here was a study that brought all the arts together. In the select bibliography each art form is listed (English, art, drama, music, dance, film), though in the study only four arts are examined according to the established categories, namely, English, drama, art and music. Malcolm Ross explained:

The project's original brief included the study of dance, film and photography. We have been unable to carry out inquiries very far in these fields. These subjects are rarely taught by specialists as disciplines in their own right – for example, photography and mass media studies generally are still in an embryonic stage of development and, despite Newsom, remain, in our view, seriously neglected in the schools.[13]

He also went on to suggest that dance 'belongs firmly to the creative and expressive arts' and recommended at least its temporary separation from PE. Here then are the arts subjects, named, differentiated, freed from the divisions of earlier curriculum structures, and placed together as a generic community.

Yet a terrible contradiction has to be recorded for, at the same time as the explicit argument moves towards the conception of a generic arts community, another argument weaving its way through the text resists and all but disowns art in its inherited and symbolic nature. Again and again in his writing, Malcolm Ross has attacked the formal arts and insisted only on the value of *expressivity* in education. In *The Claims of Feeling* he wrote:

> We were not after all advocating education in the arts – still less an apprenticeship for school children in the high western artistic tradition. Real art and real artists were all but incidental to the thesis of human expressivity that the project was advancing.[14]

It is essential to notice that 'self-expression' in *The Intelligence of Feeling* is regarded as 'the most central category'. As a consequence of this progressive notion the child's actual state of feeling comes largely to regulate the arts curriculum. The aim of the work is 'the personal development of the pupil' and assessment can only be made in terms of it. According to Witkin, the teacher of the creative arts had only the inner reality of the educational encounter from which to abstract an assessment. The teacher is cast as a kind of psychological guide and therapist, rather than educator in the great traditions of the arts. Writing about the project retrospectively in 1989 Ross claimed:

> It began by accepting that what arts teachers wanted was good: to give children access to their expressive impulses and to help them use them creatively in the interests of personal development. The project did not challenge these assumptions; it attempted to make teacher practice more effective by articulating the theory implicit in it.[15]

The psychological child-centred approach elevated the intelligence of feeling at the expense of the intelligence of art and the intelligence of the great cultural continuum. In this respect it is very close to Herbert Read's *Education through Art*, analysed later in this volume (see Chapter 10).

In brief, the idea of the arts community was almost discovered and exploded at the same moment. Perhaps it couldn't have been otherwise starting out from 'the psychology of affects' and an 'approach rooted in social science'. The art was bound to remain secondary as it lay outside the primary and defining terms of interest. Thus the contribution of the *The Intelligence of Feeling* was ambiguous and slippery; it did much to establish the arts as a family, but, ironically deprived them of their intrinsic content. It is not for nothing that Malcolm Ross called his work 'iconoclastic', for it served to devalue the living icons, the great exemplary work of the aesthetic field. What it *did* affirm, however, if for partial and limiting reasons, was the idea of the arts as a generic community within the curriculum of secondary education. It was one of the first projects to do so. That is an achievement that must be recognized.

The next major step towards a unified conception of the arts came in 1982 with the publication of the Gulbenkian Foundation's report *The Arts in Schools*. This project was chaired by Peter Brinson, while the report was written partly by David Aspin (who wrote the opening philosophical chapters) and partly by Ken Robinson (who wrote the remaining pragmatic chapters). The report located the need for a comprehensive view of the arts in the curriculum. Like *The Arts and the Adolescent* project it sought to make, once again, the connections between the broken segments of the arts more visible and to see them not only in the context of the whole curriculum but of society conceived as something infinitely larger than a series of economic transactions. In particular, it addressed a lack of coordination and continuity in arts education under the three following aspects:

> First, there *is little contact between teachers working in different arts* – even within the same schools. Second, there is little coordination between the three main sectors of education, primary, secondary and tertiary, and, as a result, too *little continuity* in children's and young people's arts education. Third, there is *too little contact between educationalists and professional artists.* We see a need to tackle these problems of liaison and want to propose some strategies for doing this and to bring attention to existing ways in which this is being done.[16]

In the report the arts are not itemized and then handled discretely as in *The Intelligence of Feeling*; rather, they are named generically and conceived as a common practice throughout the document (though film is often omitted or left in the sidelines as dance was in the Newsom

Report). The authors are explicit about their holistic intentions; they are committed to the genus and the need to conceive it whole:

> Our arguments in this report refer to all of the arts – music, dance, drama, poetry, literature, visual and plastic arts. We do not deal with them separately because we want to emphasise what they have in common – both in what they jointly offer education and in the problems they jointly face.[17]

The philosophy derived from a central European tradition in aesthetics going back through the writing of Louis Arnaud Reid, to the work of Susanne Langer and Ernst Cassirer, back to the philosophical writings of Kant.

In *The Arts in Schools* the arts are seen to provide a unique kind of knowledge of the world, in particular, a knowledge of *feeling* and *value* and hence to form an indispensable part of any complete curriculum. On this issue the report is emphatic:

> The arts are fundamental ways of organising our understanding of the world and call on profound qualities of discipline and insight. They must be included in education wherever schools are concerned to develop the full range of children's intelligence and abilities.[18]

And again:

> The arts are not outpourings of emotion. They are disciplined forms of inquiry and expression through which to organise feelings and ideas about experience. The need for young people to do this, rather than just to give vent to emotions or to have them ignored, must be responded to in the schools. The arts provide the natural means for this.[19]

In a bleak period of educational change, when abrasive materialism had taken over the minds of many influential figures, the *Arts in Schools* report gave hope to many teachers, who were beginning to doubt the value of their work because of the general failure of society to affirm the life of consciousness.

The emphasis is on knowledge and aesthetic intelligence, but the knowledge is understood as materializing through the actual practice of art making as well as through aesthetic engagement with works of art, both contemporary and traditional. What the report advocates, for the most part, is not history or sociology but *sustained practice* with all kinds of artistic media. It advocated an aesthetic education based on the arts rooted in the reality of a complex civilization. The progressivism of Malcolm Ross and Robert Witkin had been rinsed out.

The report was widely disseminated, widely read and – for England, with its deep anti-intellectualism – widely debated. It was for the arts a considerable educational triumph, though, it has to be said, that those with political power were looking in a very different direction, and they were as the tone deaf listening to the harmonies of music.

The hope and energy generated by the report was taken forward by the *Arts in Schools Project* directed by Ken Robinson. This project, which included eighteen local education authorities, was launched in September 1985 and completed under the auspices of the National Curriculum Council in August 1989. The project culminated in the publication of a set of three related books. In the most theoretical of these volumes (although none of them could be called philosophically exacting) *Arts 5–16: A Curriculum Framework*, three reasons are given for presenting the argument. Each of these reasons demonstrates the essential continuity of the project, not only with the Gulbenkian Report that had fathered it, but also to the earlier *Arts and the Adolescent* research. The first reason is expressed as follows:

> Much of the existing writing and research is about single disciplines. Work in different disciplines tends to use different terms to describe similar ideas. These differences in terminology are an obstacle to coherent planning for the arts as a whole in the curriculum. A single framework offering a common terminology is a necessary basis for dialogue and co-operation between the various arts specialisms.[20]

Not only the conception but also the formulation is close to that of the previously quoted Malcolm Ross who wrote in 1975: 'I was able to offer the prospect of a language which would enable arts teachers better to understand and control their work; a language that would have to be equally applicable to all the arts'.[21] Similarly, while the interpretation is different, there is a congruence between the two projects on the second major point:

> Existing frameworks have been developed for different purposes or phases, e.g. for assessment, or course planning or discussing methods of teaching. There is a pressing need for consistent principles to be applied across all these areas of arts education.[22]

Again, the third point only displays a further consistency between the two enterprises:

> Our aim is to offer schools a map of entitlement for all pupils in the arts: a way of conceiving the range and depth of provision to be made in arts education and of judging their success in making it.[23]

Of course, however, the contexts in which the reports worked had changed and so had a number of assumptions. *The Intelligence of Feeling* had been written in a period of progressive educational thinking and in a general period of social expansion and liberalism, even optimism. *The Arts 5–16* project, on the other hand, had emerged as a response to the 1988 Educational Reform Act and the national curriculum; it had been written in a period of growing utilitarianism, of cut-back, of general retraction. Unlike the *The Intelligence of Feeling*, which makes the liberation of individual subjectivity its key educational value, the *Arts 5–16* volumes advocate not a self-expression model but an ideological and cultural model of learning. It insists that critical understanding is necessary to correct 'self-expression' and proposes a public rather than a private view of art. In particular, it stresses the need for multicultural approaches to aesthetic education. Yet, ironically, it is precisely here that the report comes close to the same blindness as the *Arts and the Adolescent* project in relationship to the cultural continuum and, in particular, to the artistic achievement of western culture.

One encounters the old nervous unease about 'high western artistic traditions' in *The Arts in Schools* project. There lurks an unresolved and barely suppressed embarrassment before traditional European culture. There is little recognition of a need for exemplars, for cultural touchstones, for any fixed nodal points of artistic expression and formulation. It is symptomatic that the examples given in the journalistic boxes that punctuate the main text refer mainly to Picasso's *Les Demoiselles d'Avignon* (1907) that 'famous fracture in the tradition of European painting' and to the futurists, dadaists, surrealists and the Bauhaus school. Yet if one were to refer to the index for some key figures in traditional western culture – Sophocles, Rembrandt, Mozart – one would not find a single reference. Here is the characteristic silence of the liberal consensus. The traditional art makers are not attacked; they are simply not mentioned – all very English.

It is as if the project is suggesting that arts teachers need to mix iconoclastic modernism with a variety of multicultural arts practices and that, then, all will be well. This is facile for multi-culturalism is not a coherent concept. How could it be – when there are thousands of cultures, and artistic processes need to be grounded in a particular culture before they can be connected to others? Indeed, I would suggest that the idea of 'an apprenticeship for school children in the high western artistic tradition' has been dismissed, too easily, by too many arts educators, for far too long. Such an apprenticeship, *linked to those other aims and intentions* listed at the end of Chapter 3 may well provide one of the necessary elements of a true arts education and, at the same time, deepen the sense of a common European culture committed to free enquiry and continuous imaginative challenge and spiritual renewal. This is, surely, better than a general policy of multicultural eclecticism, without a centre and without an historic identity? Cultures are not counters to be rationally manipulated; they are historic forces within which people live and have their being.

Under the challenge of non-European cultures, the curriculum framework document argues for a new conceptualization of the arts, *not according to kinds but according to modes*:

> We noted above that some cultures do not distinguish as Europeans have done between separate disciplines and that a good deal of arts practice in Western European cultures also challenges these distinctions. For this reason it is inappropriate to relate a definition of the arts – or a plan for the arts in schools – to a conception of artistic disciplines which is specific to particular cultures. A general definition of the arts needs to be built on a broader base.[24]

This broader base (free from specific cultures) involves the classification of the arts into the following five modes:

- the visual mode – using light, colour and images;
- the aural mode – using sounds and rhythms;
- the kinaesthetic mode – using bodily movement;
- the verbal mode – using words;
- the enactive mode – using imagined roles.[25]

Whether this represents an advance on the traditional categories of film, dance, drama, music, literature and film must be debated, for it seems essentially ahistorical in nature, possessing a specious abstract logic. But it certainly represents a significant development in the generic argument as it comes under the influence of the ideology of multicultural education.

I have been delineating the evolution of a concept in the teaching of the arts over three decades, from James Britton's *The Arts in Education* published in 1963 to the publication of *The Arts in Schools* volumes in 1989. The Government showed little interest in the argument. What happened, in fact, is that the Government imposed a curriculum that, true to the tradition of arts education in our schools, continued to fragment the arts into isolated, unequal and competing parts. In the various national curriculum documents literature was seen as an integral part of English teaching; drama was regarded as a subsidiary part of English; dance was similarly returned to physical education; while film as an arts discipline more or less disappeared. Music and visual arts, in contrast, were first given the full status of foundation subjects and then made optional after the age of 14. At the moment the national curriculum has made structurally most difficult, if not impossible, the realization of a unified arts curriculum based on the emerging idea of the generic community. As usual in our society, intellectual formulation and practical action are widely out of kilter. Once again we identify a general lack of vision and public commitment; the notion of the arts as a generic community remains a radical conception, a disruptive notion that has still to find its fitting organizational shape in the national curriculum of our schools. The paradigm is there but not yet its collective realization.

Confronting the Opposition

Up to this point I have assumed the philosophical coherence and educational value of the notion of the arts as a generic community. But is the idea coherent? And does it carry value? It is time to excavate assumptions and submit them to critical scrutiny. This is extremely difficult to do where one is attached to a particular formulation or where one may have contributed to it in some small way. Fortunately, this is not a problem, for the philosopher David Best has entered the public arena of debate and in two essays ('Arts in Schools: A Critical Time' and 'Generic Arts: An Expedient Myth') set out to offer a devastating critique of what he sees as a blinding orthodoxy and a facile myth. I want to close this chapter on the arts as a generic community with a consideration of his outspoken critique.

David Best's critique derives, in part, from his deep suspicion of verbal generalities and his own marked predilection for particulars, for specificities, for actual cases and locatable examples. For him, high sounding abstractions can easily delude the mind and seduce its critical judgments. He sees the notion of the generic community as precisely such an abstraction, plausible on the surface, but, at the same time, bearing a number of dangerous fallacies that could have dire consequences on the arts curriculum of our schools.

Very early in his paper in the *Journal of Art and Design Education* Best gives his definition of the generic in the context of the arts. He claims that he aims to consider 'some of the more philosophical issues involved in the notion of generic, combined, or integrated arts'.[26] He makes the same point later when he writes that 'a commitment [in this case Ken Robinson's] to the notion of generic arts entails a commitment to integrated or combined arts' and 'to assert that the arts are generic is to assert a general experience of the art'.[27]

David Best then uses the dictionary to substantiate the main point involved in his own definition:

> According to the Oxford Dictionary the meaning of generic is most clearly exemplified in zoology or botany: a group of animals or plants having common structural characteristics distinct from those of all other groups.[28]

With this definition it becomes clear, Best argues, why the generic community of the arts is such a flawed concept. For in botany to understand the structure of one species is to understand the general structure of all the other species gathered under the one genus, but in the arts this is simply not so; to understand the structure, say, of music gives one no understanding of, say, the structure of painting. No such translation is possible. Thus the generic notion is a fallacy leading to conceptual nonsense and, inevitably, practical confusion. In 'Arts in Schools: A Critical Time' the example is given of the principal of a college considering terminating the visual arts teaching on the grounds that the students' 'aesthetic education' was provided for in their dance. This is also why the notion of 'generic' is not only logically unsound but 'expedient' because it justifies the cutting back of the arts to either one of the species or to some amalgam, a 'general' arts programme that would inevitably neglect all the specificities that mark out and define the individual arts disciplines. Against this he writes with characteristic directness:

> We should reject as philosophically senseless and educationally damaging the notion that there is such a thing as *a general capacity for artistic appreciation* which can be experienced of any and all art forms, rather as a muscle may be developed by any of various exercises.[29]

Against such bogus generalities, Best would have us see the distinctive characteristics of the different arts and, in specific circumstances, their possible combinations.

I would like now to consider his argument in the stages in which I have presented it. Let us examine first the definitions offered at the outset. For David Best the concepts 'generic', 'combined' and 'integrated' are virtually synonymous. Generic arts, he insists, entails a commitment to combined arts. The problem here is that the definition predetermines the outcome in advance of the discussion. The argument doesn't expand but, like a tautology, merely respeats itself. But do we need to accept the definition? Others who have used the notion of the generic have *not* understood it to mean combined or integrated. Susanne Langer, who may have been one of the first to use the term generic in this context, wrote 'art . . . is the generic term subsuming painting, sculpture, architecture, music, dance, literature, drama and film', and went on to differentiate severely between them according to their different modes of operation. Not once does she imply that the arts could be assimilated or that they were, in any conceivable way, interchangeable. The same is true of the other writers. They aim to practise a certain dialectic that observes the general (the genus) and, simultaneously, recognizes the differentiation into distinct types. This is, precisely, the logic first used by Aristotle in his *Poetics*. For these writers 'generic' has simply *not* meant what David Best would have it denote.

In such cases the dictionary is not a definitive way of resolving a definition, but it is, at least, neutral and always pertinent. The shorter Oxford English Dictionary gives the following entry for 'generic': 'belonging to a genus or class: applied to a large group or class of objects; general', while Webster's Dictionary differentiates between a logical use of the word (which it gives first) where characteristics relate to a class and a biological use (which it places second) where they relate to a genus. In brief, there would seem to be two closely related references, one deriving generally from logic, the other, more specifically from biology. Thus, all those working to uphold a common category for the arts could well adopt the logical meaning and rightfully free themselves from any critique based on a relentless analysis of the genus–species model. But even on the second reading, one could justly insist that David Best brings to it a narrow literalism of mind that is false to the nature of language and its necessary metaphoric extensions. It is perfectly reasonable to suggest that just as there is some binding connection between the species that make up a genus, so there is a binding connection between the arts that entitles us to refer to them collectively as Art. This doesn't have to involve the notion of structural *equivalence*, only the idea of common characteristics. What these characteristics might be is, of course, a complex question, but I will attempt an answer shortly.

Finally, Best attacks those who, mesmerized by the deceptive logic of the generic argument, went on to develop a general aesthetic faculty or to merely amalgamate the arts into general programmes to meet diminishing resources and allocated time. The difficulty here is to know *who* exactly he is attacking. As we have seen, these are not even remotely the concerns of Aristotle or Langer but neither are they the concerns of those who have attempted to develop the argument in an educational context. In much of his attack David Best directs his criticism at *The Arts in Schools* project but there, in what could be termed a 'David Best formulation' it is explicitly stated: 'Young people do not have a general artistic ability which can be developed equally well by work in any medium.'[30] It is as if David Best is fighting a phantom, a spectre of compromise and philosophical ineptitude, that does not exist. His formulations act in the manner of an expanding tautology but, failing to encounter the actual arguments, have little purchase and, therefore, little power.

At the end of his critique David Best affirms his own commitment to the arts:

> I must emphasise, that nothing I have said implies any opposition to the idea that we shall *all*, in *all* the arts, work together for the good of the arts in general. On the contrary, for those of us who are convinced of the enormous values of the arts in education, it is *highly* desirable, from strategic and political points of view, that we should work together, to present a solid, united front, to insist that all our children and students should be entitled, as a central part of their education, to as rich as possible an experience of *all* the arts.[31]

What is so ironic is that these are precisely the values of those he attacks. If the 'generic community' was such a dangerous concept, how could it possibly lead to the same conclusions and, as it does, what has been the point of the argument?

It remains to attempt an answer to the question: what are the essential characteristics that hold the arts together? David Best puts his challenge in the following closely related forms:

> one cannot discover a common characteristic, or a set of characteristics, which distinguishes the arts. One cannot discern

some essential characteristic underlying, a Rothko painting, Bach's *Goldberg Variations*, Michael Bogdanov's exciting production of the *War of the Roses*, the ballet *Giselle*, the film *Babette's Feast*, and Wilfred Owen's poetry . . .

What is needed to make the 'generic' case for the arts *specifically* – i.e. to mark them out as a group with some special cohesion – is to show that they possess a character distinct from all other areas of the curriculum. I challenge anyone to cite any characteristic, or set of characteristics, which is both *common to all the arts*, and *distinct from all other areas of the curriculum*.[32]

What, then, might unite a Rothko painting, Bach's *Goldberg Variations*, a production of the *War of the Roses*, the ballet *Giselle*, the film *Babette's Feast* and Wilfred Owen's poetry? To say that they are all works of art is to state the conclusion that must be demonstrated. I would propose that, at least, the three following interconnected characteristics unify the works of art listed (and any other work of art that could be named) and, taken together, give them their distinctive unity:

1 All the works of art referred to create forms *expressive of life*.
2 All of them for their various meanings *depend upon their formal constructions* that cannot be extracted or translated without significant loss.
3 All of them for their understanding require not a critical response but an aesthetic response – a response through feeling, the senses, and the imagination.

These three propositions are by no means original formulations and can be found elaborated in the writings of, for example, Susanne Langer and Louis Arnaud Reid. They provide sound reasons for seeing the arts generically while acknowledging, in the tradition of Aristotle, their very obvious diversity. Taken together, they also indicate what separates the arts from other established areas of the curriculum e.g. history, geography, physics, law.

In *Feeling and Reason in the Arts* David Best himself formulated a very similar conception when he claimed:

I argue . . . that an art form must allow for the possibility of expression of issues from life and that the object of one's attention and feeling may be fictional. Moreover, there is an important sense in which the concept of art is non-purposive, by which I mean that the supposed 'purpose' of a work of art cannot be identified apart from the artistic means of achieving it, which is the same as saying that, in the arts, there is no distinction between means and ends.[33]

Here, indeed, are fine reasons for upholding the idea of the generic community of the arts. Now with these good reasons clearly in our minds we should be ready to work *together* for the burgeoning of the new paradigm in arts education. Never was it more necessary – and never was it more necessary to make contact in our arts teaching with the whole cultural continuum, with the deep aesthetic fields of our respective arts disciplines. However, securing a whole curriculum based on the teaching of all the arts, while essential, would not of itself secure the creative teaching of the arts. To secure that we must have a much fuller understanding of the nature of creativity. This is the theme of the next chapter.

Notes

1 SUZANNE LANGER (1953) *Feeling and Form*, London, Routledge & Kegan Paul.

2 THE HADOW REPORT (1926) *The Education of the Adolescent*, Report of the Consultative Committee, London, HMSO.

3 THE NEWSOM REPORT (1963). *Half Our Future: A Report of the Central Advisory Council for Education*, London, HMSO.

4 THE SPENS REPORT (1938) *Secondary Education*. The Report of the Consultative Committee, London, HMSO.

5 THE NORWOOD REPORT (1943) *Curriculum and Examinations in Secondary Schools*, London, HMSO.

6 *Ibid.*, p. 123.

7 HADOW REPORT (1926).

8 SPENS REPORT (1938), p. 171.

9 JAMES BRITTON (ed.) (1963) *The Arts in Education*, London, The Institute of Education.

10 MALCOLM ROSS (1975) *Arts and the Adolescent*, London, Evans/Methuen Educational, p. 8.

11 *Ibid.*, p. 17.

12 *Ibid.*, p. 19 (my italics).

13 *Ibid.*, p. 54.

14 MALCOLM ROSS (1989) *The Claims of Feeling*, London, Falmer Press, p. 8.

15 *Ibid.*, p. 9.

16 GULBENKIAN FOUNDATION (1982) *The Arts in Schools: Principles Practice and Provision*, London, The Gulbenkian Foundation, p. 9 (my italics).

17 *Ibid.*, p. 10.

18   *Ibid.*
19   *Ibid.*, p. 11.
20   NATIONAL CURRICULUM COUNCIL (NCC) (1990) *The Arts 5–16: A Curriculum Framework*. Longman/Oliver & Boyd, p. 2.
21   ROSS (1975), p. 19.
22   *Ibid.*
23   *Ibid.*
24   NCC (1990), p. 25.
25   *Ibid.*
26   DAVID BEST (1992) 'The Generic Arts: An Expedient Myth', *Journal of Art and Design Education*, **11** (1) p. 28.
27   *Ibid.*, p. 41.
28   *Ibid.*, p. 31.
29   DAVID BEST (1990) 'Arts in Schools: A Critical Time', Corsham, NSEAD Occasional Paper, p. 3 (my italics).
30   GULBENKIAN FOUNDATION (1982).
31   BEST (1990), pp. 42–3.
32   BEST (1990), pp. 32, 33.
33   DAVID BEST (1985) *Feeling and Reason in the Arts*, London, Allen & Unwin.

Chapter 6

From Babble to Rhapsody:
On the Nature of Artistic Creativity

Few books have interested me more to write than *The Waves*. Why even now, at the end, I'm turning up a stone or two: no glibness, no assurance; you see, I could perhaps do B.'s soliloquy in such a way as to break up, dig deep, make prose move – yes I swear – as prose has never moved before; from the chuckle, the babble to the rhapsody. Something new goes into my pot every morning – something that's never been got at before.

Virginia Woolf in her diary on the composition of The Waves

What does the unicorn care for the premier league, the FT share index or party politics? He cares for purity, the fulfilment of our imaginative potential, the destiny of the earth. Of countless fine subjects for the artist, none can reach as deep as myth. The unicorn and I mutually recreated each other.

David Powell in his essay on the creation of Unicorn

Introduction

A return to aesthetic response, a recognition of the shaping power of the aesthetic field, an understanding of the nature of the generic community of the arts – these are essential for the proper teaching of the arts, yet the paradigm is not complete until these elements have been placed inside a Socratic context of learning and a profound commitment to the creative process. In the first two chapters I outlined the manner and style of Socratic teaching; in this chapter I want to examine the creative dynamic through which most significant works of art – whether by professional art makers or by children – get made. Recent developments in the national curriculum have rightly stressed the value of skill, but they have not emphasized the need for an often very elusive and highly motivating creative act and, in missing this, they

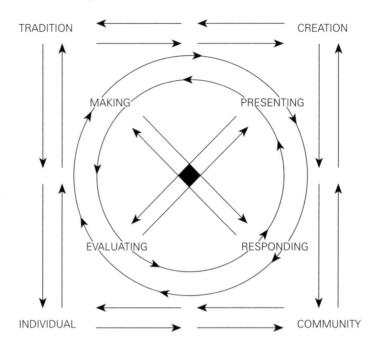

Figure 1 Diagrammatic representation of the phases of art making

have often missed the very heart of artistic activity and its deepest educational value.

In an earlier volume on the new paradigm in arts education, *Living Powers*,[1] Figure 1 was presented. It schematically indicates the four key stages in any significant art making, namely the phases of *making*, *presenting*, *responding* and *evaluating*. The frame suggests a constant dialectic between tradition and creation and the individual and the community. The arts teacher and the arts student work in the field of its creative and liberating energies. The inner circle within the frame denotes the four necessary phases of art work.

In *making* the student struggles to shape some impelling experience into form through a specific medium (through words, musical sounds, clay, bodily gesture, image, narrative or whatever). He or she seeks, but may not necessarily achieve, the creation of a symbolic form for that experience. When this symbolic realization is complete the creative process then moves to its second phase, *the presentation of the work* to an audience. The music is performed, the poem typed, duplicated and read out, the paintings mounted and displayed, the drama acted out, the dance presented, the video or film shown. This second phase releases the next two stages and takes the work away from the art maker into the community. The presented work calls for *immediate aesthetic response* (third phase) and then *considered evaluation* (final phase), where judgments are made and justified and related not only to the individual work but the whole complex field of its form (the aesthetic field).

This has become a dynamic model for the teaching of the arts. The practical implications of such a model were explored at some length in *Living Powers*, but in this chapter it will be used in another way. Does the model illuminate any significant examples of creative imagination? And, if so, what does it tell us about the nature of creative art making? The first example is the creation of *The Waves* by Virginia Woolf; the second example is the creation of the sculpture *The Unicorn* (see Plates 7, 8 and 9) by David Powell.

States of Soul in Creating

'Really', jotted down Virginia Woolf in her journal when she was in the middle of the intense struggle to find the necessary artistic shape for her novel *The Waves*, 'these premonitions of a book – *states of soul in creating* – are very queer and little apprehended.'[2] She then went on to confess a link between illness and creativity, which has since become widely recognized in the psychology of creativity. She wrote;

> These curious intervals in life – I've had many – are the most fruitful artistically – one becomes fertilised – think of my madness at Hogarth – and all the little illnesses – that before I wrote *The Lighthouse* for example. Six weeks in bed now would make a masterpiece of MOTHS.[3]

Six weeks in bed could be interpreted psychoanalytically as six weeks to move freely between the unconscious, preconscious and conscious. Ill in bed, drowsing or dreaming, lapsing out of consciousness, moving away from the formal and constraining conventions of both art and society, we are closest to the unconscious and the unchanging biological elements of human existence, sex and death. In fact, Virginia Woolf herself in a paper 'On Being Ill' (first published in 1930) deplored the fact that 'illness had not taken its place with love and battle and jealousy among the prime themes of literature. 'Novels one would have thought would have been devoted to influenza; epic poems to typhoid; odes to pneumonia; lyrics to toothache'.[4] In the same essay she claimed: 'yet it is not only a new language that we need, more primitive, more sensual, more obscene, but a new hierarchy of the passions; love must be deposed in favour of a temperature of 104'.[5] It was illness, she declared, that gave access to 'a virgin forest in each; a snowfield where even the print of birds' feet is unknown'.[6] However, in this chapter my interest is not directly with the connections between illness and creativity, maladjustment and symbolism, so much as with *the structural phases of the creative act in the making of art* (in this particular case, the making of *The Waves* which in its original conception had been given by its author the title *Moths*). What I propose to offer is a schematic delineation of the stages through which a work of art *has to pass to become a work of art.*

The First Phase of Art Making:
The Releasing of an Impulse

The first phase I want to mark rather than fully describe, for in its manifestation it is formidably elusive, entails the releasing of an expressive impulse, a being moved to utterance, *an animation towards form*, a compulsion to symbolize. Virginia Woolf in her diary gives us a simple example of this elementary desire for expression. It derives from a delight in observing that cannot remain distant and spectatorial, an act of observing that aspires to participate in the objects seen:

> The look of things has a great power over me. Even now, I have to watch the rooks beating up against the wind, which is high, and still I say to myself instinctively 'What's the phrase for that?' and try to make more and more vivid the roughness of the air current and the tremor of the rook's wing slicing as if the air were full of ridges and ripples and roughness. They rise and sink, up and down, as if the exercise rubbed and braced them like swimmers in rough water. But what a little I can get down into my pen of what is so vivid to my eyes, and not only to my eyes; also to some nervous fibre, or fanlike membrane in my species.[7]

One can quickly discern something of the power of the expressive impulse. It is an urge to join (symbol comes from *sun-ballein*: to throw together) the author to the creation she is watching. Through the impulse to find words representing what she sees, Woolf establishes a kind of inner communion with the outer object which, however, is endlessly frustrated and broken off. It is significant she uses the word 'instinctively' to mark the nature of the process as if symbolizing in this way was a fundamental characteristic of our inherited biological nature. And the symbolism, perhaps, in large measure, represents a need constantly to overcome a threatening schizophrenia where subject and object remain fatally divided. Of course, such a suggestion in the case of Virginia Woolf has an immediate pertinence – as indeed do the images of rising and sinking in rough water, for these symbols draw her own subjective fate and the outer objects almost ominously together.

My concern here, though, is with the phases of the expressive act; all I want to suggest is that for art to be created there must be some primary impulse released in the art marker, an expressive need triggered into motion by some experience or other, often quite ordinary, sometimes almost too trivial to record. There must be an unresolved impulse that demands articulation, that requires amplification and completion through the labour of artistic shaping.

On 30 September 1926, Virginia Woolf wrote in her diary:

> I wished to add some remarks to this, on the mystical side of this solitude; how it is not oneself but something in the universe that one's left with. It is this that is frightening and exciting in the midst of my profound gloom, depression, boredom, whatever it is. *One sees a fin passing far out. What image can I reach to convey what I mean. Really there is none.* I think. The interesting thing is that in all my feeling and thinking I have never come up against this before. Life is, soberly and accurately, the oddest affair; has in it the essence of reality. I used to feel this as a child – couldn't step across a puddle once, I remember, for thinking how strange – what am I? etc. But by writing I don't reach anything. All I mean to make is a note of a curious state of mind. I hazard the guess that it may be the impulse behind another book. At present my mind is totally blank and virgin of books. I want to watch and see how the idea at first occurs. I want to trace my own process. Yet I am now and then haunted by some semi-mystic very profound life of a woman, which shall all be told on one occasion; and time shall be utterly obliterated; future shall somehow blossom out of the past. One incident – say the fall of a flower – might contain it. My theory being that the actual event practically does not exist – nor time either. But I don't want to force this.[8]

The Waves would seem to have its origin in a specific image, some memories and a mood, 'a curious state of mind'. Very early on in the process there often emerges what Robert Witkin has defined as a 'holding form':[9] a working title that implicitly bears within it the whole complex import of the future work, or some kind of elementary structural schema. In the case of Virginia Woolf we find both title and schema. There is the original provisional title *Moths* (a title that for Virginia Woolf was saturated in childhood associations; the original opening actually began with the lines: 'an enormous moth had settled on the bare plaster wall').[10] On 2 July 1929 there were a number of contenders: '*The Moths?*' she wrote 'or the life of anyone. Life in general, or *Moments of Being* or *The Waves*'.[11] Very early on in the process of composition the following schema is outlined in her diary:

Monday, February 21st 1927

Why not invent a new kind of play; as for instance:
Woman thinks.
He does.
Organ plays.
She writes.
They say.
She sings.
Night speaks.
They miss.

I think it must be something on this line – though I can't now see what. Anyway from facts; free; yet concentrated; prose yet poetry; a novel and a play.[12]

Here one notices a number of elements characterize the final work: the present tense, the eternal present tense, as it were, the tense of an immediate and polyphonic simultaneity. One notices the impersonality: 'he', 'she', 'they'. One notices the cosmic: 'night speaks'. One notices the emphasis on music and song: 'organ plays', 'she sings'. One notices also the opening insistence on female gender: 'woman thinks' and the sense of some fundamental dislocation and failure: 'they miss'.

At this point, too, in the early stages of deep incubation and initial expression there is a preoccupation with the form of the work: 'prose yet poetry; a novel and a play'. Elsewhere in the journals, struggling to name the art she is about to make, she calls the book a 'playpoem', 'a drama', 'lyric poetry', 'autobiography' and even something as broad as 'a mind thinking'. In her critical essays, written around the same time, she explores the same issues. Her creative act provides her with fresh critical concepts, sharp acts of hermeneutic perception. On Jane Austen she writes that in order 'to develop personal relations to the utmost, it is important to keep out of the range of the abstract, the impersonal'.[13] After a discussion of Proust and James she asserts: 'Poetry, it would seem, requires a different ordering of the scene; human beings are needed, but needed in their relation to love, or death, or nature rather than to each other'.[14] It is that 'different ordering of the scene' in terms of a cosmic principle that she is most after in *The Waves*, most struggling with in the first stages of her own intense creative preoccupations.

The Second Phase of the Art Making Process

This first phase of the art making process begins as the impulse for symbolic representation (materializing often in guiding metaphors, working titles, possible schemas), engages more and more fully with the medium of expression, in the case of Virginia Woolf's *The Waves* with the English language and its intimate and necessary connections with the whole field of literature, the inherited symbolic order of art. It is important to notice that the word 'medium' can generally suggest 'neutrality' or a 'free space', but in our context of art making 'medium' refers more to the manifold invitations and resistances that the words make, both the opportunities they offer and the possibilities they close down, as well as the happy and unhappy accidents they engender. The language the writer struggles with is neither neutral nor that open; it is laden and striated with various deposits of past achievements and failures. Some years after the completion of *The Waves*, Virginia Woolf wrote that she was thinking of 'taking sentences from great writers and expanding them'.[15] But she also wrote most emphatically about women writers, 'the very form of the sentence does not fit her. It is a sentence made by men; it is too loose, too heavy, too pompous for a woman to use'.[16] The ambivalence between the two formulations marks an essential tension in the relationship between the creative intention and the existing medium through which it has to work towards artistic transformation.

An essential part of the expressive medium is the dynamic field in which it operates. For art not only derives from biological and affective impulses, it also comes out of other art, in the most subtle almost undetectable ways as well as in the most obvious ways, as when a writer employs an established genre or works through a series of allusions to prior narratives. Now Virginia Woolf claimed in her diary that her novel *The Waves* had 'kept stoically to the original conception',[17] that the final form of the art had faithfully embodied the originating impulse. Yet, at the same time, we know from the same journal that her style had also evolved through an awareness of and contact with Ibsen, Shakespeare, Racine, of Byron and the Elizabethan poets and by listening to Beethoven's *Quartets*. For example, on 22 December 1930 she wrote:

> It occurred to me last night while listening to a Beethoven quartet that I would merge all the interjected passages into Bernard's final speech and end with the words O solitude.[18]

At another time she referred to the emerging conception of the work as 'all to be very *Arabian Nights*',[19] and commented at another stage: 'I rather think the upshot will be books that relieve other books: a variety of styles and subjects'.[20] *The original work formed itself substantially in the great matrix of the received culture*, 'relieving other books', other works, reliving them and eventually transforming them into a new imaginative synthesis.

The notion of a fidelity to the original conception may not be false but it is oblique and inherently problematic; at best that fidelity was achieved through the mediating power of many other literary and creative works, from Shakespeare to Beethoven. *The Waves* emerged out of a prolonged struggle – beginning seriously around 10 September 1929 and ending in the summer of 1931 – to articulate some personal moment of vision and mystical feeling through the assiduously internalized high traditions of European literature.

Here, once more, one senses the power of active connection and recreation but this time as well as a knitting together of self and nature, there is a profound joining together, a coupling of self and history, self and culture.

In the late stages of the first phase of art making, in this prolonged struggle between impulse and the vast subterranean matrix of language animated by the diverse expressions of past literature, the essential and exacting movement is from working approximate formulation to definitive formulation – from babble to provisional utterance to divine rhapsody. Virginia Woolf exclaimed: 'I think I am about to embody at last the exact shapes my brain holds. What a long toil to reach this beginning'.[21] Such an engagement leads to preoccupied reflections on form and structure and also often devastating inner self-doubt and deep emotional unease. Virginia Woolf's diaries testify to both these states. During the composition she wrote:

There is something there (as I felt about *Mrs. Dalloway*), but I can't get at it squarely.

The difficulty of digging oneself in there with conviction.

Yesterday I had conviction; it has gone today.[22]

She complained of 'blundering on' with her 'arrant nonsense'. At the same time, the emotional unease is intimately related to the active questioning of expressive possibilities, not in general, but as they actually impinge on the specific work of art being desperately and uncertainly created. These reflections often create the conceptual terms that will be later necessary for the understanding of the new work. This is how, for example, Virginia Woolf struggles to define in her diary what she is after, the kind of style that will hold the *multiplicity of shifting meanings, her plural vision of being-in-time*:

The idea has come to me that what I want now to do is to saturate every atom. I mean to eliminate all waste, deadness, superfluity: to give the moment whole; whatever it includes. Say that the moment is a combination of thought; sensation; the voice of the sea. Waste, deadness, come from the inclusion of things that don't belong to the moment; this appalling narrative business of the realist: getting on from lunch to dinner: it is false, unreal, merely conventional. Why admit anything to literature that is not poetry – by which I mean saturated?

Is that not my grudge against novelists? that they select nothing? The poets succeeding by simplifying: practically everything is left out. I want to put practically everything in: yet to saturate. That is what I want to do in *The Moths*. It must include nonsense, fact, sordidity: but made transparent.

What it wants is presumably unity; but it is I think rather good (I am talking to myself over the fire about *The Waves*). Suppose I could run all the scenes together more? – by rhythms chiefly. So as to avoid those cuts; so as to make the blood run like a torrent from end to end – I want to avoid chapters; that indeed is my achievement, if any, here: a saturated unchopped completeness; changes of scene, of mind, of person, done without spilling a drop. Now if it could be worked over with heat and currency, that's all it wants.[23]

And then towards the end of the long labour of birth she wrote:

What interests me in the last stage was the freedom and bold-
ness with which my imagination picked up, used and tossed
aside all the images, symbols which I had prepared. I am sure
that this is the right way of using them – not in set pieces, as
I had tried at first, coherently, but simply as images, never
making them work out; only suggest. Thus I hope to have
kept the sound of the sea and the birds, dawn and garden sub-
consciously present, doing their work under ground.[24]

Virginia Woolf's grudge against novelists, her animosity towards
the appalling narrative business of the realist, worked against the dominant tradition. At the time she was preparing to write and during the
actual writing of *The Waves*, she wrote a number of critical essays that
retrospectively we can now read as barely disguised manifestos, as
thinly veiled apologias. The most significant of those essays are: 'Women
and Fiction', 'The Narrow Bridge of Art', 'Impressioned Prose', 'De
Quincey' and 'Phases of Fiction'. In these eloquent essays Virginia
Woolf advocates an imaginative mode of writing which, while possessing a metaphysical coherence, yet houses the elusive fluidity of
inner narratives; she seeks a literary equation that combines formal
order and eternal flux. Her critical reflections clarify the nature of the
novel-poem-play-myth she is actually struggling to create. In her criticism she is critical of the main tradition of the novel yet she also names
exemplars and exceptions; she lists on her side Sterne, De Quincey,
Proust, Dostoïevsky; she praises *Wuthering Heights* and *Moby Dick*. Her
literary-critical preoccupations also run explicitly into some of the
working drafts that were later discarded or modified, as into the final
text itself.

The Last Phases of the Art Making Process

'I think it is possible', she wrote, 'I have got my statue against the sky',
and continued, 'I have at any rate the feeling that I have wound up and
done with that long labour: ended that vision.'[25] At this point the work
is moving towards its completion; the work is becoming 'a statue
against the sky' – a public artefact in a landscape where others can see.
The text is beginning to shed its author and stand in its own right
requiring the imaginative work of others. It is this stage, the realization
of final form, that begins the second phase of the creative act, but it
does not end the process, for the work requires immediate aesthetic
response from others, and then *evaluation*; and response and evaluation

may well be of the greatest importance to the development of the author. Virginia Woolf wanted her work to be read, first by an intimate audience and then, with a kind of intense dread, she awaited for the general critical evaluation.

The second phase of the creative act marks the moment of presentation to 'the intimate other' and releases, almost simultaneously, the third phase: the immediate response to the work. Virginia Woolf always showed, with trepidation, her work to her husband Leonard Woolf and awaited, in fear and trembling, for his first reactions. On Sunday 19 July 1931 she wrote in her journal:

> 'It is a masterpiece,' said L., coming out to my lodge this morning. 'And the best of your books.' This note I make; adding that he also thinks the first 100 pages extremely difficult and is doubtful how far any common reader will follow. But Lord! what a relief! I stumped off in the rain to make a little round to Rat Farm in jubilation.[26]

The third phase moves *imperceptibly* into that final phase (of which we too are a part) where the work is not quickly responded to but slowly and cumulatively evaluated. Virginia Woolf's diaries also record key moments in this transition towards formal appreciation (or rejection) and its crucial importance in the development of the art maker. The following entries reveal not only the pleasure the author receives from sensitive appreciation but also the way in which it can promote the desire to write again, to develop the craft of words and the vision of life even further:

Monday, October 5th 1931

A note to say I am all trembling with pleasure – can't go on with my Letter – because Harold Nicolson has rung up to say *The Waves* is a masterpiece. Ah Hah – so it wasn't all wasted then. I mean this vision I had here has some force upon other minds. Now for a cigarette and then a return to sober composition.

Monday, November 16th 1931

Here I will give myself the pleasure – shall I? – of copying a sentence or two from Morgan's unsolicited letter on *The Waves*: I expect I shall write to you again when I have re-read *The*

Waves. I have been looking in it and talking about it at Cambridge. It's difficult to express oneself about a work which one feels to be so very important, but I've the sort of excitement over it which comes from believing that one's encountered a classic.

I daresay that gives me more substantial pleasure than any letter I've had about any book. Yes, I think it does, coming from Morgan. For one thing it gives me reason to think I shall be right to go along this very lonely path. I mean in the City today I was thinking of another book – about shopkeepers, and publicans, with low life scenes: and I ratified this sketch by Morgan's judgement. Dadie agrees too. Oh yes, between 50 and 60 I think I shall write out some very singular books, if I live. I mean I think I am about to embody at last the exact shapes my brain holds.[27]

The communal evaluation of the work, in brief, invariably leads the artist back to the first stages of creativity, with the indomitable desire to make again, to renew the exacting contract with the language and the culture, to further formulate the elusive shapes of primordial impulse and pre-semantic experience. The loss of such an audience during the years of the war, severely curtailing the last two phases of the creative process, may well have been a major factor in Virginia Woolf's suicide. On 27 June 1940, nine months before her suicide, Virginia Woolf wrote in her journal:

the war – our waiting while the knives sharpen for the operation – has taken away the outer wall of security. No echo comes back. I have no surroundings. I have so little sense of a public that I forget about Roger [her biography of Roger Fry] coming or not coming out. Those familiar circumvolutions – those standards – which have for so many years given back an echo and so thickened my identity are all wide and wild as the desert now.

I mean, there is no 'autumn', no winter. We pour to the edge of a precipice . . . and then? I can't conceive that there will be a 27th July 1941.[28]

Virginia Woolf drowned herself on 28 March 1941.

In this account of the composition of *The Waves*, based largely on the diaries of Virginia Woolf, I have suggested that there may be four typologically distinct but experientially overlapping phases to the creative act. First, there must be the release of an expressive impulse; this impulse then has to work in and through the active medium (full of invitations and resistances) of the art form chosen. Second, in this encounter, it must struggle towards a formal symbolic completion, the realization of final form. Third, it must be presented to an audience inviting an immediate aesthetic response. Finally, it has to be evaluated, made sense of, judged, related, taken into the collective imagination of the culture or, for various complex reasons, left on the edges, either to wither and die or to be reclaimed by another generation, another age. The reader might here find it useful to refer to the diagram at the beginning of the chapter.

The Case of the Unicorn

I have taken literature, specifically the composition of *The Waves* as my example, but essential to the argument is the notion that these four phases characterize the sequence of movements attending any serious artistic creation in any art form from music to dance, from film to sculpture. To extend the analysis I would like now to examine the case of *Unicorn* (see Plate 7); a remarkable sculpture by David Powell submitted as his creative project for the Language, Arts and Education MA at the University of Sussex, in the summer of 1993.

Initially, David Powell was beset by a bewildering number of possibilities for the project – an autobiographical three-dimensional box, a sculpture relating to the natural environment, a Madonna and child in stained glass – but his choice crystallized, suddenly and dramatically, around the archetypal image of the unicorn. Almost at once, the compulsion to create a sculpture of this fabulous animal led to the resonant field of the unicorn and the primordial beast (see Plate 8).

The very first phase of creativity, the eruption of an impulse demanding symbolic articulation, rapidly moved into the known world of cultural exemplars and inherited icons. In an account of his own creative process David wrote:

> I had already borrowed a book from the university library called *Romanticism*, simply because I wanted to understand what the term really meant. The book afforded immediate availability of good reproductions of paintings of lively horses by Eugene Delacroix, Theodore Gericault and George Stubbs. For horses, read unicorns. This was a lucky coincidence which gave me a solid pictorial start.[29]

The search for images led to the sixteenth-century *Dame à la Licorne* tapestries in the Musée de Cluny, Paris as well as to the photographs collected in a volume, *Horses and Ponies.*

From the outset there were two main concerns; one to remain true to the emerging spirit of the unicorn, the other to interpret that image into two dimensional shape and then into three dimensional sculpture. The first stratagem was to cultivate a profound state of negative capability. David surrounded himself with a personal selection of compelling images:

> I decided to surround myself with all the useful images from my books, care of my college photocopier, set at 141%. I densely covered the walls inside my house with pictures. My theory was that in this way I could just assimilate the build of the beast, merely by being, rather than needing to actually learn it. Set up as a subliminal possibility, I do not know of course if this was effective.[30]

In this state of vulnerable immersion, David began to perceive the world through the single polished lens of his obsession. Nothing was truly observed except that which conformed to the lineaments of the emerging archetype. In London, he discovered in the Institute of Contemporary Arts some plaster casts of cattle's hoof-prints; at Picadilly Circus he spotted the *Horses of the Helios* by Rudy Weller; in both cases he sketched what he saw with absorbed attention, wondering: 'Is this Unicorn already affecting my perception?'.[31]

Slowly, the precise image of his unicorn became clearer; it was to rear up (not unlike Delacroix's *Horse Frightened by a Storm*, 1824); it was to be around six feet in height (in fact, it was to be considerably taller); it was to be free standing and it was to be constructed of rough wood simply dismantled from builders' pallets. The form became even clearer as David actively experimented with possible structures; this included the making of pipe-cleaner models, large charcoal drawings, and a lay figure (jointed with the aid of split pins) that made visible the spatial articulations of the animal as it moved. Eventually the first stage of the unicorn's creation culminated in a large two dimensional image. David wrote:

> The drawing eventually satisfied me. From the base of the spine sprang a line which arched down to the level of the cloven feet. This indicated the tail, effectively the third leg.
>
> So where's the hair? The mane, the tail? A unicorn's tresses go beyond this. He has a beard, like a goat, and fine switches

at his fetlocks. On draught horses these are called feathers. I applied collages of torn newspaper to represent streaming hair. The racing pages of the *Guardian* seemed appropriate. [For David had already appointed his unicorn as 'a defender of our potential space'.]

Finally, the crowning glory, the horn, which I made as long as the distance between forehead and ceiling allowed, out of paper folded to a point.

I've spent days working on this picture. It has been tiring, at times nervous-making, and it has fully engaged me. I've been aware of time slipping by, and often rued the fact that this piece is not the end product.

Not the final piece but nevertheless vital, the wall-drawing forced me to consider every part of the posture and the anatomy. Two-dimensional mistakes preclude three-dimensional ones and are a lot easier to rectify. It was a problem processor, if not solver. Most importantly of all, the wall-drawing was my entrée to the unicorn. After seven weeks preparation, I feel ready to begin the sculpture.[32]

The formal struggle now was to convert the two dimensional image into a compelling three dimensional sculptural form. Working under considerable stress David made a working structure that represented in sculptural space the equivalent of the two dimensional image:

That evening I put together a very quick and crude structure, based on the drawing. The legs had one joint each, no ankles, no feet, just stumps. The back pair screwed to either end of the hip board, at the bottom of the rigid spine, the front pair to the shoulder board at the top. The neck-piece was also fixed to the top of the spine, which supported a rough head, triangular if viewed from above. As in the drawing, the head pointed backwards, for drama, and, now, balance. The horn was just a great spike; and the tail, jointed once, like a leg, propped the whole thing up. The day had been a hard won battle.

The 'sketch sculpture' held its promise overnight. The unicorn on the wall had generated another in space. The shift from 2-d to 3-d has taken place, but there can be no bridge between the two, for there is nowhere in between. There is no transition, it has to be a leap.

This must be of immense importance to a sculptor, but I had never really seen it before. Along with this discovery, now crystal clear, comes the realisation that my task is definable again, having crossed the void.[33]

The resources, he went on to write, 'have all come from my centre, and I am allowing the task alone increasingly to possess me'.[34] Each part of the body's soaring structure – the limbs, the feet, the spine, the shoulders, the pelvis, the neck, the head, the open mouth – represented at once technical and artistic problems of the highest order. 'Everything must be part of the whole', David wrote; more practically: 'My saw is indifferent. It does not care where it cuts. You need strong magic to get the inanimate on your side'.[35]

Work on the unicorn's tail revealed further spiritual and artistic possibilities:

> As I made the tail it came to me that I did not need to shape every piece. If I incorporated, splintered or smashed wood this would highlight the process and the material, and also surprise and engage the mind of the viewer. Since all unicorns must be created, this *is* a unicorn.[36]

After days of labour – time perfecting the spiritual head of the animal, of resolving the boxed-in chest, the fine tapering horn, the flying mane – there was one further decision to make, a decision that profoundly affected the ultimate meaning of the work. It is interesting at this stage, also, that the artist now considers his future audience, whereas in the earlier stages it is *too intense* and *too unrealized* to engage with the viewer's apprehension. As the work reaches symbolic form, the maker is already considering his audience. The decision involved using a broken pallet as part of the whole piece:

> I decided to include the pallet. I carefully sawed and broke into it as if it was being consumed. The smashed wood, I imagined, suggested noise to accompany the movement. The audience would witness and participate in the genesis of the myth.[37]

At last the work was complete. From its first inception to its final form it had gone through a series of transformations; it had drawn imaginatively and compulsively from the field of the unicorn; it had moved from two dimensional image to three dimensional sculpture; it had presented technical problems of a seemingly insurmountable kind that, in turn, gave way to higher levels of artistic integration, each new integration presenting a further challenge; and, right to the end, fundamental decisions with regard to its inner significance had to be taken

– the last one, the inclusion of the broken pallet in the composition of the work being of crucial significance to the power of the sculpture.

The next phase of the creative act moves to presentation. In the case of David Powell's work, a context was already waiting. On a Saturday Day Conference at the University of Sussex the sculpture was exhibited in a room of its own. The other students on the course, as well as the tutors, gathered round the *Unicorn* in a breathless silence. It was clear, at once, that the work, in its urgency of articulated movement, in its spiritual nobility, had deeply affected everyone present. This was the moment of immediate aesthetic response, of that preverbal recognition that says 'yes' to a work of art, without quite knowing why. Later these responses work their way into approximate language and critical evaluation. Later formal reports were to follow. Later still, there were further exhibitions of the piece. So it is that the art creation moves away from the creator and enters the collective life of the imagination.

Reflecting later on what he had created, David wrote:

> At the very centre of this individuality seem to be the archetypal, atavistic inner visions, collective memories of myth . . . Mythology seems to be magnanimous. It has a greatness of soul too big for trivia. It is so beautifully, exquisitely general. Its auspices are non-specific, universal, stepping far back to allow for a wide or panoramic view.
>
> What does the unicorn care for the premier league, the FT share index, or party politics?
>
> He cares for purity, the fulfilment of our imaginative potential, the destiny of the earth.
>
> Of countless fine subjects for the artist, none can reach as deep as myth. The unicorn and I mutually recreated each other.
>
> I have boldly claimed that work (art) is more fun than fun is. More quietly, it brings us moments of epiphany.[38]

In brief, this unicorn was created for our own bewildered but dynamic twentieth century. Deriving from collective myth, it finally returned to it. In this respect, the artist is midwife to the universal and, having given birth, waits impatiently for the next sign of creation and for the creative act to begin again.

On Creativity in Education

In the past many theories of creativity have derived from the model of scientific activity. In 1926 Joseph Wallas put forward the following four stages:

Preparation
Incubation
Illumination
Verification

In 1953 Osborn expanded these stages to include the following seven movements:

Orientation
Preparation
Analysis
Ideation
Incubation
Synthesis
Evaluation

These categories offer useful conceptual schemata for abstract and scientific acts of creative formulation and understanding. They do not fit artistic activity so neatly. In this chapter I have indicated the distinctive phases of creativity in the making of a work of art. It is only a rough schema, a working schema, but if in broad outline it corresponds to the nature of the creative process, it could have value in improving the quality of arts teaching. It could heighten the teacher's awareness of how to pace and space, of when to intervene, and on what terms, and of what formal and informal conditions may be necessary to complete whatever expressive activity has been set in motion. It also confirms the existence of an aesthetic field as described in Chapter 4, the need for a dynamic background, for exemplars and models, not only from which to learn actively but also to struggle against, to overcome, and to transcend. In Chapter 9 I will outline a programme of work in creative writing based on both the Socratic principle of reflection and the four phases of the creative act as exemplified in the creation of *The Waves* and *Unicorn*.

Here my intention has been to explore the schema in relationship to two fine creative arts. The assumption is that something of the same dynamic is at work in the creation of all art, at whatever level or stage of development. We need to develop a style and structure for teaching the arts that allows for both the babble and the rhapsody or, rather, that moving from babble to rhapsody (and back to babble) allows profound acts of inner liberation and transcendence to take place. For we all have a profound inner need to place our statues and unicorns (often buried, fractured and lost) against the sky. The new paradigm in arts teaching exists, in large measure, to secure that inner liberation.

Notes

1 See PETER ABBS (ed.) (1987) *Living Powers: the Arts in Education*, London, Falmer Press, pp. 56–62.

2 (1984) *The Diaries of Virginia Woolf* (ed.) ANNE BELL (five volumes) 1980, London, The Hogarth Press.

3 *Ibid.*

4 VIRGINIA WOOLF (1966), 'On Being Ill', in *Collected Essays*, vol. II, London, Hogarth Press, p. 193.

5 *Ibid.*, p. 195.

6 *Ibid.*, p. 196.

7 WOOLF (1984).

8 *Ibid.*

9 See ROBERT WITKIN (1974) *The Intelligence of Feeling*, London, Heinemann Educational Books, pp. 180–3.

10 The first manuscript notebook of *The Waves* (New York Public Library, Berg Collection).

11 WOOLF (1984).

12 *Ibid.*

13 WOOLF (1966).

14 *Ibid.*

15 WOOLF (1984).

16 WOOLF (1966) 'Women in Fiction', p. 195.

17 WOOLF (1984).

18 *Ibid.*

19 *Ibid.*

20 *Ibid.*

21 *Ibid.*

22 *Ibid.*

23 *Ibid.*

24 *Ibid.*

25 *Ibid.*

26 *Ibid.*

27 *Ibid.*

28 *Ibid.*

29 David Powell in his own account of the creation of *Unicorn*, 'Angels are Something We Have to Wrestle with', essay for Language, Arts and Education MA, submitted summer 1993 unpublished.

30 *Ibid.*

31 *Ibid.*

32 *Ibid.*

33 *Ibid.*
34 *Ibid.*
35 *Ibid.*
36 *Ibid.*
37 *Ibid.*
38 *Ibid.*

Section III

On the Practice of Arts Education

Chapter 7

Educational Drama as Cultural Dispossession

Of all the arts in schools drama and movement are the least encumbered with a corpus of techniques which teachers feel they must impart to pupils. Drama has emerged and grown in schools at a much later time than the other arts and its 'youth' is touched with the spirit of the times which is for the relaxing of constraints and the release of personal initiative and expression. Some of the most pressing doubts about the value of what the drama teacher is doing stem from this very freedom, this lack of imposition of formal control.

Robert Witkin

It began in the Sixties when we tore down proscenium arches and turned our backs on the classics, those hated symbols of the bourgeois culture. What we threw out was the craft of playwrighting; classic narrative structure. New, young writers were taken up who had no knowledge of what makes a play work, and placed in the hands of directors and actors who had no ability to guide them towards the basics of their craft. A couple of generations of would-be chair-makers have produced a vast array of bean-bag seats. Without any guidance within their trade, they learned from the only instructive form available: the television. If any one thing characterised the new writing of the Eighties it was the short-scene, episodic 'naturalism' of the TV. For writers, with no wider influences, this has been disastrous.

Noel Greig

Introduction

This chapter takes an unconventional form. It consists of three documents in which I make the case that educational drama over the last three or four decades has badly neglected the aesthetic field of drama, namely the continuum of theatre. It has operated in exile from its own traditions and thus deprived its students of any living sense of a tradition involving plays, actors, performances and interpretations. Fortunately, there are now signs of a return to the continuum of theatre. The opening paragraph, for example, of the Arts Council *Drama in Schools* (1991) begins:

> Drama is an art, a practical activity and an intellectual discipline. It involves the creation of imagined characters and situations which are enacted within a designated space. A drama education which begins with play may eventually include all the elements of theatre. Like all the arts, drama helps us to make sense of the world.[1]

In 1993 a frustrated student completing a PGCE drama course at a university wrote to the *Times Educational Supplement* and concisely put his case for drama as an arts specialism:

> As a drama student on a Postgraduate Certificate in Education course, can somebody tell me what is the role of drama in the curriculum?
>
> As far as I can see when we are not 'doing issues', we seem little more than a service-subject to English, history and pastoral studies.
>
> Isn't it time that drama stood up for itself and carved out a place for itself in the curriculum, assuming the importance that it has always been denied?
>
> To me it seems quite simple. Instead of English worrying about teaching Shakespeare, why not let drama do the job? After all we are specialists in the subject and know about teaching the Bard in more than the two dimensions it is mostly taught in now.
>
> I'm sure I needn't mention the usual 'these-are-plays-to-be-acted' argument, but with myself and others chasing after the decreasing number of drama jobs (state sector) we want to be respected for teaching drama and be recognised as specialists in the same way that science teachers are specialists.[2]

Both these positions are close to the one developed in the three following documents and both are signs of a significant change in the

Plate 2: Rembrandt van Rijn: Self-Portrait, *1669 Like Socrates, Rembrandt explores the meaning of his existence but through the gestures, tones and textures of vibrant paint.*

Plate 3:   Vincent van Gogh: Self-Portrait, *1889. van Gogh remorselessly continues the tradition of Rembrandt in his search for self-knowledge (Paris, Musée d'Orsay).*

Plate 4: Martha Graham in Strike, 1927. Meaning can be symbolized through kinaesthetic movement and gesture as much as through verbal language (photographer Soichi Sunami).

Plate 5:   Jane Lapotaire: MA Language Arts and Education master-class at the University of Sussex in 1992. Drama must involve the knowledge of theatre and be ready to use the apprenticeship model of learning again.

Plate 6: Painting by Katrina Schwab, aged 6 years, Daubeney Primary School, Hackney. The work demonstrates the spontaneous aesthetic sensibility of a young child. To be developed further it must be taken into the aesthetic field of art.

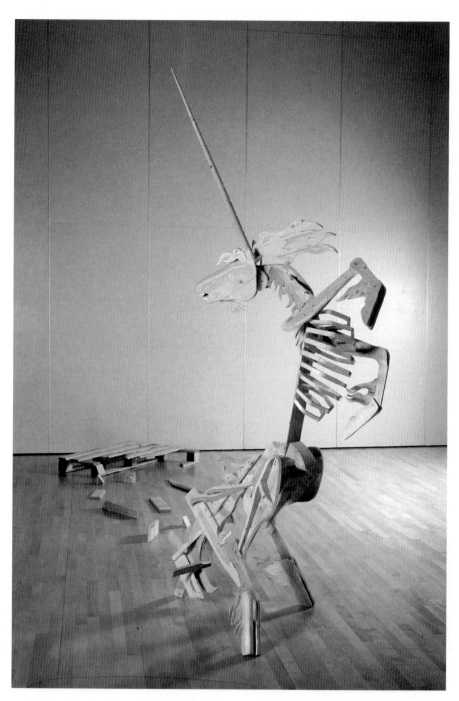

Plate 7: David Powell: Unicorn. *'Of countless fine subjects for the artist, none can reach as deep as myth'.*

Plate 8:   Eugene Delacroix: Tiger Attacking a Wild Horse. *Delacroix's work entered the field of the unicorn.*

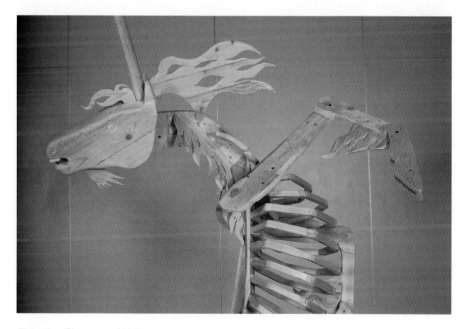

Plate 9:   Close up of Unicorn.

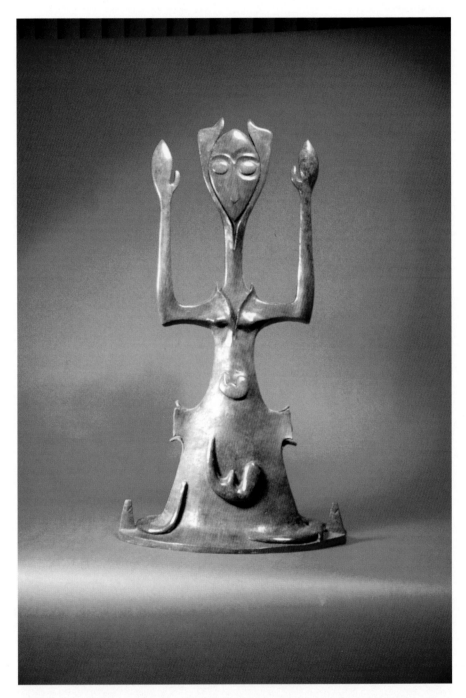

Plate 10: Sculpture by John Meirion Morris: Modron. *If art is to disturb and fulfil us, it must return again to the repressed realm of the sacred.*

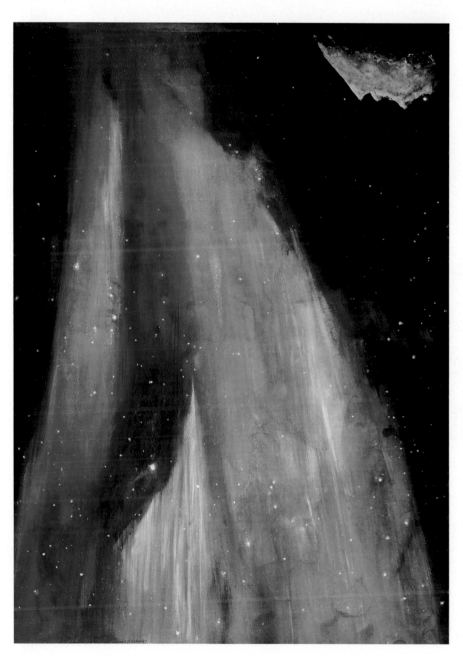

Plate 11: Keith Grant: Aurora Borealis, Mountain and Stars (1992). A celebration of the cosmos as seen through the spirit of awe and tranced contemplation.

Plate 12:   Herbert Read 1960, influential art critic and educationalist.

Plate 13: Peter Fuller, iconoclast and conservationist.

teaching of drama. Unfortunately, the national curriculum has left little room for such a major reconstruction. That is a structural problem that will call for a dedicated politics and philosophy; what is important first, though, is some agreement about the strengths and weaknesses of the drama in education tradition and a better understanding of the basic elements in the new configuration of drama as an arts discipline within the emerging arts paradigm.

The three related documents are as follows. The first one was a challenge to drama teachers written and published in *London Drama* in 1987. The arguments used here were to be rephrased in my preface to David Hornbrook's *Education in Drama* (1991) and this preface provoked a challenge from Gavin Bolton (a leading theoretician in the educational drama world) to justify my attack. This I did in the second document *An Open Letter to Gavin Bolton*.[3] The third document is based on an open seminar given at the University of Sussex in 1992 to elaborate some of the points made in the letter. Taken together, I hope they form a coherent critique of educational drama and indicate the nature of drama as an arts discipline in accord with the new emerging paradigm of arts education.

The Dilemmas Confronting Educational Drama: First Critique 1987

At the moment, I suspect, many drama teachers would be opposed to calling their discipline 'aesthetic' and 'symbolic'. The tradition of drama teaching has been largely child-centred and psychological in orientation. The titles of two key books in the tradition, *Child Drama* and *Development through Drama* display well the dominant preoccupations – preoccupations which have worked against collective notions of culture and tradition and against the place of theatre. Not only that, but the current notion of 'drama as a learning medium' also works powerfully in an opposing direction. Many teachers now see drama as a kind of instrument either to bring about ideological change or, more frequently, some form of adaptive behaviour in relationship to social needs. Both these uses of drama have one major premise in common. They assume that drama is a technique to secure an end – political understanding or well adjusted behaviour – which lies *outside the actual drama*. This instrumental concept in the present political climate has become extremely powerful and extremely popular, yet it means that one can have drama in the classroom in which there may be virtually no aesthetic or symbolic content, no critical interpretation, no sense of any tradition, no sense of any art form. This is a disturbing state of affairs.

One of the problems with educational drama has been its excessive reliance on too few 'gurus': on Peter Slade, on Brian Way, on Gavin Bolton, on Dorothy Heathcote. Four decades of practice virtually determined by four individuals! It is not that those individuals have not been original pioneers (it is obvious that they have) it is, rather, that it is impossible for so few individuals to create that complex community of *perspectival understanding and dissent* necessary for the vitality of any arts discipline. If one compares English to drama, the point becomes quickly clear. There are now so many schools of literary interpretation that there is no room for any easy piety and also, at the same time, considerable room for acts of intellectual and imaginative synthesis. The situation itself engenders argument, complexity and, in particular, an awareness of a long and rich tradition. Drama teachers, in contrast, have tended to move, euphorically or uneasily, from one dominant trend to another, without always seeing the possible narrowness or the inevitable partiality of the prevailing faction.

Such conditions have not provided teachers of drama with a synoptic and critical understanding of a distinctive symbolic field. Nor has the profound anti-intellectualism of the progressive movement in education (which provided the conceptual matrix for the birth of educational drama) given most drama teachers the necessary conceptual equipment. I still remember a well known drama teacher saying: 'I *never* recommend a book . . .' As a result there has not been sufficient concern for those comprehensive principles which would integrate, for example, drama and theatre, process and performance, innovation and tradition, the child and the inherited culture, the open space as well as the closed stage. These simple and falsifying dichotomies have plagued and impoverished the history of educational drama. Thus what is needed in drama teaching is a conceptual revolution which would begin the careful delineation of all the elements that constitute drama in order to forge a better synthesis, *a comprehensive and structually demarcated totality*. Such a revolution might bring about, at least, three major shifts.

First of all, it might bring about a recognition of the place of the whole of drama in education, in particular, a formal recognition of *the inherited practices of all known cultures*, particularly our own. This reclamation would necessarily include both 'high' and 'low' drama, the drama of the street and that of the theatre. A theory of 'types' might clarify the variety of symbolic modes and formally indicate the missing elements in drama teaching. Without doubt such a movement, *seeing the whole of the drama of the past as the basis for critical appreciation and dramatic improvisation and performance*, would bring about a long over-due reunion with theatre. It would also parallel the movement now taking place in dance studies and dance teaching.

The second shift, intimately related to the first, would be that of a renewal of interest in the symbolic and aesthetic dimension. In Dorothy Heathcote's work there are two radically divergent preoccupations, one with drama as a technique for learning and the other with narrative action and the understanding of the symbolic and universal. It is the latter which needs greater elaboration for it is in 'narrative' and in 'non-discursive symbol' that much of the aesthetic power of drama and theatre lies. An aesthetic of drama would attend particularly to the metaphoric rather than the literal modes of delineation – those mo-ments in improvised work, for example, when an ordinary object or a simple gesture resonate with multiple meanings, all of which sym-bolize the emotional core of the drama being created. Such high aes-thetic moments in improvisation could then be linked to those in the tradition of theatre. And in this way a sense of an aesthetic field and a tradition could be established.

The third shift would entail a greater appreciation of *theory*. Any delineation of a living tradition would have to be *qualitative* and *critical* or it would only give birth to a new sterile academicism, contradicting all the best things that educational drama has actually achieved in the last three decades. The categories which selected the inherited material (and its plurality of conventions) would have to be open to constant debate and, through debate and dissent, change and development. This requires philosophical acuity, historical sense and a critical cast of mind. Furthermore, as in most of the other arts disciplines, surely it is essen-tial that pupils in their drama-work acquire greater powers of evalua-tion of their own drama, as well as the drama of others? This doesn't happen *naturally*. It is dependent on *the conscious forging of an interpretive language*. It depends on the creation and sensitive application of a range of critical concepts. In this context, it is vital that drama teachers engage more fully with intellectual theory, with psychoanalysis, with structuralism, with philosophical anthropology, with the history of the theatre, and, in particular, with aesthetics – with, for example, the writings of David Best, Roger Scruton and Peter Fuller. Concepts allow one to reflect on the status quo, to see above it and beyond it and, thereby, to envisage other and better possibilities.

These are deliberately contentious reflections. They arise from a collective study of all the arts in the curriculum. It is our view that now is the time for 'educational drama' to reclaim its aesthetic identity, to renew its connection with theatre and tradition and to enter more unequivocally into the arts community. Chris Havell in his essay on drama in *Living Powers* concluded:

> One can only hope that the emerging interest in the aesthetic nature of drama and its place in a coherent arts education will encourage teachers and students to reflect on the final inadequacy of any instrumental view. If we don't attempt to place drama squarely in the aesthetic field then narrow and partial influences will determine its nature. We can only hope drama teachers' interest in the aesthetic has not come too late.[4]

We now need to provide a framework for the aesthetic renewal and unification of the six major art forms. We hope drama teachers will seriously consider our case.

An Open Letter to Gavin Bolton: Second Critique 1992

May I begin by reminding you of the passage which has given so much offence to some members of the educational drama world and to yourself? It comes from the preface to David Hornbrook's new book *Education in Drama*. There, in order to put his argument in context, I offered a brief historical survey of drama in education. Having glanced at the work of Peter Slade and Brian Way and the practice of child drama, I went on as follows:

> In the 1970s and 1980s drama changed again and the conception of 'drama as a learning medium' became, largely through the energetic work of Dorothy Heathcote and Gavin Bolton, hugely popular. But once again the new developments excluded any significant reference to actors, theatre and plays – what, in this study, David Hornbrook names the three conceptual outcasts. Drama was converted into an effective tool for enquiry which could be extended across the curriculum but, cut off from the aesthetic field, it forfeited any sense of intrinsic identity. Devoid of art, devoid of the practices of theatre, devoid of artistic and critical terminology drama became a method of teaching without *a subject*.[5]

These then are the offending remarks. And in this letter I want to stand by them and expand them.

But first it must be clear that my central target is drama as a learning medium and its deficiencies from an aesthetic and artistic point of view. It is simply not a 'condemnatory dismissal' of your work. A movement, as you yourself must know from your own experience in educational drama, is always larger than any of its individual protagonists, however influential. In my preface to David Hornbrook it is quite explicit that my highly critical analysis relates *to the whole movement*, is not personal in orientation and does not refer exclusively to your own contribution. In this letter, then, I want to elaborate my remarks on educational drama and also make *some* references to your own work for, as I understand it, your work with all its virtues does largely bypass what I call the aesthetic field and, to my knowledge, nowhere offers a convincing or comprehensive view of drama as an arts discipline.

You will probably have noticed that in the offending passage I *do* indicate the positive aspect of educational drama. I do say it went across the curriculum (and here I would add particularly the primary school curriculum) as an 'effective tool for enquiry'. Indeed, I would suggest that for twenty years the dominant notion of drama (deriving partly from your own work and that of Dorothy Heathcote, but by no means exclusively) has been that it exists to activate learning of a social and psychological kind. Most typically, a drama teacher would select an issue, often suggested by the pupils (family violence, school conflict, rape, poverty, etc.) then he or she would guide it into narrative action (with the whole class or in groups) and then (either during the creation of the narrative or afterwards or, both) encourage reflections on the action and its human and ideological implications. At best, this activity was Socratic in nature and marvellously effective. It worked from the immediate 'now' of the pupils' experience and through the operation of a number of dramatic techniques ('hot seating', 'the mantle of the expert', 'the teacher in role') moved towards an engaged enquiry into a certain kind of 'problem' or 'theme' or, as you generally call it in your early writing, 'topic'.

The main purpose in all this was to change the pupils' understanding. *Educationally* I believe there is a great deal to be said for this kind of pedagogy; it can open up the discursive curriculum and release highly engaged and enactive modes of learning. It can; and it did; and it will continue to do so. The problem arises, however, when such a pedagogy is itself equated *with being an arts discipline or when (more often) it subverts the place of drama as an arts discipline.*

The problem is brought out well in the following quotation from *Issues in Educational Drama* (1983) where Haydn Davies reflecting on 'learning *through* drama' (his italics) writes:

it will be clear that learning, that is, changes in behaviour, will be looked for not in the area of mastery over the medium, but rather in that area of outcomes resulting from the use of acting out and its attendant activities.[6]

Thus, the art is *incidental* to the learning gained. In an arts discipline, in contrast, the learning cannot be extricated from the art form. The increasing mastery of the medium is *in itself* the chief way to greater freedom and greater understanding. Hence, in the arts the primacy of the expressive act and the realized symbol. Those who believe in drama as an arts discipline would espouse, in other words, a notion of learning *in* drama, not *through* it. And *that* difference is crucial for it exposes the difference between a general pedagogy and a distinctive discipline of the imagination.

It is here in this distinction between drama as a device to facilitate learning and drama as an arts discipline *centred on art* that any critique of educational drama, from an arts perspective, must begin. In fact, the critique began some time ago. In 1979 John Allen was sounding the warning note. In his important but somewhat diffuse *Drama in Schools* he wrote:

> The repeated emphasis on drama as 'learning by doing' is to devalue drama until it is virtually unrecognizable as an art . . .
>
> We are selling our children short when we limit drama to role-playing and the exploration of personal relationships . . .
>
> [Drama is] a subject that must be allowed to stand on the basis of its own integrity.[7]

John Allen was right. For there was every reason to believe that as educational drama advanced across the world, drama as a distinctive arts discipline (with its many genres, texts, techniques, modes of performance and reception and its many commanding imaginative and expressive achievements from Greek tragedy onwards) went underground and became woefully neglected. Indeed, the subject became so repressed that notions relating to genre, performance and classical texts became all but unthinkable and, certainly, unsayable. As a result, it stood no chance of being located as an identifiable discipline when the national curriculum was being formulated.

Significantly, Jonothan Neelands wrote in 1984 in *Making Sense of Drama* that:

> Drama is seen as an active process which is useful to learners if it is appropriately introduced. It is not seen as a subject or as a

distinct curriculum area (we will not be considering theatre arts) . . . It is seen instead as a classroom resource.[8]

By the end of the 80s the Government had made precisely that conception of drama a curricular reality.

It was this shocking disappearance of drama as a distinctive arts discipline that urged me to write the trenchant preface to David Hornbrook's volume. That was, in fact, some time ago. Now, I believe that all that was repressed and split off in educational drama must be reclaimed and given primacy; and, furthermore, that it should be placed, unapologetically within a new matrix of understanding which makes creative sense of the teaching of all the great and distinctive arts disciplines: art, music, dance, film, literature, as well as drama. That is why David Hornbrook's book is in a library of twelve volumes on *aesthetic education*. This task of profound systematic reclamation will not be easy for the inhibitions and blocks (and the anxieties that fold around them) are many and deep. But the movement is underway and is, I believe, now unstoppable. For it is part of the contemporary postmodernist impulse to transcend the cultural amnesia of the last decades and to rehouse ourselves culturally, to reanimate, to recreate, to retell, to inwardly and imaginatively possess all that has gone before us. It is to do with inscribing ourselves into a historic culture, not as passive but as creative agents. It is to do with a conservationist (though not uncritical) aesthetics which has been absent in drama teaching (with some fine exceptions) for far too long. After child drama, after educational drama, we want a radical poetics of drama based on a continuous historic culture and the dynamic power of the imagination. That is the agenda, I believe, for the 90s. And it is an agenda that goes across the arts, disrupting settled practices in other arts disciplines to extend their range.

I would like now before returning to the specific points raised by your letter to explore these general points a little further. Take, for one moment, from a cultural and aesthetic point of view, the very term 'educational drama'. Can you not see what a desperate mutant it is? Envisage the whole intricate evolved world of drama (from Sophocles to Caryl Churchill) with all its connections with mime, with carnival, with *commedia dell'arte*, as well as its obvious contemporary relationships with video, radio and television, not to mention its characteristic forms in Japan, China, India and other non-western cultures and, then, repeat the term 'educational drama'. At that moment you may suddenly see how I look at it. What an immense contraction is involved; what a severe blinkering of vision. Or, if you prefer it, invent the following hybrids: 'educational music', 'educational literature', 'educational ceramics', 'educational film'. I would suggest that all of these terms strike our linguistic imagination as lean and impossible monsters. *For an art maker or an arts teacher, committed to the cultural continuum, they are virtually unthinkable.* And yet we have had this term 'educational drama' with all its artistically self-mutilating tendencies elevated as an all but definitive concept in most of our thinking about drama in schools for over two decades.

I know that in your own writings, as you say in your letter, you have taken some of your concepts ('tension', 'contrast', 'symbolisation' etc.) from the tradition of theatre and arts discourse. Here, indeed, it is true that *your* work has not been devoid of 'the practices of theatre'. But, as I see it, you hardly ever return them to the aesthetic field, put them back in that infinitely broader matrix from which they have derived. (There is a wonderful exception when in *Drama as Education* you talk about the prismatic device and relate it to *Hamlet*, Peter Brook's production of *A Midsummer Night's Dream* and the *Marat/Sade*.) Nor does it seem that you have felt under much obligation to introduce pupils in our state schools to, say, the compelling achievements of Greek theatre, medieval theatre, Elizabethan theatre, naturalistic theatre, modern theatre in all its variety, Noh theatre, Kathakali, etc. Nor have you thought fit to explore in detail the diverse techniques they employ as creative devices for the elaboration of form and meaning in the drama studio, nor the artistic possibilities of a rich cross fertilization between different cultural traditions. Analysing the educational drama literature it seems to me, as I implied earlier, that educational drama has worked in a kind of hermetically sealed bubble in which has resided the thin air of topics, issues and themes. Certainly, as an investigative tool it has forged or adapted some successful dramatic techniques and given an animating shape to group enquiry, but this has been gained at the price of an astonishing neglect of one of the finest artistic forms ever evolved for the exploration of human consciousness. Whatever happened to that formidable challenge on arts teachers to bring the symbolic achievement of the culture into living conjunction with the expressive energies of their pupils? And who else in the absence of the drama teacher could possibly do it? How is it that such a task in arts education became all but entirely eclipsed by the notions of topics and interdisciplinary enquiry?

Of course, you may think I exaggerate. We are in desperate need of a national survey of drama teaching in our schools, but, if we take the literature of drama education seriously, the evidence *there* is massive and largely unambiguous. I gave some examples earlier. Here is another. It is from *Dorothy Heathcote: Drama as a Learning Medium* (a book which must have the dubious distinction of being the most hyperbolic book ever written on educational drama) where we find Betty Jane Wagner claiming:

> As Heathcote sets up a classroom drama and trains teachers, she relies on her theatrical sense. *However, she is not in theatre ever. She thinks we tend to press children far too early to grow the art form of theatre* – the making of an overly explicit statement with one's gesture, and body and voice. . . . *Whether her students ever go into theatre is irrelevant to Heathcote.* Her concern is that they use drama to expand their understanding of life experiences, to reflect on particular circumstances, to make sense of their world in a new and deeper way.[9]

One might have anticipated that someone, somewhere, would have grasped a culturally dispossessed pedagogy and turned it euphorically into a kind of dispossessed educational world religion. Well here it is, under the name of Betty Wagner; and the outcome for theatre is clear. *Educational drama has nothing to do with it.* Indeed, we must not press our children 'to grow the art form'. It is strange, but the idea that there is something slightly dangerous and wayward about theatre permeates much of the education in drama literature. At best (as in the earlier passage from Jonothan Neelands), it is allowed to lurk like a caged animal in embarrassed parentheses. Well, I believe the time has come to lift, without apology, those equivocating parentheses. The time has come to let the animal out of its cage.

Again, if we apply the principle of educational drama to teaching *any of the other art disciplines* the narrowness of the approach becomes swiftly apparent. Imagine, for example, teaching creative writing by using only a free-association exercise and with no reference to any other writers, or imagine teaching the art of painting by allowing only a kind of abstract expressionism, and that without any reference to its practitioners. To attempt such a thing experimentally, that is laudable, but to make it the rationale for the whole troop of arts teachers that is little short of cultural kamikaze.

It is symptomatic of educational drama's exile from its own artistic field that in its defence it has, with the exception of some of your own writing, rarely drawn on aesthetics or on the leading theoretical literature from Aristotle's *Poetics* onwards. Rather, it has tended to draw on passing educational fads and fashions, particularly on communications, sociology and psychology. As Richard Courtney pointed out in *Drama Contact* (1977):

Whereas Slade and Wethered assume the work of Jung, Witkin bases his work upon Piaget. Many of Heathcote's assumptions have similarities with those of Rogers and Maslow, while G.T. Jones has a basis in behavioural psychology.

Social assumptions can differ from writer to writer. Adland, for example, tends towards a group theory, Hunt towards Marxism, while Burton, Heathcote and Way proclaim the dignity of the individual inter-acting with society.[10]

Drawing on such eclectic sources it is not altogether surprising that educational drama lost sense of the primacy of the artistic, of the great cultural continuum, of the power of the imagination and the abiding pertinence of European theatre. What was spun was logically loose, an *ad hoc* 'philosophy' *without a tradition*; an eclectic theory not only provincial (and quickly dated) but also extrinsic to the art.

If you have persevered thus far, I must now return to your letter. I want in conclusion to make three points in relationship to your various comments and challenges. The first one relates to your own artistic claims for drama, the second to my concept of the aesthetic field and the final one to the future of drama.

While, as I said at the outset, my preface was not written as an attack on either your writing or your teaching but on educational drama in general, I *do* see why you are perplexed, for more than most of the other educational drama theorists, you *do* emphasize the aesthetic and artistic in your writings. Yet, at many key points, you too seem often uneasy and equivocal in relationship to art and theatre, you almost get to the point of perception and then generally veer off into the world of topics and discursive learning. Let me give two examples.

In *Towards a Theory of Drama in Education*, talking about symbolization, you give a telling example of how an orange can take on a fully symbolic significance in a drama narrative but then, against the full import of your own argument (based on Susanne Langer) you write:

> An interesting point to note here is that whereas at first the dramatic form controlled and indeed modified the expression of anger, at the end of the lesson their feelings were further contained and *harnessed for the exploration of historical subject matter*. In these terms therefore this illustration represents for me a classic instance of the practice of education. I wish we were able to train teachers to help children 'feel their way into knowledge'.[11]

Now here I believe the educational imperative *to get on with the historical learning* undermines your own insight. It is as if, in the end, you do not trust the primacy of the artistic symbol. You want to put it to use. You want to make the art instrumental to curriculum learning. If you believed in the primacy of art you would see the orange transformed into symbol *is* the very heart of the enterprise. *The art created is the meaning*; it does not have to be extricated to serve propositional knowledge. The tendency to use drama to get *somewhere else* must involve the weakening of the art form and the loss of the power of the symbol. For as Malcolm Ross has claimed, 'dramatic art is a way of knowing which needs neither exegesis nor paraphrase'. Certainly, there is an unresolved ambiguity here in much of your writing.

In *Drama as Education* a similar equivocation emerges. There you *do* affirm community theatre but then, most revealingly, you go on to claim:

> Many pupils in our secondary schools will benefit from a theatre experience just as many enjoy being in a school orchestra. As a performing art, however, drama can make no claim to a higher status than dance or music. They are all equally important as celebration. A special case for drama can only be made in regard to its potency as a model for learning that is both psychological and social.[12]

There is something depressingly negative in your formulation 'drama can make no claim to a higher status than dance or music'. Do you think that dance and music are only for celebration and cannot explore, just as well as drama can, the human condition and its possibilities? Why this *educational* need to make a special case for drama? Are not all the arts engaged with understanding? It seems to demonstrate that you are *not interested in drama as an arts discipline within the generic community of the arts*, but as an instrument for interdisciplinary learning. In the same book you move on to define what drama as an arts discipline would look like: you call it 'the view of drama as celebration of a communal identity' and refer to 'the school play' and 'Community Drama'. But this is hardly a convincing conception of drama as a complex and systematic arts discipline. It is much too narrow. You write: 'In placing a great deal of emphasis on pedagogy, the alternative view of drama may become neglected'. Indeed, it did; but the irony is that your alternative view of drama is not the alternative view of drama at issue. Indeed, any comprehensive view of drama as an arts discipline

built on the constant creative and critical interaction between the imagination of the student and the entire field of dramatic art never seems
to surface in your writing.

This brings me to the notion of aesthetic field. 'Drama', I argued
in that offending preface became 'cut off from the aesthetic field' and
'forfeited any sense of intrinsic identity'. Now, if you consider the
particular meanings I give to this term you will see that it is quite
reasonable for me to state that educational drama operated, for most of
the time, outside it. For me aesthetic field denotes both the four phases
of art making, namely, making, presenting, responding and evaluating
and the symbolic system in which individual art work is always constituted. The latter is a structuralist point. You will find this conception more fully elaborated in my entry on 'aesthetic field' in Trevor
Pateman's *Key Concepts* where I write 'the primary task of arts teachers
is to initiate their pupils into the vast interactive symbolic system of
their disciplines and to do so in the manner of engaging aesthetic
experience, not inert knowledge'.[13] Educational drama, as I have tried
to show throughout this letter, denied the place of theatre and in so
doing disowned its own symbolic matrix. In this very real sense it thus
bypassed the aesthetic field. While in terms of making, presenting,
responding and evaluating, it was always reticent, to say the least, on
presenting (to an audience) and *evaluating* (on artistic criteria). In your
own work your frequent reiteration that educational drama must be an
'art form in process not product' is merely one expression of this denial
of formal performance and artistic evaluation.

Yet, I *do* believe there is a way forward for drama as an arts discipline. What I think has happened over the last four decades is that *one
genre of drama based on improvisation* has been turned into a self justifying
totality. What is needed now is to place that segment back into the vast
circle of drama, with all its genres, all its techniques, with all the
commanding work in our culture and across cultures, with all its
actors, texts, authors, designers and directors and the artistic and intellectual movements and countermovements of which they are a vital
part. The pupil must still remain one central player in this recasting of
drama and improvisation one essential technique for exploration and
the trying out of ideas. Thus in the reconstituted arts discipline there
is no need to jettison what has been created in educational drama;
rather, it is a matter of taking that contribution into an infinitely larger
compass. The *dynamic approach* fostered by educational drama (and child
drama) must be kept. It is the map which needs radically enlarging; it
is the subject which needs reclaiming. If the Arts Council guidance on
drama education *Drama in Schools* and the burgeoning of theatre studies

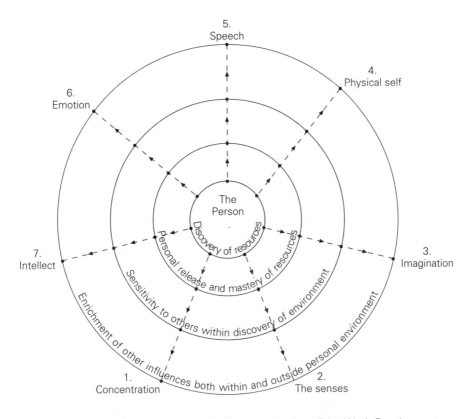

Figure 2 *Diagrammatic representation of self-expression. From Brian Way's Development through Drama, 1967*

are symptomatic of recent developments then the future of drama as an arts discipline may not be as grim as it looked two years ago. Perhaps the full circle of drama is slowly becoming visible? Perhaps, then, it will fit more happily with the other arts in the curriculum and find its proper place there?

Educational Drama as Cultural Dispossession:
Third Critique 1992

Let me begin, at once, by examining Figure 2. It is taken from Brian Way's once highly influential book *Development through Drama*, first published in 1967. It is designed to represent graphically the nature of 'person-centred' or more commonly named 'child-centred' education in relationship to drama.

You will notice how the approach represented through the circles of Figure 2 makes the individual person the single justifying centre of educational activity. *First* the person, it would have us think, and *then* culture and history. This is a specious abstraction with consequences which we will shortly consider. An immediate result of the tabulation is that the teacher becomes secondary; there to *release* what is within the person but not to *inform*, to *follow* but not to challenge or initiate. Brian Way went on to express the teacher's role as follows:

> The teacher's function is not that of imposing a whole new set of (possibly) artificial factors, but of starting with facets of human beings that exist from birth in all people.
>
> All possible points of the circle exist in each person. The diagram below shows the points on the circle that are considered in this book. At this stage, only the inner circle really concerns us, as at the beginnings of drama we are concerned with helping each individual *to discover and explore his or her own resources, irrespective of other people.*
>
> . . . what is valuable is for each person to discover for himself his own way of doing it. This is genuine freedom of opportunity.
>
> It may be that we shall be less satisfied with what comes from the class than we would be if we saw a shadow of our own effort – *but we must console ourselves that it is of them and from them and this is ultimately what is important. The imitation of another person's experience is never as deep as our own experience*, even if, through lack of practice, our own experiences are on the shallow side in the early stages of the work.[14] (my emphasis)

The orientation is clear enough. What is cherished is personal expression; what is critically held back is the received culture and the demands of 'other people'. Significantly in the generation before Brian Way, Peter Slade had coined the word 'child drama' to designate his own practice – a practice which had exerted a profound influence on Way as Way's was subsequently to exert a deep influence on Gavin Bolton's.

But do we need to accept the tenets and the diagram of child-centred education? Or does it represent a fallacy? Is it possible to formulate a view which would enable us to envisage the person *at the outset* not as a self-contained circle but as already a member of a culture who achieved something like a true identity within (and, at times, against) the real pressures and real potentialities of that culture? This is not a difficult position to hold. Indeed, most anthropologists and sociologists would hold some version of it. At a highly abstract level, it would seem to offer a simple working definition of the human condition. In our language it is not easy to connect individual words, but what is needed is a hyphenated compound like 'being-in-culture' or 'being-in-society' to capture the reciprocal nature of human experience. Where else could a child exist but in an encompassing culture? But if this is anthropologically sound, then to hold the resources of the culture back or to confine them to one social class, is to unwittingly commit a social injustice of the first order. To leave children where they *naturally* are is *educationally* to betray them.

Education must eternally beckon to new ground, the promise of possibilities as yet unknown to the pupil or student. Protection of the child from the culture becomes a form of dispossession; and dispossession the pathology of a culture which had lost faith in its own historic existence. As Michael Oakeshott eloquently phrased it:

> Selves are not rational abstractions, they are historic personalities, they are among the components of this world of human achievements; and there is no other way for a human being to make the most of himself than by learning to recognize himself in the mirror of this inheritance.[15]

It is this conception of the historic nature of human existence, of being-in-culture, which enables us to see some of the limitations of educational drama. For while in its *first phase* (Peter Slade and Brian Way) it may have offered possibilities of expression and exploration and in its *second phase* (Dorothy Heathcote and Gavin Bolton) forms of social understanding and Brechtian reflexivity, it seldom offered a living initiation into the collective culture of drama with its playwrights, its actors, its forms, its techniques, its critical terminology; nor did it assiduously connect the aesthetic field of drama with the drama-making potentialities of the individual child.

As I have argued, the dominant educational dramatists have made such a programme virtually *unthinkable*. Let us glance at some of their formulations across three generations. Here, representing the first generation of educational drama teachers, is Peter Slade:

> Drama is part of real life and has its deep origins in the activity and nature of Man. It is quite different from any conception of theatre, which is a small – though attractive – bubble on the froth of civilization.[16]

Here, representing the second generation, is Brian Way:

A basic definition of drama might be simply 'to practise living'. The same definition might well be both adequate and precise as a definition of education; for this reason it is suggested that opportunities for drama should be provided for every child and should be the concern of every teacher. However, for both child and teacher this becomes possible only *if we discard the limitations of theatrical conventions and consider drama as a quite different activity, calling upon different skills, different standards of judgement and entirely different results.* The aim is constant: to develop people, not drama. By pursuing the former, the latter may also be achieved; by pursuing the latter, the former can be totally neglected, if not nullified. By pursuing professional theatre conventions – some dating back more than three hundred years [*sic*] – the point may be missed altogether, the activity reduced to one of interest to only a few, achievable by fewer still, and all quite outside any fundamental aspect of general education. Ultimately, theatre may always remain the concern of the few – drama will increasingly become a way of teaching and a way of learning for everyone.[17]

And here, describing the approach of the third generation of educational drama teachers, is Betty Wagner in her book *Dorothy Heathcote: Drama as a Learning Medium*:

As Heathcote sets up a classroom drama and trains teachers, she relies on her theatrical sense. *However, she is not in theatre ever. She thinks we tend to press children far too early to grow the art form of theatre* – the making of an overly explicit statement with one's gesture, and body and voice . . . *Whether her students ever go into theatre is irrelevant to Heathcote.* Her concern is that they use drama to expand their understanding of life experiences, to reflect on particular circumstances, to make sense of their world in a new and deeper way.[18]

In brief, educational drama through three generations essentially denied *the aesthetic field* of drama, the symbolic field of its own form. It elevated one valuable genre, *improvisation*, and made it the totality.

In discarding the art form of theatre, drama became not a subject within the generic community of the arts, but 'a method of learning' and gave birth to a number of dichotomies which further severed it from the arts. These dichotomies, hardly worthy of close examination, were as follows. Drama teaching it was claimed had to:

a)   be a *process* and not move towards *product*,
b)   be *child-centred* and not *teacher-centred*,
c)   have its source in *child play* or *enquiry* but not *theatre*.

However, all these 'dichotomies' are not essentially antithetical; they are not mutually exclusive. For example, in the arts *a process of making* invariably leads to *the creation of a form or product*; in the teaching of the arts one invariably moves from being *child-centred* to being *teacher-centred* to being child-centred etc. The elevation of so many dubious distinctions in the literature of educational drama only increased the narrowness of the discipline and gave birth to endless divisions and dogmas.

In brief, educational drama has been culturally provincial. It now needs to widen its range and open itself fully to the whole circle of theatre. It needs to bring a wealth of philosophical conception from the long European tradition to its reformulations; not only the mandatory Brecht and Boal but also Aristotle's *Poetics*, Nietzsche's *The Birth of Tragedy* and the formulations of, say, Strindberg, Lorca, T.S. Eliot, Arthur Miller, Jonathan Miller and a hundred others. Students of drama, at whatever level, need more technical terms, more abstract concepts, more awareness of names, movements, genres.

The aim is to open up drama, to conceive in an educational context its furthest boundary lines. Here are some questions which come immediately to mind:

• What about a new taxonomy based on genre: from Greek tragedy to the circus, from medieval theatre to a Japanese Noh play?
• What about identifying all the great dramatic works (not only of western culture) to delineate the continuum?
• What about editing the key texts on dramatic representation from Aristotle's *Poetics* onwards?
• What about bringing all three elements described above into productive and exacting relationship with the expressive powers of the child?
• What about an ambitious mapping of dramatic form and dramatic theory for the comprehensive classroom?

There is only one answer to cultural dispossession; and that is cultural reappropriation. As David Hornbrook has phrased it: 'if drama teachers are to be serious egalitarians then they must give their pupils access to the narratives of our historical consciousness'.[19] Quite so. And the questions above are designed to provoke the remedy. There is no need, of course, to reject what educational drama has done well (brilliantly well, at times); it is rather a question of taking its established practice into an infinitely larger symbolic universe and into the new arts paradigm. As I said at the beginning, there are strong signs that this has already started. Drama in education is, it would seem, at last coming back to the arts.

Notes

1 (1991) *Drama in Schools*, The Arts Council, p. 1.
2 TONY HARRIES (1993) letter page, *The Times Educational Supplement*, 2 April.
3 PETER ABBS (1992) 'An Open Letter to Gavin Bolton', Drama, **1** (1) summer. Gavin Bolton's reply is in the same issue.
4 CHRIS HAVELL (1987) 'Rifts and Reunions: a Reconstruction of the Development of Drama in Education', in PETER ABBS (ed.) *Living Powers: the Arts in Education*, London, Falmer Press, p. 180.
5 PETER ABBS (1991) 'Preface', in DAVID HORNBROOK, *Education in Drama: Casting the Dramatic Curriculum*, London, Falmer Press, p. ix.
6 HAYDN DAVIES (1983) 'An operational Approach to Evaluation', in CHRISTOPHER DAY and JOHN NORMAN (eds) *Issues in Educational Drama*, London, Falmer Press, p. 111.
7 JOHN ALLEN (1979) *Drama in Schools: Its Theory and Practice*, Heinemann, p. 106.
8 JONOTHAN NEELANDS (1984) *Making Sense of Drama A Guide to Classroom Practice*, London, Heinemann Educational Books, pp. 6–7.
9 BETTY JANE WAGNER (1979) *Dorothy Heathcote: Drama as a Learning Medium*, London, Hutchinson, p. 147 (my italics).
10 RICHARD COURTNEY (1977) 'Goals in Drama Teaching', in *Drama Contact*, Ontario, Ontario Institute for Studies in Education.
11 GAVIN BOLTON (1979) *Towards a Theory of Drama in Education*, London, Longman, p. 87 (my italics).
12 GAVIN BOLTON (1979) *Drama as Education*, London, Longman, p. 186.
13 PETER ABBS (1991) 'Entry on "aesthetic field"', in TREVOR PATEMAN, *Key Concepts*, London, Falmer Press, p. 5.
14 BRIAN WAY (1967) *Development through Drama*, Longman, p. 12.
15 MICHAEL OAKESHOTT (1989) *The Voice of Liberal Learning*, New Haven, Yale University Press, p. 48.
16 Peter Slade (1954) in *Child Drama*, London, London University Press, p. 337.

17 WAY (1967) (my italics) p. 5.
18 WAGNER (1979) (my italics) p. 147.
19 DAVID HORNBROOK (1991) *Education in Drama: Casting the Dramatic Curriculum*, London, Falmer Press, p. 111.

Chapter 8

The Teaching of Literature as an Arts Discipline

Art has its own language and illuminates reality only through this other language. Moreover, art has its own dimension of affirmation and negation, a dimension which cannot be co-ordinated with the social process of production.

Herbert Marcuse

The novelist makes no great issue of his ideas. He is an explorer feeling his way in an effort to reveal some unknown aspect of existence. He is fascinated not by his voice but by a form he is seeking, and only those forms that meet the demands of his dream become part of his work. Fielding, Sterne, Flaubert, Proust, Faulkner, Celine, Calvino.

Milan Kundera

Introduction

My aim is to affirm an arts approach to the teaching of literature. In this chapter I will concentrate on principles for the most part; in the next I will concentrate more on practice, and on one specific pro-gramme of work in relationship to creative writing. As with the earlier analysis of the concept of the arts as a generic community, so here I will begin with some historical excavation and then move towards more radical formulations for the future. I am out to establish an approach to the teaching of literature which actually fits the nature of literature as an art form, *a discipline of the imagination*. I will begin with two highly influential approaches, now both more or less defunct, which have limited literature either to social themes (for discursive discussion) or sets of structures (for computation). I will conclude by placing the teaching of literature within the emerging arts paradigm and examine the consequences for the creative teaching of the subject.

English as Sociology and Communications

The major preoccupation of English teaching during the late 60s and the 70s was with *language* and *learning*. Excited by concepts deriving from linguistics and sociology, many English teachers became preoccupied with the intersections between language and social class, language and politics, language and the curriculum. References to different kinds of language (Was it poetic? Was it transactional? Was it expressive?) and to different kinds of coding (Was it in the so-called restricted code of the working class or the elaborate code of the middle class?) were ubiquitous and began to predetermine the issues that characterized the serious discussion of English. The titles of some of the most widely disseminated books – *Language, the Learner and the School* (Douglas Barnes, 1969), *Language and Learning* (James Britten, 1969), *Language and Class* (Harold Rosen, 1972) – revealed the breadth of interest and the major unifying concerns that were *linguistic*, *social* and *educational*. Some of the most influential formulations were those relating to oracy (now rightly such an important part of GCSE work) and the notion of 'language across the curriculum' (given the formal imprimatur by the Bullock Report of 1975 which devoted a whole chapter to it).

It can be demonstrated that the real contribution of the sociolinguistic school was not so much to English as an individual discipline in the curriculum as to educational thinking. The sociolinguistic school developed broad theories of learning and social interaction; it heightened an awareness of class, of ideology, of materialist history; it promoted among teachers a finer perception into the intimate, reciprocal relationship between language and understanding, between the symbolic act of knowing and the individual participant, the learner. Many of the trenchant arguments, many of the intellectual and social insights were of value but they were, for the most part, *general* insights into *general* educational conditions and possibilities. It is wholly consistent with its broad conceptual framework that, arguably, its greatest achievement was a now forgotten 'language across the curriculum policy' which, simultaneously, involved *all* teachers but left *teachers of English* a little uncertain as to their precise responsibilities.

It is difficult to determine the exact relationship between the sociolinguistic theory of the 60s and 70s and the daily classroom practice of teaching English. What seems certain is that there was a strong connection between the general social and ideological orientation of the philosophy and the emerging method of teaching English through themes, selected according to their social relevance and their ideological content. Here, I believe, the achievement of the sociolinguistic movement, in its broad influence, in its tacit structure of mediation, was little short of a disaster – for under its power, English (not unlike educational drama) became, for the best part of two decades in many comprehensive classrooms, a species of sociology, a kind of current affairs, using literature as documentary evidence for a general case against society. What was lost was a sense of a continuous literary tradition, with its own self-justifying value, and its own quite particular ways of structuring experience.

The guiding model for nearly all thematic teaching of English during the 60s and 70s was the textbook *Reflections*, put together by Simon Clements, John Dixon and Leslie Stratta, and first published in 1963. As late as summer 1980 – nearly two decades later – it was still being proclaimed by Anthony Adams in *English in Education* as the best model for any further development in the teaching of English. *Reflections* was, certainly, in 1963 an innovative textbook and it was to exert a steady and a profound influence on the reconstruction of English for the new comprehensive system of secondary education. In their handbook to their classroom text the authors wrote:

> The material in this book has been chosen as a springboard for reading, discussion and writing on a wide variety of topics, integrated here into three major themes . . . These three themes are 'The Family, Community and Work', 'The Mass Media' and 'Questions of Our Time'. They were chosen because we felt they were central to the pupils' lives; indeed they form part of a cultural heritage we all share.[1]

'A wide variety of topics, integrated . . . into . . . major themes'. *There* was the central unifying method of new approach to the teaching of English. The *theme* became the direct means of integration and of control. Invariably, work on these lines began with a short extract (from a novel or a document) which raised the predetermined theme; from there the theme was quickly developed through open-ended discussion *outwards* into general issues; these issues were then finally clarified through a mixture of research and writing tasks. Following this pattern of organization *Reflections* offered 'a year's English lessons' for 14–18-year-olds.

The book began with the major theme 'Family, Community and Work'. This is, in turn, subdivided into the following series of subthemes: 'Old Age', 'Parents and Children', 'The Home', 'The Neighbourhood', 'Work'. The middle section then opens up the theme of 'Mass Culture' (which includes advertising, newspapers, comics, magazines and television) and concludes, in the final section, with 'Questions of Our Time' (starting with the 'pay-packet' and ending with 'A doctor from the USSR goes to India'). A single schematic glance at the whole programme reveals both the social developmental progression that informs the text (moving from the home, to the environment, to the 'global society') and also just how ideological and political its categories are.

I do not want to explore here complex problems about ideology and education, but I do want to raise the problems of the effects of such a view as the one I have outlined on the meaning of English. The significant question is: what happened to literature under such a guiding ideology? In *Reflections* literature is seen as a transparent window onto a social universe. It is seen as a means by which certain themes can be directly raised only to be resolved outside the artistic work in group discussion and group praxis ('collect statistics on the cost of various forms of social services in your area' or work out 'how you would budget on a pension'). The function of literature is to dramatize the social theme, to act as an initial stimulus for the subsequent thematic exploration. *Reflections* is a perfect example of the outcome of such a conception – and, furthermore, became a powerful model for innumerable other textbooks that quickly followed from the publishing houses. Consider some of the inevitable consequences, in no particular order of importance.

First, *Reflections* consists almost entirely of *excerpts*, short pieces taken from whole works. In other words, the excerpt, because it is sufficient to provoke the required theme, is seen as self-justifying totality.

Second, *Reflections* consists almost entirely of prose. Only two poems are presented formally in the programme of work, and only *one* of these is actually complete (Philip Larkin's *Toads*). One complete poem in a year's work in English!

Third, *Reflections* offers no examples of literary work, of prose or poetry, before the twentieth century. The excerpts are taken only from modern or contemporary writers and the only genre favoured, for obvious reasons, is social realism.

Fourth, *Reflections* offers no serious questions on stylistics; no questions on the metrical form of the poem or the particular construction of the fiction. There is no attempt to establish a language other than 'what does it say?' and 'do you agree?' for the understanding of literature.

All of these consequences are the logical outcome of a theory that gives no value to literary form or to the aesthetic and imaginative 'otherness' of art. *Reflections* as a classroom textbook represented, in effect, the negation of literature as a symbolic universe and its reduction to excerpts for social exegesis. During the 60s and 70s this model of English teaching, linked with the general values of the sociolinguistic school at large, led to the steady erosion of literature in many classrooms. The Bullock Report of 1975 complained that 'we have a definite impression that fewer full-length novels are read' and strongly urged 'where anthologies are used we commend those that include complete pieces of substantial extracts, virtually artistic units on their own, rather than merely short snippets clipped out of their context'.[2] The tradition of rhetoric (still mechanically present in the earlier textbooks of Ronald Ridout) and the sense of a high literary tradition (such as had been advocated and developed by F.R. Leavis and T.S. Eliot) all but disappeared from the map. Many learning activities developed but, with regard to literature, a general amnesia, a loss of a sense of cultural continuity and a unique imaginative and aesthetic structuring of experience, set in.

Symptomatically, Leslie Stratta, co-author of *Reflections*, for example wrote in an article 'Language and Experience' in autumn 1972:

> Twenty years ago a teacher of English might have confidently asserted that his main concern was to introduce his pupils to literature. Today he might less confidently assert that his main concern is with the process of helping his pupils to develop their abilities in using language for a variety of needs and purposes . . . But part of this change results from the realisation that using literature almost exclusively is too abstract an approach for many pupils, which rather than engage their interests may well prove to be a barrier . . .
>
> Reading, especially of literature, presents all pupils with a number of problems. Books are frequently long or longish, the language used, especially of poetry, is often dense and difficult, more so if the work is from the heritage, the vision of life presented comes from the mature imagination of an adult mind.[3]

The informing concern is, quite explicitly, not with English as *a distinctive symbolic discipline*, not with a *particular way of apprehending and formulating human experience*, but with the *general process of learning through language*. It is, of course, a positively philistine position, a disturbing act of cultural abnegation.

What, in retrospect, we can now see is that the achievements of the sociolinguistic school, both at a theoretical level and a practical level, primarily involved *process* and *pedagogy*. In particular, they developed a richer sense of language in action, a greater appreciation of oracy (and, therefore, of group work in classrooms) and an awareness of the connections between language and learning (and therefore, a recognition that all teachers should be directly implicated in the teaching of language). These were broad and valuable insights, generalized perceptions into the nature of learning, of relating and developing, not to be quickly dismissed. What was tragically excluded was any sense of a unique symbolic order characterizing English, any sense of the intrinsic value of literature, or any sense of the power of the aesthetic, any awareness of the vast field of literary creation.

The Rise of Structuralism

Yet it is a remarkable paradox that at about the time of the publication of *Reflections*, at a higher level of education, a movement was beginning which gave primacy to the symbolic and formal nature of literature. *As secondary English became thematic, university English became structuralist.* In 1961, for example, Wayne Booth published his enormously influential *The Rhetoric of Fiction*. In this book he wrote: 'we have seen that the author cannot choose to avoid rhetoric; he can choose only the kind of rhetoric he will employ'.[4] Such a conception, the polar opposite of that developed in *Reflections*, led Booth to criticize 'the widespread abandonment of the notion of peculiar literary kinds, each with its unique demands'[5] and to call for *the return of genre.*

At about the same time in France, Roland Barthes' work was also attacking the notion of 'theme' and pure content. Barthes wrote: 'the labour does not consist of starting from forms in order to perceive, clarify or formulate content . . . but, on the contrary, of scattering, of postponing, of gearing down, of discharging meaning through the action of a formal discipline'.

To take one final example of this dramatic severance between secondary and university English, in 1975 (the year of the Bullock Report) Jonathan Culler in another influential work *Structuralist Poetics* argued that the work of fiction should not be seen mimetically (or, in our context, as bearing an unambiguous social theme) but 'as a structure which plays with different modes of ordering'. Again, countering the idea of instant relevance and easy referentiality, Culler asserted the notions of interior structure, genre and intertextuality, the symbolic play *between* works. In the movement inspired by the structuralists it is possible to locate many of the elements which had been jettisoned by the once fashionable practice of thematic English. It is time to examine more fully the return to rhetoric and poetics.

On the Strengths of Structuralism

It is now said at universities that structuralism is over. As generalizations go, this is true. But we must not forget that as a theoretical enterprise structuralism, like psychoanalysis, has been in the central arena of European culture for the best part of this century, time enough for its major strengths and weakness to be discerned and placed. Yet, at the same time, English teachers at secondary level have remained largely unaware of its intellectual challenges and have still to consider its implications for their own teaching and their own subject. It is my aim to outline the structuralist movement as it relates to literature, to indicate some of its failings and to suggest, finally, how its more positive notions could give the teaching of English in our comprehensive schools greater artistic coherence and autonomy, give back to English all that it lost in the two decades from 1960 to 1980.

Jonathan Culler's book *Structuralist Poetics* (1975) did much to bring the structuralist conceptions of French intellectuals, which had been so fashionable in France during the 60s, into the academic life of English and American universities. Geoffrey Strickland's more critical analysis *Structuralism as Criticism* (1981) had its origin around the same time. Then in 1980–81 the much publicized affair at Cambridge concerning the structuralist Colin McCabe brought structuralism unexpected publicity and an incredulous coverage. At the time, English teachers in school, developing thematic discussions based on the literal content of literature or developing the individual sensibility of their pupils through 'creative writing', must have felt a dizzy abyss open before them, dividing them from their university counterparts.

Yet a better date with which to begin is 1957: the year in which the influential Canadian critic Northrop Frye published *The Anatomy of Criticism*. With a mixture of dry academic humour and intellectual determination the book quietly sought to put an end to literary criticism as it had developed from the romantic revolution onwards and to inaugurate a more formal analysis of literature based, in many ways, on the neglected principles of Aristotle. Frye was in search of a synoptic understanding of literature, a theory of criticism that was at once *comprehensive*, including all the main types of literary expression, and *autonomous*, grounded, that is to say, on the principles of its own operation. Frye wanted to establish a study of literature that was not concerned with the individual interpretation of individual works but with the formal understanding of the whole of literature and the ways in which it was constructed.

The aim of *The Anatomy of Criticism* was to renew Aristotle's enterprise as announced in the *Poetics* for the twentieth century; to make, using the paradigm of biology, a comprehensive classification of literary forms as they interacted within their own distinctive symbolic field. 'Criticism', Frye wrote, 'seems to be badly in need of a co-ordinating principle, a central hypothesis which, like the theory of evolution in biology, will see the phenomena it deals with as part of a whole'.[6]

Yet a similar desire for a systematic theory had united a number of literary critics in Russia around the years 1913–30. These critics, often known as the Russian formalists, advocated the organized examination of the internal structures of literature as the necessary means of understanding its nature. A work of literature was seen as a construction whose meaning resided not in its apparent referentiality but more in the interior and invariant workings of the artefact itself. For example, in 1928, Vladimir Propp in his *Morphology of the Folk-tale* argued that all folk-tales broke down into thirty-one possible narrative functions released by seven main characters. The work, confined to one specific genre, was out to establish a *grammar of narrative*, to discern and schematically to delineate the structure that underlay the obvious surface content. This book was to exert a seminal influence on later structuralist analyses. Perhaps the most brilliant member of this cultural milieu (while himself an opponent of strict formalism) was the critic Bakhtin, whose work, still being rediscovered and translated into English, is now having a profound influence on literary study.

Unlike Northrop Frye, Bakhtin thought it essential to consider the historical and ideological dimension of literary production but, like Frye, he too regarded the notion of *genre* as axiomatic. 'By definition', wrote Bakhtin in *The Formal Methods in Poetics*, 'the world is unlimited, genre makes a selection, sets up a model of the world and breaks up the infinite series'.[7] In aphoristic style, Bakhtin asserted: 'the artist must learn to see reality through the eyes of the genre' – and insisted that 'poetics must begin with genre'[8] – for each literary genre represented a way of simultaneously apprehending and rendering some portion of human experience.

At around the same time as Russian formalism, French structuralism was coming to birth. This complex movement has its origins in Ferdinand de Saussure's *Course in General Linguistics* published in 1916. In Saussure, as in Propp, the overriding preoccupation was to look at *the phenomenon of language in terms of the underlying system that governed it.* Saussure wrote: 'A science that studies the life of signs within society is conceivable . . . I shall call it semiology . . . Semiology would show what constitutes signs, what laws govern them.'[9]

It is not possible here to examine the French structuralist movement – that movement to locate and delineate the interior elements shaping the work of art – but I have said enough to show that what Northrop Frye was calling for, albeit in a different cultural context and under somewhat different philosophical premises, had already taken place. The notion of a new comprehensive poetics, informed by the study of linguistics, was in Europe well under way and indeed has become, by now, an academic commonplace. Concepts like 'rhetoric' and 'poetics' have become essential, even liberating, terms in the advanced study of literature.

The major concern of the structuralists in the literary domain was with *the conventions of literary form.* In the *ABC of Reading*, Ezra Pound had claimed that prose was about the world, but the structuralists' argument was that this could not be unambiguously so, for the language is determined not by the objects in the outside world, but more by the laws governing its own formulation. Content can never be divorced from the syntax and the syntax does not owe its structure to things but to its own system of internal relations. The lucid French structuralist critic Todorov expressed the position as follows: 'Poetics . . . aims at knowledge of the general laws that preside over the birth of each [literary] work. It seeks those within literature itself. Poetics is therefore an approach to literature at once "abstract" and "internal" '.[10]

It is ironic that in the teaching of English at secondary level nearly all the 'internal' and 'abstract' relationships had been removed from literature from the 60s onwards. Indeed, many university tutors teaching in the last decade, following in the wake of structuralism, have discovered with consternation that their students have never learnt either the figures of rhetoric of the formal devices of poetry. Terms like: metonomy, synecdoche, oxymoron, litotes, elegy, iambic pentameter (terms which had been systematically presented in earlier textbooks like Ridout's *English I–V*) were no longer used in the teaching of English at secondary level. As I suggested earlier, neither the practice of theme teaching, dating back to the early 60s, nor a teaching based on a notion of individual growth required their assimilation or application. Structuralism, in reviving and extending traditions of rhetoric, had unintentionally rendered dramatically visible the poverty of literary discourse and symbolic practice in the secondary classroom. It also possesses certain vivifying principles for its renewal as a discipline.

Before turning to this possibility a number of severe reservations about structuralism must be recorded.

The Failures of Structuralism

Severe criticisms have ultimately to be brought against the structuralist enterprise. It was not infrequently informed by a drab materialism, a mechanistic nineteenth-century positivism of the rational mind. In the Russian formalists, for example, one often encounters that language of pseudo objectivity – of hard 'facts' and clear 'data' – which has shown itself to be so cumbersome in the definitive formulation of any aspects of human consciousness or cultural experience. Structuralism tended to envisage literature as impersonal material that could be clinically tabulated without prior response, without any prior dialectic of exploratory and reciprocal engagement. *Structuralism often reified literature.* Even in Northrop Frye (who one could not accuse of materialism), there is the underlying assumption that botany, the science from which key word 'genre' derives, forms the best kind of paradigm for critical theory. Structuralism, like Freudian psychoanalysis, never quite freed itself from the model of natural science and the flawed language of objective investigation.

As a movement structuralism formally excluded the fertile and incalculable subjectivity of the individual reader in relationship to the individual literary work. It tended to deny or omit that complex aesthetic response between reader and work in which all literature (as *literature*) exists and can only exist, that field in which literary work is tirelessly recreated and so constituted. Because it envisaged itself as a materialist science – 'a science of signs' – it also excised the notion of worth, of value. It dimmed and made remote that hierarchical sense that marks all alert human consciousness, that some things are made and done better than others, and require recognition. Implicitly, by its mode of study, and explicitly, by the ends it set itself, it negated the primary need for judgment, for discrimination, for evaluation, both celebratory and critical. Tellingly some of the most convincing analyses of the structuralists were made in relationship to inferior, mass-produced, counterfeit works of 'art': to Ian Fleming's *Goldfinger*, to advertisements, to covers of journals and popular films. It forced the variegated achievements of literary production into a single reductive category of 'texts' and saw these texts as the mere outward example of the impersonal laws governing all sign making. In this way, it denuded art and made what was variegated, uniform and uninteresting. In the pursuit of an impossible objectivity it eclipsed the existential sources and existential outcomes of literature.

'Knowledge', according to Gabriel Marcel, 'is contingent on a participation in being for which no epistemology can account because it continually presupposes it'. The materialist epistemology of structuralism had constantly suppressed the ontological dimension in all cultural matters. And yet without it what *value* can such analysis have? A common student response to structuralist analysis is: so what? So what if those schema are at work? Why does it matter? Other traditions of literary analysis, the tradition of Arnold, Leavis and T.S. Eliot, had provided better answers to that question.

What then, can English teachers now learn from structuralism? Surprisingly, the answer remains a great deal. First of all, it offers a brilliant and necessary critique of teaching literature solely through themes. To teach literature, in any sense, must include a detailed attention to the form of the work. The illusion of common reality created by 'social realism' is an achievement of artifice, of device, of construction. *Pupils need to know what the literary devices are.* Contemporaneity of text and a simple-minded reference to 'issues' is simply not enough. They resulted in the severe truncation of literature in our classrooms.

In more positive terms, structuralism provides us with *the principle of genre.* Informed by this principle, the teaching of literature becomes, in part, a living and formal initiation into the various genres that comprise it. The most elementary structural demarcations show that the universe of literature has many symbolic galaxies: myth, poetry, short story, the novel, drama, autobiography, biography, documentary, the essay, etc. A careful enumeration of the genres could help to provide English teachers with the elements necessary for a coherent curriculum.

Second, structuralism provides English teachers with the *notion of aesthetic field.* This means that the English teacher needs to create an awareness not just of 'set texts' but of 'texts in relationship', of a dynamic intertextuality. The concept of 'aesthetic field' – described earlier in Chapters 3 and 4 – gives a new principle of organization that allows for a vast range of related work to be brought structurally together. 'Set texts' should give way to 'related texts'. The teacher of English should strive to open up the whole intricate symbolic field of literature and encourage an awareness of its diverse forms and of its manifold interconnections.

Third, structuralism provides the English teacher with *the concept of autonomy.* Nobody else in the curriculum is directly concerned with teaching *poetics* or even *rhetoric.* These are the *intrinsic* concerns of the teacher of English – concerns which, if developed, could provide a much needed philosophical resistance to the encroachments of the mindless utilitarians. In these three ways, at least, structuralism has much to offer English teaching. It serves, simultaneously, to extend and unify the nature of a literary discipline.

Towards a Synthesis

I have suggested that structuralism offered a much needed corrective to the thematic teaching of English. If the sociolinguistic school of English expanded pedagogic possibilities to include both the dynamics of collaborative group work and the process of rehearsing ideas through the process of talking and drafting, then structuralism (seen broadly as a return to rhetoric and poetics) urged English teachers to identify some of the formal and distinguishing elements of their subject. Is it possible that we can bring the two movements together and placing the negative features to one side, locate the necessary elements for a further synthesis? What would such a programme for the study of literature look like? A coherent programme for literature coming out of the two traditions of English teaching I have here examined would offer the pupil:

1 A structured initiation into all the main literary genres.
2 A growing appreciation of the terminology needed to understand those genres.
3 A study in depth of some individual works but kept in relationship to the whole aesthetic field of literature.
4 The experience of working collaboratively in groups built up on the principle of group amplification and provisional understanding.

The reader will see, at once, that the first three propositions concern *curriculum content* and derive from my analysis of structuralism while the fourth proposition concerns *pedagogy* and derives from the work of the sociolinguistic school.

To these propositions I would add four more, deriving from the pedagogy of the other arts established in the earlier chapters of this book, namely:

5 A constant practice in imitating and experimenting with the various genres and their conventions.

6   Continuous first-hand experience in rendering and performing literary work so that it is experienced in and through its own medium, the power of articulate sound.
7   The experience of publishing, reviewing, proofreading, editing so that the techniques of composition are mastered by *doing* and the best critical and creative work given an audience.
8   A growing recognition of the practical and theoretical connections between literature and the other five art disciplines: art, drama, dance, music and film, as outlined in Chapter 5.

Such a programme is both demanding and distinctive. It is in intimate relationship to the symbolic form studied and comes out of engagement with some of the recent contested traditions in English teaching. It is neither structuralist nor sociolinguistic. It is a fusion and development of both these movements, and takes the teaching of literature into the arts. This calls for a transformation of the subject, making it more imaginative, more expressive, more physical. It is to these *aesthetic qualities* that I now wish to turn.

An Arts Approach to the Teaching of Literature

An arts approach to literature is committed to establishing and making current those kinds of knowing most appropriate to what is being studied. Rather than using literature as a means to abstract speculation and linear formulation it would encourage an indwelling in the literary text – in the rhythm, in the metaphor, in the associations, the mood, the texture, the non-discursive energies of the work. Thus the aim would be to bring the student's feelings, sense-perceptions, imagination – and the intelligence active in all of these – inside the pattern of the words in order to comprehend it. What is being asked for is a refining of the mimetic imagination, an anchoring of thinking in the aesthetic response. The approach is committed to finding non-discursive ways into the essentially non-discursive meanings of literature and doing this on the supposition that discursive methods, used prematurely, could only result in the effective bypassing of the rich potential *presence* of the poem, story or novel. What we are out to establish is a thinking *within* the actual medium rather than an immediate thinking *about* the explicit content that leads to the abstract intellectual discussion of 'themes', 'issues', 'causes', 'ideologies'. The first emphasis of an arts approach would be towards promoting a formative experience of the artwork as *aesthetic embodiment*.

This may be realized by placing more weight on *the oral recreation of literature*, particularly of poetry. It is a depressing fact that many university seminars on a poem do not even *begin* with a reading of the work. The dead print has been read privately and in the teaching the aim is often to reach theory almost at once. In contrast, an arts approach to literature might well experiment with various oral renderings of a poem in order to establish (within the medium) its possible range of meanings. *Reading, as expressive rendering, is critical evaluation, kept within the aesthetic experience of the art form.* Many writers have insisted on the hermeneutics of oral presentation. T.S. Eliot referred to the 'auditory imagination' with its 'feeling for syllable and rhythm, penetrating far below the level of conscious thought'. Henry James, in his preface to *The Golden Bowl*, wrote about 'the finest and most numerous secrets' of the artwork yielding themselves up only under 'the pressure of the attention articulately sounded'. Paul Valery went so far as to claim: 'Poetry has no existence at all . . . It comes to life only in two situations – in the state of composition in a mind that nominates and constructs it, and *in the state of recitation*'. In the act of reading aloud the poem becomes part of the body, part of the breath, part of the tongue, throat, lips. The poem is articulated as expressive sound; that articulation links the poem *physically* to the memory, feeling and imagination of the reader. The intellectual conception of the poetry is thus most fully released through a physical engagement with it. Without that physical contact, perhaps, we cannot reach the full meaning of the work. In aesthetic education, meaning emerges through the senses, imaginatively centred. Robert Lowell found what we, tellingly, call 'his voice' through *listening* to William Carlos Williams's *reading* and through his own experience of *reciting* to large audiences, where slowly he found the lines that married his own breath and his own metabolic rhythms. Listening and performing, he came to his own style. In academic study, have we neglected the very elements that take us into the heart of literary understanding and response?

A formative experience of literature could be further developed through the method of creative amplification, where there is no premature desire for explicit meaning and explanation, but more a sensitive ambulation of the work, a spiral movement, going up and down, from level to level, from surface to depth, from immediate naive response ('I like . . .', 'I dislike . . .') to focused insight. Creative amplification involves a communal working into a poem, a Socratic process where interpretation condenses in the actual investigation, in the meandering, in the apparent culs-de-sac of response as much as in the apparent main routes. Responses can only be deepened and connected after they have been expressed. So often in seminars personally felt responses are banished because the student suspects they are not 'right', not intellectual enough, not what the tutor wants; as a consequence, emotion and intellect part company and a condition of mind is fostered that excludes existential involvement, inner growth. The method of creative amplification, in contrast, rests on collaboration, a sharing of all responses, a gradual deepening, a cumulative creating, constantly tested by being brought back to the words, and hence the possible meanings, of the literary work. A Japanese stroll-garden unfolds as one moves through it; as one meanders along its paths symbols recur, but always from an altered perspective and at different levels. To know the garden one has to be inside it, lost in it, found in it and lost again as the same symbol changes, offering yet another portion of meaning. In our classrooms we should enter literary works, particularly poems, as we enter stroll-gardens.

An arts approach to English would also include, centrally, and not as a peripheral option, the actual discipline of writing, not just writing in the analytical mode (though that would have its place) but in *all the main forms of expressive utterance*. The student would be expected to experiment with the writing of poetry, autobiography, fictional narrative and documentary, and to be guided, wherever possible, by established practitioners. There are a number of reasons for including the practical experience of making literature in any course on English studies. First, such work has intrinsic educational value. Second it brings about an acute awareness of the medium and its formal possibilities. (How better to know the nature of the sonnet than to try and shape a personal meaning within its form?) Third, the practice of writing connects the student's experience with the aethestic field and, in so doing, makes that culture no longer a distant object of study but a contemporary force. It is in this encounter between existential impulse and literary tradition that the deep educational value of an arts approach resides. I will give further examples of this in the next chapter.

What is required is a form of 'creative mimesis'. Through creative mimesis the need to create our own meaning (our own 'voice') within the symbolic possibilities of the culture (in this context, literary culture) is satisfied. The mimetic imagination lies at the heart of all arts disciplines. Under the power of the mimetic imagination the work of art transcends its specific historical context and becomes contemporary, a symbolic energy in the mind *now*. We reconstitute past literature according to our existential needs; but that literature also, in the encounter, changes us. In expressive disciplines the primary concern is neither historical nor critical, it is rather aesthetic and mimetic. The structuralists speak of intertextuality; what I am trying to describe is a kind of intertextuality lifted up into the creative form-seeking life of the psyche, intertextuality as a creative *method* rather than an analytical tool. Of any literature, the initial questions are: How do I imaginatively respond to it? How can I recreate it as living form? How does its meaning impinge on my experience? And can I make from it? Moral and political questions may well be latent in such activity but the important thing to note is that they are mediated *through the expressive work*, rather than turned into justifying categories which then raid the literary tradition for evidence and mere example.

Some of the forms for the teaching of literature emerge from the above description. The discursive essay would continue to have a valid place but only as part of a much broader configuration. Other forms might include: the experimental journal, the folder of original work, the cassette of readings, the formal production of an established text, the formal performance of the original work. These forms would be kept in some kind of intimate and reciprocal relation. For example, the journal might document the process of staging *King Lear* and the discursive essay explore, say, the role of the Fool in the play. These are suggestions; in the next chapter I will present a more carefully documented programme in the teaching of literature in relationship to creative writing.

A new principle makes sudden unified sense of a mass of previously disconnected perceptions, isolated observations, momentary hunches and by bringing them into telling relationship generates further insight, both into the limitations of existing practice and into possibly richer and more subtle patterns of working. The principle of literature as an arts discipline strikes me as just such a principle; it draws many conceptions together and offers a richer approach to the teaching of literature, more in tune with the nature of literature itself. Its realization will be difficult at the present time, when most of the dominant forces transpire against the imaginative and the existential, but once the idea exists it makes action possible and under its power much that now exists under English studies will have to be dissolved and recast in the name of intellectual fidelity, expressive need, and the new paradigm in arts education. It is time for the study of literature to return to the imagination and the community of the arts.[11]

Notes

1 Handbook to SIMON CLEMENTS, JOHN DIXON and LESLIE STRATTA (1965) Oxford, *Reflections: an English Course for Students 14–18*, Oxford University Press, p. 3.

2 See DEPARTMENT OF EDUCATION AND SCIENCE (1975) *A Language for Life: The Bullock Report*, London, DES.
3 LESLIE STRATTA (1972) 'Language and Experience', *English in Education*, **6** (3) autumn, pp. 99–100.
4 See WAYNE BOOTH (1983) *The Rhetoric of Fiction*, Chicago, University of Chicago Press.
5 *Ibid.*
6 NORTHROP FRYE (1957) *The Anatomy of Criticism*, Princeton, NJ, Princeton University Press, p. 13.
7 TZVETAN TODOROV (1984) *Mikhail Bakhtin: The Dialogical Principle*, Manchester, Manchester University Press, pp. 80–1.
8 *Ibid.*
9 See FERDINAND DE SAUSSURE (1974) *Course in General Linguistics* (translated by Wade Baskin) Peter Owen.
10 TZVETAN TODOROV (1981) *Introduction to Poetics*, Harvester Press.
11 For a further study of English as an arts discipline see, 'English as an Arts Discipline' and 'The Aesthetic Field of English', PETER ABBS (1988) *A is for Aesthetic*, London, Falmer Press.

Chapter 9

The Place of Creative Writing in the Development of Teachers

The development of experience is largely unconscious, subterranean, so that we cannot gauge its progress except once in
every five or ten years; but in the meantime the poet must be
working; he must be experimenting and trying his technique
so that it will be ready, like a well-oiled fire-engine, when the
moment comes to strain it to its utmost. The poet who wishes
to continue to write poetry must keep in training; and must do
this, not by forcing his inspiration, but by good workmanship
on a level possible for some hours' work every week of his life.

T.S. Eliot

Today a poet faces a practical problem in trying to define a
common cultural tradition available to both him and his readers.
The difficulty originates in contemporary society, where the continuous proliferation of information has increasingly fragmented
audiences into specialized subcultures that share no common
frame of reference.

Dana Gioia

Introduction

In this chapter I want to examine an approach – both Socratic and
aesthetic – to the teaching of literature in relationship to the practice
of writing in the context of the training of English teachers. I have
decided to present one term's fairly concentrated work in writing with
a Postgraduate Certificate in Education (PGCE) English group at the
University of Sussex. I will describe, briefly, what my intentions were,
how the work was structured, what was written and what was claimed,
at times, by some of the students. Such descriptions are, of course,
inherently problematical. After all, any workshop involves the varied,
sometimes volatile, always changing, perceptions of all its members; a

workshop group is an extraordinary complex psychic web, impossible to represent fully in words. What I am after in this description is to evoke some feeling of the kind of activity one is seeking to generate, what it can produce in terms of written work and some indication of certain procedures, the practical 'what and how' of a workshop approach to writing committed to the aesthetic, the practical and the imaginative, committed in short to the new paradigm in arts education.

My general aim before the course commenced could be defined roughly as follows: I wanted the PGCE English students to have ample experience of writing. I wanted to engender through practice rather than theory a living sense of the process of composition, moving from first hesitant jottings to something like a realization of final form. I wanted them also to have some direct experience of performance (of finding a public voice) and practical criticism. I knew they would all have had years of apprenticeship at writing critical essays, of shaping words to present a discursive argument, and would be masters of the academic apparatus for presenting such arguments, but I suspected that, for the most part, they would be much less at ease with more personal and imaginative forms of expression. It was time for the students to have first-hand experience of the poetic rather than the discursive; experience of thinking through image, narrative, the poetic power of language when it arises out of engaged emotion and imaginative play.

Nietzsche somewhere suggested that in the elevation of conceptual theory lay the roots of nihilism. Was the effect of literary criticism (particularly under the influences of structuralism and poststructuralism) to create a widespread dissociation between the intellectual and the personal? Where there is a near complete division between theoretical abstraction and the psychological·life of the one who abstracts, then perhaps the possibility of personal development or of cultural renewal has been rendered all but impossible? This is not an attack on theory, but on theory, spinning theory, spinning theory . . . I hoped the workshops might counter any such dissociation by joining the life of memory, association and feeling to the practical tasks of literary creation and appreciation: by bringing, for example, the material of inherited myth to the material of one's own imagination or by inviting free association and then bringing to the work all the organizing power of an accepted literary convention, the aesthetic field of the subject. Furthermore, I wanted the workshops to act as a model for teaching in the comprehensive school where for three days in each week the students would be doing their teaching practice.

The art critic Anton Ehrenzweig has written:

> The intellect must be enlisted as a potent helper of spontaneity
> . . . The students must be taught by coercion if necessary – not
> to wait on their inspiration and rushes of spontaneity, but to
> work hard at being spontaneous through choosing tasks that
> cannot be controlled by analytic vision and reasoning alone.
> We would . . . call on intellect and reason in order to sting into
> action the powers of the deep.[1]

To develop exercises that promoted imaginative and poetic thinking,
to develop mundane methods for releasing imaginative language, to
reflect on this process and to consider its educational import: these
were the main intentions when the autumn term started.

The Programme of Work

In the PGCE university induction week two workshops were set aside
for writing. The workshops were to operate from opposite poles. The
first was to be open with regard to form and directly personal with
regard to content. The second was to be formally prescriptive in that
it was to begin as an organized exercise, presenting one poetic form
for the structuring of the writing. It was also to be collective in nature in
that the work was to be shared and discussed by the group.

Before coming, all the students, as a requirement of the course,
had written a fairly sustained piece of discursive autobiography, reflecting on their own education. Now in the very first writing workshop I asked them to select an autobiographical event and to present it
not as *abstract* reflection but as embodied symbol, to convey, that is to
say, the feel and full specificity of the experience: *how it was*. I read a
few pieces of autobiography by comprehensive school pupils and then,
without commentary, keeping them in the room, dictatorially set ten
minutes of time for the mind and the pen to scratch around in the dry
ground for those buried seeds and roots from which the later work
might grow. Such prescriptive time-counts can be extremely important in the formal releasing and directing of spontaneity; they seem to
create, simultaneously, an inner anxiety and a set context for overcoming
that anxiety and producing work that otherwise would never have
been created. Ted Hughes has written:

> These artificial limits create a crisis which rouses the brain's
> resources; the compulsion towards haste overthrows the ordin-
> ary precautions, flings everything into top gear, and many things

that are casually hidden find themselves rushed into the open. Barriers break down, prisoners come out of their cells.[2]

When the ten minutes were up, I gave twenty minutes for the students to begin the more formal shaping of whatever material they had located. Perhaps, at the end of twenty minutes, they would have, at least, a working first draft if not the completed artefact? At the end of the session I asked them to submit the work, anonymously if they wished, in two days' time, and to add some brief reflections on the actual experience of writing. Here are two of the passages which came in:

First autobiographical passage

This is a moonless night;
Darkness, thick, impenetrable, surrounds me.
Outside the elm trees creak and strain in the rising wind,
Here the loneliness and fear pervade the dark stairs.
At the bottom there is a door:
If I can reach it, lift the latch, I will find sanctuary.
Another world, glowing gold,
Tranquil, warm, secure: fire hissing, clock ticking, mother
    knitting.

Commentary by the author

I wanted to write this episode in prose, but it didn't work – neither does this really, but in some ways it comes closer to my feelings. The language is fairly banal. I can see the scene and feel the emotions in my imagination but I can't convey it in words – the contrast between the dark, forbidding world behind the door and the security that the open door promised me, as a small child awoken on a stormy night. (Maureen)

Second autobiographical passage

Sussex Downs

Seen from afar, soft breast-curves rolling,
    tree-filled hollows,
    promising joy;
Encountered closer their pains disclosed
    mean sharp-flint grazed knees,
    wind-whipped wet knickers and cheeks

– Sham comfort
In summer they yield tenderest beauties
    yellow gorse flowers,
    blue fritillaries;
Beauty-eager fingers clutch prickles with the blossoms,
    dead dust on wings,
    life's patterns crumbling.
– Counterfeit beauty.
Lines of young children hold hands on the flint-paths,
    teacher-training,
    a chattering throng;
Yet secretly mean fingers pinch, push and scratch,
    cruel words are uttered,
    friendless despair
– Sentimentalised infancy.

Sussex Downs – bleakness-bleak, beauty-bleak, childhood-bleak,
Chalk-hearted, sharp-flinted, cold-fleshed downs
– Archetypal betrayers.

Commentary by the author

So Wednesday arrived; the subject matter was fine, there was a dominant theme of alienation in my education. My second school/'home' was Rottingdean, the Downs unconsciously imprinted on my mind/body, to such a degree that when I returned to Sussex aged 26 I wept quiet tears of suicidal despair on seeing them – never dreaming why, as I had blocked it all off. Some of the horror peeps through my poem.

But the poem is totally unsatisfactory and incomplete: for lying in one of the tree-filled clefts of the Downs in the University – my second education. Here the Downs yielded their treasure without betrayal. Here I conquered the alienation of my childhood Downs. I wanted to write about the Downs that beat me, and the Downs I conquered. The polar opposites were too complex for the time allowed. I could only sustain one image, one agony, one emotion in 20 minutes or so. There is much to do with the poem – or perhaps with a parallel poem. The problem posed and the intensity of the despair meant I did not try to rework it – I avoided it until handing-in time.

As to the session: I found it totally easy to separate myself from my surroundings, to concentrate 100% on the poem. The 'super-ego' was irrelevant. The subject was fine; the structure of the session excellent. I loved the model poems and if I had to imitate the form more-or-less, that didn't worry me; I have so little knowledge of poem forms and no aspiration to originality or genius.

Of the week the poems seem the most meaningful thing at one level. I want to learn to write better and better poetry. I don't want anonymity – I want good, valid criticism. I can't wait for next time. (Pat)

One of the characteristic rhythms of creativity is to move from *free association rhythmic play* to the identification *of an emerging pattern* to its *elaboration into a satisfying symbolic form.* Attempting to analyse the elusive nature of the creative act, Einstein wrote:

Taken from a psychological standpoint this combinatory play seems to be the essential feature in productive thinking – before there is any connection with logical construction in words or other kinds of signs which can be communicated to others.

The above-mentioned elements are, in any case of visual and some of muscular type. Conventional words or other signs have to be sought for laboriously only in a secondary stage, when the mentioned associated play is sufficiently established and can be reproduced at will.[3]

Yeats described the same process more imagistically:

Those masterful images because complete
Grew in pure mind but in what began?
A mound of refuse or the sweepings of a street
Old kettles, old bottles and a broken can.[4]

The second workshop was structured to release this rhythmic movement, moving from free combinatory play to conscious construction and, finally, communication. We began with some simple free-association exercises, carefully timed. A word or word cluster was given:

Underground at Rush Hour
Hospital at Midnight
Water
Bride in a Church
Autumnal Tree

In one minute the students had to scribble their immediate associations. Thus within five minutes there was a mass of fairly inchoate material created out of free verbal associative play. The students were then asked to consider their own spontaneous free associations to look not only within one stream but also across streams to see if they could discern any distinct patterns emerging out of the half-random chaos. They were asked to work consciously with these patterns, to see if they could be expanded, to see, as it were, where they would go. For this expansion and elaboration ten minutes were given. At that point I introduced the haiku form with its economic three lines and formal 5/7/5 stress pattern and asked them in a short period of prescribed time to reduce the material they had expanded to a haiku. At the end of the session the small haiku poems were written up anonymously and handed round for a public reading.

Thus in one short session all the stages of art making had been formally included and, at a simple level, experimentally encountered, from first impulsive jottings ('combinatory play') to conscious shaping into a poetic form, through to performance and communication. Graham in his journal entry for 7 October 1983 wrote up his haiku and commented on the process of composition:

The pantomime bride
Bids a forlorn farewell to
Her summer lovers.

I'm really very pleased with this. Today was – I think – the first time I had encountered the 'haiku' and having criticised the artificiality of the writing exercise (but not the intention) in the last meeting I was a little suspicious as to how today's exercise would go. However, I can now see more clearly the idea behind such 'control' – *that deliberate experimentation with prescribed structures provides the possibility to experience and experiment with different forms of writing; an approach to finding one's own style.*

The writing and rendering of haiku in the second workshop suggested a further development in collaborative art making. Writing about the related Japanese form of *renga* Toyoko Izutsu has pointed out:

The particular feature of this poetic art, renga, is that it is composed not by one poet but by a group of poets gathered together in a party. The units go on being created one by one on the spot and are placed one after another in serial form by the participants taking their turns.

The starting verse, the very first unit of 5/7/5, assumes technically a particular significance in renga so that it is composed usually by an honoured poet in the gathering, known for his conspicuous poetic attainment.

Hokku, the very first verse in the whole renga is the only fixed point stably established under the direct control of one individual poet to mark the departure for the whole course of a yet unknown creative voyage, in which functional fluidity and relational mobility play a great part, preventing any one of the participants from steering its course at will. The participants know only afterwards the whole scope extending from the starting point to the end, recognising it as a wake they themselves have left behind in their group voyage of creation.[5]

In their third workshop (after the students had returned from a longish period in the schools in which they were now placed, for the best part of the year, for three days in each week, with two days at the university) sheets of the haikus, typed up, were handed out. We looked at some translations of Japanese haiku and noted the way they invariably move from a cluster of particular images to hint at a universal, the way in which the concrete object is envisaged as a manifestation of the metaphysical, the way in which also, sometimes, a contradiction is established, an opposition, which is then delicately rooted in the ground of Non-Being:

The sea darkens
The voices of the wild ducks
Are faintly white.

Then I asked the students to take any haiku on the sheet, preferably not their own, and to write, while keeping the structural form of the original, its antithesis in mood and meaning. After ten minutes, the students were asked to exchange with their neighbour the double haiku and now the task was to find, in a third stanza, the resolution, the synthesis.

The pantomime bride
Bids a forlorn farewell to
Her summer lovers.

A summer lover
Preparing his next encore
Grows into autumn.

Off the stage of life
Our dramas enacted
Meet reality.

The brown leaves lie still
Embalmed in the clear water
Reflecting dry death.

The green leaves sparkle
Reflecting in the water
Moist vitality.

Green-striped, muddied brown
Leaves splashed by fungoid fingers
Purity mouldered.

Lindsey, who wrote the resolution of the last sequence wrote in her journal:

Thursday – after a whole week at Seaford Head. It's so strange being back on campus – University life looms large and slightly artificial. It's taxing leaping from one context to another. I feel like a chameleon.

I do enjoy the seminar today though. Peter has had the haiku printed up (my hateful haiku), and we try an experiment. Choosing a haiku, we write an antithesis for it, it is then passed on and someone attempts a reconciliation. Thus, it is a three stage process. Subtly the exercise has prompted us to consider someone else's work critically and also involved us in a co-operative scheme. It really works.

The last three lines are mine and I feel satisfied with them. It falls into place for me. The exercise has a complete feel about it.

Karen, who wrote the original thesis confessed:

What made it difficult for me was resolving somebody else's antithesis and previous thesis. I was amazed to feel a pang of possessiveness as I handed my work to another member of the group.

More than a structural exercise was taking place it would seem!

For the second half of the session we worked with four reproduced self-portraits: two from Stanley Spencer, two from David
Bomberg. According to my notes I said something like:

> Take one of the pairs. Look at it carefully. You are the person
> painting. Each stroke expresses a disposition, a moment of
> declaration, of unease, of self-discovery. Express the move-
> ment of the mind in words as the portrait is painted. Now look
> at the second painting. Do the same. Now finally see these
> immediate rough jottings as the material for a unified piece of
> writing.

Lindsey's reaction to this command was interesting in the light of
Ehrenzweig's comment on 'work[ing] hard at being spontaneous'.
Lindsey wrote in her journal:

> Peter hands us a choice of self-portraits and we are to write in
> whatever form we wish feelings and thoughts that occur to us
> when we reflect on them. I feel rebellious. I don't like the
> pictures. They do nothing for me. However I mull over them
> and suddenly almost miraculously I'm fascinated and threads
> start unwinding in my mind zig-zagged and haywire. It's like
> a giant puzzle and it excites me.

It may be that at times the material creates the mood and sets the
mind off from its peripheral preoccupations into something deeper. I
am sure, as I will show later, this is certainly often the case reworking
mythical material. Something more than 'self-expression' takes place
in such unexpected encounters from which conversations grow.

This was Frank's work in response to the two portraits by Stanley
Spencer:

Two Pictures

I

Black on white. Strange how the face of youth
Should look so like a fingerprint,
A mass of whorls and eddies on the cheek.
An assertion of identity, the ink
Rocking weightily downwards
On lip and jawbone. Round the neck

A loose fold, like a rope,
Knotted. The glint of his reflection
Caught only on the hair
(it will grow in the coffin); none in the eyes.
The stare says: 'Mine is the confidence
Of the innocent, and the resignation
Of the condemned man.' Entered into freely.

This the newly-stamped, a seal of approval.

II

Then, so many years later, another identity parade.
Again the paper is saturated, again
The pressure evenly applied. Yet
Here the pattern has been rubbed away
As if glasspapered; only the eyes
Are polished by the process, shrunken but magnified
Under dead lenses. At the crown
A crop of autumn flax, bent double
Before it breaks the skin, waits on the sickle.
Each line offers over our heads
The stillness of the solitary: a mute lip worn
Like a convict suit, the jaw locked around it.
And that open throat, yielding its scare,
Is the most and least human part,
A withered root for the head.

Now he is released into silence;
Once hung already.

In his journal, Frank commented:

Today's writing: the poems from portraits. I recognised the
Stanley Spencer, but tried not to let it interfere with my perceptions. Unfortunately I've lost my original notes from which
Two Pictures was drawn: but there is a first and second draft
before the 'finished' thing. I was pleased (and amazed) at the
way the poem emerged (so quickly) from the notes – in the
end, it took maybe a couple of hours to reach its typed state.
It's the first substantial piece of writing that I've done in a few
years – that, in itself, is enough justification (from my selfish
point of view) for the practical component of these workshops.

One note about it: Graham criticised what he felt was the overplaying of the scarf-as-rope motif. However, much of my thinking about the art-as-hanging theme came from the fact that the second picture of Spencer bears (to me) an uncanny resemblance to John 'Babbacombe' Lea, the man who was 'hung' three times in 1913, commuted to life imprisonment. Hence the 'art' = 'death' ('a living death') idea playing through the poem, and made explicit at the end.

A question: how effective/valid would the poem be without the pictures to accompany it?

I began the next workshop by asking the group to respond immediately and imaginally to the following propositions:

On the horizon a city burns
The jester looks out from a pack of cards
The painter faces a blank canvas
Sadness came
The old woman considered her death
Love entered

Some of the responses were as follows:

On the horizon a city burns
A scarlet sunset killing the day

On the horizon a city burns
A lion roars in its cage

Love entered
Celestial light spilling from the sun

Love entered
Like a kingfisher dipping the surface of a tranquil stream

The old woman considered her death
A knot in the thread, her sampler finished

The painter faces the blank canvas
Pondering a field of perfect snow

Sadness came
The noise of the last train over the bridge

The jester looks out from a pack of cards
Leering at the slow shuffle of humanity

As with many of the imagist poets, it was discovered that the
easiest movement was from the abstract or general to the specific and
imaginal (consider Ezra Pound's 'faces on the underground/petals on a
wet black bough' or T. E. Hulme's 'Sounds fluttered/like bats in the
dark'). Thus the statement 'love entered' was easier to complement
with an image than the already imagistically suggestive 'the jester looks
out from a pack of cards'.

The students were then asked to take the ones they felt they could
develop further. These were some of the results:

Love entered
An Astaire pirouette across marble flights
that laced me in the orbit
Of your dancing passions.

Sadness came
Like dipping leaves in a pool
One by one.

The old woman considered her death
The dust and disappointment of years
Twinkled in the evening sunlight
Then fell grey, shrouding the darkening room
Muffling her gentle sighs.

A 'great way of generating creative play with language', wrote
Kevin in his journal, but Graham's commentary was, in the light of
my earlier remarks about the reciprocal relationship between image
and emotion, particularly revealing;

This was an interesting exercise and one which I look forward
to trying with a class (I think my top-band 3rd years could
handle this well). I think this exercise worked ultimately for
me because I tend to write in sharp, dense images. But I find
it so difficult to begin with – I really didn't feel that I got on
with the first three initial impulses. I must admit that I didn't
feel particularly interested at the start of yesterday's lesson anyway (we all have our off days). But it is very interesting how
I was suddenly able to synthesise the fourth and sixth ideas. All

of a sudden these ideas struck a very personal (and emotional) note in me, and the exercise suddenly took on a very intense and significant meaning, emotionally rather than intellectually.

Love entered
The visitor left her calling card
You took away my life in your suitcase.

> I'm proud of that poem; it may be 'one from the heart' but I think it is direct and unequivocal in its effect as the (really good, even though I say so myself) image of the first two lines is dramatically realised in the final line. I wasn't too sure about reading it out in class – the creation of it and seeing it on the page in front of me really shook me up – but I'm glad I did . . . Apart from the educational significance of the exercise it was a great opportunity for me to resolve some feelings – thank you!

For the next workshop I distributed round the room a mass of photographs. The students were invited to select one and use it, in whatever way seemed 'right' as a starting-point for their own writing. I followed this workshop a week later with mythical images. I selected some striking images from the strange myth of Perseus and Medusa. Then I asked the students to consider ways in which the images could be developed or adapted in terms of their own experience and our own age. In his book *The Witness of Poetry* Czeslaw Milosz has pointed out the advantages of using such material:

> Perhaps there is a good craftsman concealed in every poet who dreams about a material already ordered, with ready-made comparisons and metaphors endowed with nearly archetypal effectiveness and, for that reason, universally accepted; what remains then is to work on chiselling the language.[6]

Milosz is surely right in saying that the writer in using myth can concentrate more easily on style knowing that the given story possesses some kind of universality. But it is also true that mythological symbols possess a great and multifarious energy and can excite the imagination to extend or, in some minor or major way, alter their references and so create new meanings yet still mythically charged. In this way the great myths can be endlessly recreated to meet personal and collective needs. Does Prometheus become Frankenstein at the beginning of the nineteenth century and Pincher Martin in the middle of the twentieth century?

In the workshop I was stumbling towards some kind of concentrated exercise in which powerful mythical images could be contemplated and elaborated. I read twice a number of loosely related passages about Perseus' journey, his shield, Medusa, the snakes, the power of Perseus with the head of Medusa to turn others to stone. The first time I asked them just to listen; the second time to make notes about any particular image that struck them. Then I asked them to engage with and amplify their notes, and to see what happened.

Alan scrawled down the memory of a disturbing experience while on a bus journey:

> I knew that if I only stared forwards, out into the world, I should remain free. Hot irons, red beams were burning in straight parallel lines through my head, carving out my head like sculpture, taking on my gaze and making it her own. There was no question of leaving the bus, for I was on a journey. A woman, behind me on a bus, looking through my head and controlling my eyes.
>
> I know I must not turn my head because if I only glimpsed her look then I would do all she commanded. From the point of sight I would be her own body, an extension, a strange limb whose movement could be traced purely to her eyes. I looked up into the night sky, now black and coagulated and I saw it was no longer the sky of my words, the movements of my possibilities but had become a black hood, carefully and eternally her shadow.

Alan then brought the experience and the ancient myth together in the following notes towards a poem:

Medusa

I knew that you could only take on my self
if you could match my gaze with yours,
map onto my look, onto my making
and make them your command.

I knew that if I turned to face your self
It would be war and I the loser,
For I have no shield
or mirror to protect me.

Only air between us,
egg thin light shattered
penetrating beams of sight
search my head,
carving throught-like-sculptures
turned to stone;

swallowed in its mist
your making me an Other
the body of a dead man.

Alan's response to the mythological images brings out in dramatic form the encounter between personal experience and inherited mythic symbolism. In his journal Alan wrote:

The Medusa story has never been one which has interested me in any way in the past, but in this seminar I suddenly cottoned on to something about it – the idea of the Other, the 'look' – which gave me some insight into why it remains such a powerful myth.

The force of the story derives, I feel, from the sense in which it reifies 'the look', makes the existence of one's self contingent upon the creative minds of other 'lookers'.

Also, the way in which Perseus then goes on, after slaying Medusa, to have such total power, is frightening . . . This idea springs mostly, for myself, from the writing of Sartre on others, on being-in-itself and being-for-itself.

I then wanted to use the experience which I once had of being in a bus and of feeling the stare of the woman behind me penetrating through the back of my head, tempting and almost seducing me to turn around and to meet her eyes. But the atmosphere of the seminar was a difficult one in which to control and contain in any poem a sense of something so fundamental, and essentially disturbing . . . Still, it was good for me because it connected this important notion to a myth which had been hitherto remote and opaque to me.

For Maureen a story was suggested:

A man marries the sort of woman who freezes all feeling in those around her, although like Medusa she had once been a human being. It is a long journey of realisation for the man that people turn to stone at his wife's presence and he feels that together they live 'isolated at the end of the world'. The only way he can manage to keep living with her is by not looking directly at her but by holding an image in his mind of the way he remembers her when they first met. He decides that carrying this memory in his mind he will defeat her, and while she lies sleeping, kills her and cuts off her head. But although he buries the body he keeps the head – there is still a terrible fascination in it even after death. Gradually as he lives with his guilty secret, he becomes aware that the strange power of the head has passed to him: he becomes hard, shrivelled, with the force to freeze others. People's reactions change towards him: from being a nonentity he becomes respected and feared, from being weak he enjoys power, but from being warm and alive he becomes dried, frozen himself, unable to feel, cast in stone. The head has become a curse as well as a power.

Maureen wrote the opening paragraph to the story in the workshop:

Medusa

The visitor's voice trailed off into cold silence; his body felt hollow, lifeless, and yet his feet appeared to have grown steel claws which fastened him to the ground preventing escape. The sudden slamming of the door shut the face from his sight and spelt his release. Inside the house the husband listened to the footsteps fade into the distance. He carefully averted his eyes as the woman swept past him, knowing the power of that terrible face: the hair barbed and fortified, the mouth a slash in frozen marble and the eyes, above all the eyes, pitiless diamond lozenges which spoke only death. It had not always been thus. Once long ago she had been a human being, but since that time they had travelled a great distance together, almost it seemed to the end of the world.

In her journal she commented as follows:

I had time only to make a beginning on actually telling the tale. I was quite pleased with my introduction for the story and the first few lines came to me fairly easily. I wished very much that there was time for us to complete projects like this – far more satisfying than preparing endless lesson plans. This is what I wrote as my introduction to what looks as if it could be classified as a 'horror' story.

I hope to have given some conception of a practical workshop approach to English. The aim was to promote creativity in a disciplined context working in the manner of the art, drama and dance teacher. Although at the end of the last workshop the possibility of story writing was beginning to emerge, most of the writing was confined to poetic forms.

Conclusions

What, then, was the connection between the workshops described and the students' teaching in the classroom? What I was trying to present was a way of working which (with necessary modifications) could be eventually tried out in the classroom. I was out to offer an experience which could be slowly integrated by the PGCE students and extended, by degrees, to their teaching practice. The journals of the students reflected on this connection, sometimes with a certain unease, sometimes with a new angle of perception (as in Fiona's remarks about 'précis' below), sometimes with a great sense of identification and excitement. Here are some characteristic reflections:

> Imagistic work. Very satisfying to play with oneself (myself) – probably very interesting as a basis for school work; the big question being the age groups with which this would be constructive to try. My sureness of touch with regard to the vastly differing cognitive abilities of different age groups, particularly in relation to 2nd and 3rd years, is definitely not yet adequate to introduce these sorts of 'stimuli' it may well be . . . and I certainly don't feel up to effectively communicating the nature of the activity yet. But . . . definitely a great way of generating creative play with language though. (Graham)

> I liked the idea of working up to a small finished idea through the attempt to complement and amplify initial images. I would very much like to use this approach in class as I think I would probably have the right balance between structure and freedom to allow the children to feel absorbed and yet free to write as they pleased. (Alan)

I have used haiku in the classroom on several occasions. Not always successful, but the students seem to enjoy working with the form. With one third year class I arranged for them to do paintings in their art lessons so that the haikus could be super-imposed. The art teacher responded well and combined the exercise with the experiment of colour. The paintings are nearly finished and when mounted they should look quite impressive. (Susan)

If a teacher is going to engage his/her classes in this activity at all (apart from perhaps once or twice a year) then it must be known intimately by that teacher at first hand. To a teacher who never writes him/herself, or who has never written as an adult, I shouldn't imagine that creative writing 'enters into it' at all. (Kevin)

Thinking today about the fact that I was made to do so much précis at school it has now occurred to me that writing poetry, if an amount of discipline and thought is applied in its process could be as 'beneficial' as précis in developing a concise but at the same time evocative picture or presentation of an original idea. By constantly refining our words and phrases for the desired effect we are exerting as much self-discipline as if we were required to reduce a page to 150 words. A ridiculous reduction of the purpose of poetry? Maybe an argument to counter the 'free expression as catharsis' view of writing. (Fiona)

The purpose of our doing this sort of thing is that it will give us a better idea of what we want from the children and of what we want them to get from the exercise. Not the least of which is self-value for by encouraging children to speak about them-selves you are tacitly informing them that they are important. This is not to be under-estimated when you remember that the examination system holds people to be important only in so far as they are capable of attaining 'O' and 'A' levels. (Garry)

I have quoted at some length so as to bring out the different ways in which a very strong connection *was* made between the university workshop and the school classroom. Alan's remark about getting 'the right balance between structure and freedom to allow the children to feel absorbed and yet free to write as they pleased' goes to the heart of the matter and also shows the internalization of our common work-shop practice into his teaching. This is exactly what one is hoping will take place, that the students will transfer their experience of the creative discipline of imaginative writing within a literary tradition to their own developing teaching. Other related university work, such as the discussion of lesson plans, the bringing in of creative work from the classroom for evaluation and the critical and open examination of the best ways of teaching literature at different levels, further extends and strengthens this crucial connection.

The workshops I have described were limited in range and took place over one autumn term. However any adequate creative course for PGCE English students would have to include, *at least*, the informal awareness of many genres and modes of literary expression including not only poetry and myth (vital as these are), but also the story and novel, autobiography, diary and journal, playscript and documentary, essay and sketch, as well as some exploration of film, video, radio and television. This is a daunting agenda, not dissimilar from the one proposed for drama at the end of Chapter 7 yet if it is the necessary agenda because it defines the nature of the subject, then we have no choice, educationally, but to prepare ourselves to teach it and, in so doing, take our students further and further into the depths of their own culture.

I see human beings as creative agents who, through contact with the best elements of a living culture, and through their own expressive and imaginative acts, can develop lives of inner significance and communal value. In *political terms*, it is a matter of people possessing their lives and securing the power and means to participate in a cultural democracy. In *educational terms*, it is a matter of individuals being continually open to further truths, further configurations of meaning discovered either through direct creative work or through a kind of submission to the power of other imaginative work in the literary tradition. In *spiritual terms* it concerns a sense of interior transcendence impossible to describe fully, but which is often sensed in the engaged acts of imaginative writing or creative performance. It takes the form of a sensation of being 'there' in some transpersonal space resonant with silent meaning. The kind of experience I am trying to denote was described by students in relationship to the aesthetic moment in Chapter 3. 'The eternity of vision lives on and I am in it', wrote one student in relationship to Monet's garden. These three categories of concern, political, educational and spiritual, are not, of course, mutually exclusive or in any kind of competition. They are all, in their manifold implications, necessary to any concept of human wholeness, whether personal or communal, and on their difficult and exacting integration must surely depend the survival of our culture and our species.

Notes

1   ANTON EHRENZWEIG (1953) *The Psycho-Analysis of Artistic Vision and Meaning*, London, Routledge and Kegan Paul. See chapter 1.
2   TED HUGHES (1967) *Poetry in the Making*, London, Faber and Faber, p. 23.
3   Einstein, quoted in ARTHUR KOESTLER (1966) *The Act of Creation*, London, Picador.
4   W.B. YEATS (1963) from 'The Circus Animals' Desertion', in *Collected Poems*, London, Macmillan, p. 391.
5   TOYOKO IZUTSU (1982) 'An Aspect of Haiku Aesthetics', *Temenos*, (3), p. 112.
6   CZESLAW MILOSZ (1983) *The Witness of Poetry*, Cambridge, MA, Harvard University Press, p. 65.

Section IV

Tributes and Evaluations

Chapter 10

Herbert Read, Modernism and the Dilemmas of Self-Expression

'School' is an emancipation achieved in a continuous redirection of attention. Here, the learner is animated, not by the inclinations he brings with him, but by intimations of excellence and aspirations he has never yet dreamed of; here he may encounter, not answers to the 'loaded' questions of 'life', but questions which have never before occurred to him; here he may acquire new 'interests' and pursue them uncorrupted by the need for immediate results; here he may learn to seek satisfaction he had never yet imagined or wished for.

Michael Oakeshott

Introduction

Where in arts education do our conceptions and inspirations come from? Often from seminal writers who by their insights, their commitment and their power of expression, persuade us to enter and take possession of their vision. In the 60s and 70s many students rushed into teaching inspired by Sybil Marshall's *An Experiment in Education*. I, for my part, was greatly influenced by the writing of David Holbrook and Herbert Read, and then in the 70s and 80s by the work of Peter Fuller. It is difficult to assess how fully such writers influence one. Their voices become internalized; they become part of our conversation until, slowly, as we add our own voices to their voices, we assimilate their way of seeing and go beyond, not necessarily to a better understanding but, at least, to a more personal understanding, a position that one has the right to call one's own.

The three sketches that follow are therefore a mercurial mixture of autobiography, of near uncritical admiration and of evaluation. They are not offered as definitive appraisals; but rather as living reflections on three cultural thinkers who have influenced our times and shaped many of the arguments put forward in the earlier chapters of this book.

I begin with the two art critics, Herbert Read and Peter Fuller, and conclude with the poet, literary critic and educationist, David Holbrook.

Herbert Read: Some Autobiographical Reflections

I first came across the writings of Herbert Read when I was about 17. I had started my A levels at what was then known as Norwich Tech. One day, on my way back to Thorpe Station, I had dropped into the city library and taken off the shelf, for no good reason, a volume called *Anarchy and Order*. I took the book back with me to Sheringham and read it with a growing sense of excitement and identification. It was to have a formative influence on my thinking.

I now know it was not a great book, not even one of Herbert Read's best, but it was a great book *for me* at that moment in my life. There had been no books in my own home; at 17 I had not heard of Marx, Darwin or Freud. *Anarchy and Order* opened the windows and doors of my enclosed rural consciousness. It put me in immediate touch with another society, another landscape, another universe. It provided me with some of the elements necessary for a kind of inner liberation; the book gave me a lexicon of names (of philosophers, essayists, poets, artists, movements and debates) as well as a firm cluster of intellectual and moral issues worth living for. No teacher had ever given me that. In our pragmatic culture, teachers, for the most part, fail to present intellectual maps, fail to show typologies of influence or to disclose those radical disruptions and those radical re-establishments of continuity that together comprise the actual symbolic field of any study. I did my 'set texts' at A level, but I had no idea of the historic or aesthetic matrix to which those texts belonged or, indeed, why, existentially, they mattered. The names of the writers were isolated, the approach atomistic, the purpose of it all very elusive: set texts for set exams; objects to be classified for certification.

Herbert Read helped me to see beyond the *ad hoc* pragmatism of the typical English attitude. He offered me, at a highly impressionable age, an almost magical litany of literary names and some keen insight into why those names mattered. After my adolescent devouring of *Anarchy and Order* my A level essays began to grow in length. They became as exuberant and unwieldy as tropical plants. Most pretentiously, they quoted such continental thinkers as Pascal and Kierkegaard. I never acknowledged the secondary sources of my quotations and, fortunately, my teachers (no doubt somewhat alarmed) never asked.

For me, the name Herbert Read did not denote an actual person, subject to the frailties of ordinary existence; the name referred to a distant voice of prophecy, whose words mysteriously materialized as printed pages bound in covers with the imprimatur of Faber stamped clearly on their bold jackets. When, later, I met people who had known Herbert Read, I felt a sense of shock and incredulity. Most of our spiritual heroes live in some other dimension in constant inner relationship to us, but unseen and leaving no tangible traces in the material world. Yet at the same time, I listened, avid for whatever details I could gather. One story moved me particularly.

Apparently, Herbert Read had given one of his last lectures, 'The Limits of Permissiveness', in Puerto Rico on 1 February 1968. He was then suffering badly from cancer of the mouth. He found great difficulty in speaking. A devoted audience sat patiently through a virtually inaudible lecture. Then, when it was clear that the lecture was over, the audience spontaneously stood up and gave this shy, courageous intellectual a standing ovation, such was the profound respect of Puerto Ricans for Herbert Read's literary and political achievement. It was a story that satisfied all my expectations, particularly as the lecture was, in essence, a spirited attack on much of the modernism he himself had done so much to set in motion.

Then later I discovered *The Innocent Eye*. Surely this book remains in our age of autobiography one of the most lyrical and affirmative autobiographical sketches of our century? And yet it was the autobiographical extensions to this first sketch that were the cause of my first becoming somewhat distanced from my intellectual hero. As I read the extended autobiography, I became uneasily aware of the conscious and often unconscious elevation of 'the natural child' over the more exacting achievements of the cultural order. I began to detect what I came to regard as a fallacy: the conceptual splitting off of the child from the necessary historic and cultural continuum. And it is here perhaps, that I should end this tribute but, in truth, I have already revealed too much. For the crack in the edifice that I have mentioned has continued to deepen and has now permanently altered the original relationship to the master. It is in Herbert Read's *Education through Art* that one finds the fallacy of the natural child most strongly at work. The direct consequence of Read's romantic misreading of the nature of cultural existence was, I am now convinced, *a desperate poverty of practice in the teaching of the arts at primary and secondary level for the best part of three decades.* In attending to the supposedly autonomous natural child, a multitude of arts teachers came to neglect, even to deny, the place of technique, of artistic exemplar, of continuous tradition, of the need for a coherent grammar of creative expression. The romantic elevation of the child ushered in a period of 'self-expression' and cultural autism.

It is, then, a moving paradox that it was Herbert Read who was one of the first writers to put me in touch with those cultural traditions that transcend our local patch of soil, that connect us to a larger symbolic world and of which, at 17, I had virtually no knowledge. That was precisely *why* I valued him so greatly, why he became an intellectual hero. My developing criticism of him, therefore, is based on the very thing he gave me. It also explains why now, before developing the critique any further, I feel impelled to put the record straight. Whatever I may say against *Education through Art* I want to acknowledge openly a sense of cultural debt to its author. He gave me an inconceivably larger world to live in.

Herbert Read, Modernism and Progressivism

I want now to examine the case against modernism and progressivism with a single focus, namely the work and influence of Herbert Read. He is an essential figure, not only because his work had a seminal influence on education during his own lifetime, but also because it is still frequently evoked and listed in most bibliographies on arts education. First I will consider the partial and disfiguring elements in Read's aesthetic for education and then go on to consider his own critical responses to much of modernism in the later years of his life.

In a lecture given at Liverpool University in February 1981 considering the educational influence of Herbert Read, Ernst Gombrich had this to say:

> When I once lectured to a teachers' training class I was firmly told in the discussion that no teacher must ever show what he personally likes since he must not influence the child. I was even told elsewhere that visits to art museums by schoolchildren were frowned upon by teachers, who alleged that the late Sir Herbert Read put freshness and originality above every other concern. But why allow oneself to be influenced by Herbert Read and not by Rembrandt? Why teach the child the words of our language but not the images of our tradition?[1]

Gombrich's target was in no way arbitrary. For decades Read had expounded on the necessary principle of modernity, a principle that became in his writings more and more eclectic and elastic. In the 30s his position had, however, been openly revolutionary. In 1933 in *Art Now* Read had declared 'the aim of five centuries of European effort is openly abandoned' and then in 1935 he claimed: 'everywhere the greatest obstacle to the new social reality is the existence of the cultural heritage of the past'. In the same address Read applauded Walter Gropius' conception of a new architecture based not on memory but on a pure functional geometry. Later, as we shall see, Herbert Read was to express considerable disillusionment with the artistic achievement of modernism, but before examining the nature of that unease, expressed in a number of essays and particularly in the last lecture he gave in 1968, I want to examine Read's conception of progressive arts education. This will involve a short digression on the general nature of modernism and progressivism.

There is, of course, a certain affinity between the concepts of modernism and progressivism; both words bear within them *an orientation to time*, a positive forward-looking disposition. The word *modernism* derives from the word *modo* meaning 'just now'. In the lexicon of modernism this orientation to time is invariably celebrated and dramatized. It can be seen in the concept of the 'avant-garde' (deriving from the French for the vanguard, the military spearhead at the front of the assault) and in the name of, for example, a movement like futurism (in February 1908 Marinetti declared in his *Futurist Manifesto*: 'but we will hear no more about the past, we young strong Futurists'). It set up in our language and made febrile and judgmental such polarities as: 'progressive' and 'reactionary', 'forward-looking' and 'backward-looking', 'contemporary' and 'archaic', 'in fashion' and 'old-fashioned'/ 'out-dated'/'old-hat'.

Modernism is most characteristically described as a movement based on disruption, severance, a breaking with past practice. Defining modernism in *The Oxford Companion to English Literature* Margaret Drabble wrote:

> Modernist literature is a literature of discontinuity both historically, being based upon a sharp rejection of the procedures and values of the immediate past, to which it adopts an adversarial stance; and aesthetically.[2]

In a similar vein, the Marxist critic Jurgen Habermas in an essay entitled 'Modernity: An Incomplete Project' wrote:

> In the course of the 19th Century there emerged out of this Romantic spirit that radicalized consciousness of modernity which freed itself from all specific historical ties. This most recent Modernism simply makes an abstract opposition between

tradition and the present; and we are in a way still the contemporaries of that kind of aesthetic modernity which first
appeared in the midst of the 19th Century. Since then the distinguishing mark of works which count as modern is 'the new'
which will be overcome and made obsolete through the novelty
of the next style.[3]

A good example of a modernist position, in its pure and dogmatic
form, can be found in the American critic Hayden White who claimed:

One of the distinctive characteristics of contemporary literature
is its underlying conviction that the historical consciousness
must be obliterated if the writer is to examine with proper
seriousness those strata of human experience which is modern
art's peculiar purpose to disclose.[4]

The imperative is clear: obliterate the collective and historical memory.
In this respect modernism uncannily resembles certain elements in
progressive educational theory.

The very word 'progressive' has, indeed, that explosive word
'progress' at its centre. The last two meanings of the word progress
given by the Oxford English Dictionary are particularly pertinent: 'fig.
To make progress, to advance, to get on; to develop; usu; to improve
continuously 1610; trans: to cause to advance; to push forward.' A
commitment to thrusting through space and time towards the next
development would seem to mark out the common ground between
the modernist and the progressivist. And yet in education progressivists would tend to work with a different set of assumptions from the
typical modernist. The former would invoke nature, biology, the
innate unfolding of an inviolate identity. Progressive educators offer
a country rhetoric, not a cosmopolitan one. The great inspiration and
the major source of this movement remains Rousseau's *Émile* (1762).

To achieve the ideal education Rousseau removed the child from
what was seen as the malign influences of civilization and placed him
in the remote countryside. Émile was to grow up in and through
communion with his own nature in relationship to Nature. 'In my
view', Rousseau declared, 'everything ought to be in conformity with
original inclinations, the innate inclinations of the body prior to the
distorting influences of society'. The progression, then, refers not to an
inevitable historic unfolding but to the innate unfolding (without overt
influence or formal restraint) of the interior nature of the individual

child. Rousseau's ferocious attack on civilization and inherited culture is at once highly eloquent and deeply fallacious:

> Man's wisdom is but servile prejudice; his customs but subjection and restraint. From the beginning to the end of life civilised man is a slave. At birth he is sewn up in swaddling bands and at death nailed down in a coffin. All through he is fettered by social institutions . . . *The result is that the inner urge to bodily growth finds an insurmountable obstacle in the way of movements that are imperatively needed.*[5]

So, in this tradition progress tends to denote not the continuous advances of a Promethean civilization but the progressive unfolding of the unique individual removed from what are conceived as the falsifying influences of received traditions, the whole spiritual and cultural inheritance. While modernism and progressivism have different starting points and concerns, they yet both share a common disdain for the collective and historic past. In Rousseau's *Émile* nature is set up in opposition to civilization and interpreted as the justifying and primary category. In typical modernism, as demonstrated by the earlier quotation from Hayden White, the past is seen as an impediment to expression and to the full and fitting response to the spirit of the age. 'Start from zero', urged the great modernist and founder of the Bauhaus, Walter Gropius.

In our century the two very complex movements come together in the figure and writing of Herbert Read, especially in *Education through Art*. It is to this book or rather one central chapter of this book that I must now turn. The chapter is, significantly, titled 'The Natural Form of Education' and, as significantly, quotes beneath its heading: 'remember that childhood is the sleep of reason', an exhortation from Rousseau. In this chapter Herbert Read offers his typology of arts teaching; he divides it into three areas: 'the activity of self-expression', 'the activity of observation', 'the activity of appreciation'. A good initial classification of tasks, one is tempted to say; but it is his *interpretation* of these three areas, informed by his progressivist notions of the child, that are of the greatest interest. First of all, he states that each activity is best seen as a distinct subject, requiring separate and unrelated methods of approach. Then he comments on each activity in turn. Of *self-expression* he writes that 'generally speaking' it 'cannot be taught'. Elaborating on this position he claims: 'Any application of an external standard, whether of technique or form, immediately induces inhibitions, and frustrates the whole aim. The role of the teacher is that of attendant, guide, inspirer, psychic midwife'.

Observation, the second field of activity, in contrast is, according to Read, one that is almost entirely 'an acquired skill'. Having said it can be taught he then goes on to severely demote it: It is the usefulness of such acquired skill as an ancillary to the normal logical and scientific curriculum of the school which has led to the fanatical defence of naturalistic modes in art teaching, and a preference to 'craft' as opposed to 'art'. Then, finally, Herbert Read comments on *appreciation*. He insists that appreciation *can* be taught, but then goes on:

> But in so far as by appreciation we mean a response to other people's modes of expression, *then the faculty is likely to develop only as one aspect of social adaptation, and cannot be expected to show itself much before the age of adolescence. Until then the real problem is to preserve the original intensity of the child's reactions to the sensuous qualities of experience – to colours, surfaces, shapes and rhythms. These are apt to be so infallibly 'right' that the teacher can only stand over them in a kind of protective awe.*[6]

In brief, for Herbert Read – as for Rousseau – the essential task of the art teacher is to hold back the various conventions of the culture so that the children can naturally unfold out of their own uncorrupted natures. 'The adult's relation to the child', he wrote, 'must always be that of a collaborator, never that of a master'. All that the teacher might formally introduce is devalued in comparison with what *the child has to give to the teacher*. This is child-centred education.

In Herbert Read it is possible to locate two main modern sources for the child-centred pedagogy. First, there was his discovery of Carl Jung's writing on the collective unconscious, on a dynamic and creative conception of the psyche with its autonomous creativity. This promoted a view that interference from outside could only hinder or often distort the natural psychic process towards expressive symbolization. In *Education through Art* Jung is quoted as saying: 'Consciousness is forever interfering, helping, correcting and negotiating, and never leaving the simple growth of psychic processes in peace'. In 1940 Herbert Read himself came across a drawing by a Cambridgeshire working-class girl, aged 5. It was called by the girl, 'Snake round the World and a Boat'. (It is reproduced as figure 1b in *Education through Art*.) According to Read it had been drawn by the child at home and was spontaneous in origin:

I was deeply moved because what this child had drawn was one of the oldest symbols in the world – a magic circle divided into segments and known as the mandala, the symbol of the self as a psychic unity, a very ancient symbol found in Egypt and the Far East and throughout Europe in the Middle Ages . . . This child of five had given me something in the nature of an apocalyptic experience.[7]

If so much was given by nature, then what was the need for an inherited culture? Indeed, was there not the constant danger that any received culture would suppress the innate biological fund of symbolic images? From a different position, Rousseau's pedagogy of non-interference was thus reaffirmed.

Read's growing commitment to the work of Jung and the notion of a dynamic unconscious fused with those elements in modernism that advocated a return to the immediate, the unpremeditated, the innocent. In *The Truth of a Few Simple Ideas* Herbert Read tells us how, in organizing some children's exhibitions abroad, he met in Paris Picasso who, after examining the children's work, said: 'When I was the age of these children I could paint like Raphael. It took me many years to learn how to paint like these children'. For a moment the formulations precipitated by child art and those proclaimed by the avant-garde seemed to be identical. The aim thus became clear; it was to liberate the expressive impulse; to create an open space untouched by the images of Raphael or Rembrandt or any previous art. It was to be an education devoted to the primacy of self-expression.

Similar versions of child-centred education, rooted often in further notions of 'play' deriving from psychoanalysis, can be found across the arts, particularly in the period between 1940 and 1970. It is strongly present in drama (in the writing of Peter Slade and Brian Way) which disowned theatre; it is present in dance (particularly in the popularization of Laban's work) and, in a less focused and more diffuse way, it can be discovered at work in music and English teaching. What the believers in self-expression valued was spontaneity, improvisation, orginality, process; what was *largely dismissed* was the collective symbolic field in which the creation should have been taking place. There was little or no reference to achieved work in the artistic medium, especially from the past. Few conventions, if any, were explicitly introduced. There was a general poverty of terms, critical and practical. What was missing was the historic symbolic and spiritual background and the recognition of a wider cultural order to which all the work produced belonged. The public nature of artistic production was entirely absent. There was no poetics or rhetoric to sustain, to extend, to connect and deepen the expressive act that easily grows repetitive and predictable from want of variety, outside challenge and the mature intervention of the teacher.

During this same period of progressive experimentation in education modernism had entered its second and more negative phase. In *Living Powers* (1987) I differentiated between the first vital movement of modernism (1900–40) and the second jaded movement of late modernism (1940–80). The two influences of progressivism and late modernism working together, consciously and unconsciously, led to a state of symbolic anorexia from which most visual art teachers are only now slowly recovering. We are now, almost by force of historic circumstance, cultural conservationists, not revolutionaries. For what now could possibly be 'next' in any self-proclaimed artistic revolution? Rather, we feel compelled to repair the bridges, to re-establish dynamic and creative lines of communication with all that has gone before, especially with that which relates to the collective spiritual narratives and the mythic images of the world.

Herbert Read's Late Work: The Attack on Modernism

What, then, are we to make of Herbert Read's paradoxical attack on the achievements of modernism made at the end of his life; paradoxical because Read had been one of the greatest champions of artistic modernism in Britain? It was as if, in his last writing, he was throwing his many manifestos into the fire as worthless prophecies, as proclamations of hope that could no longer withstand the test of passing time. It was as if Herbert Read, in the last years of his life, came to see many of the fruits of modernism (and especially of late modernism) as withered and poisonous, as if he could sense some inversion at work in modern artistic expression, could sense the loss of a sacred dimension, but could not adequately locate their cultural causes.

In 1962, in 'What is There Left to Say?' Herbert Read had indicated his sense of isolation from his times. Commenting on the corroding cynicism and despair of most of the major authors of his period he wrote: 'I was born with an innocence that is abashed by such cynicism, and for this reason alone I must retire into silence, or into the sacrificial busy-ness of committees.'[8]

The paper ends with a dismissive reference to 'pop' artists and 'drug-addicts' and to the conclusion that the last phase of disintegration had set in. Yet only two years before, in 1960 in a further preface to *Art Now* Read had expounded in true modernist style:

> People forget that the artist (if he deserves that name) has the acutest sense of us all; and he can only be true to himself and to his function if he expresses that acuteness to the final edge. We are without courage, without freedom, without passion and joy, if we refuse to follow where he leads.[9]

Here we find the rhetorical assertion of the conception of the avant-garde on which so many 'isms' of the twentieth century were to be quickly created and as quickly discarded. Yet Read's formulation is quintessentially vague. For what was 'the final edge' to which the artist was moving in 1959, just as the 60s were about to explode? And what was 'the final edge' to which many of the earlier modernists had come? These are not speculative questions. They are the actual questions that Herbert Read came to ask himself in one of the last lectures he gave, on 1 February 1968, a few months before his death. The answers he provided were as aesthetically critical as they were ethically bleak. They disclose, unambiguously, that Herbert Read had come to feel that 'the final edge' was not the right place for the arts to be. Significantly, the lecture was entitled 'The Limits of Permissiveness' (it was the lecture given in Puerto Rico, mentioned earlier). Here is a brief summary of this important document in the history of the rise and fall of modernism.[10]

Herbert Read began his lecture by defending the principle of modernism and then plunged, unexpectedly, into the negative element. He attacked James Joyce's modernist masterpiece *Finnegan's Wake*, quoting with approval Stanislaus' judgment that it represented 'the witless wandering of literature before its final extinction'. Its influence, he asserts, 'has been disastrous'. He then moved on to damn the experimental work of Samuel Beckett. From 'a stylistic point of view, it has led to an apotheosis of futility and to a permissive logorrhoea . . . with so little aesthetic reward'. Having dismissed Beckett, he then dismissed the anti-novel of Alan Robbe-Grillet, Nathalie Sarraute and Marguerite Duras. They, he claimed, had none of the movement, tension and resolution found 'in the great literature of the past'.

Next, Herbert Read turned his critical eye on Ezra Pound and, while claiming that Pound must remain one of the great poets of our time he went on to quote with approval Yeat's judgment, referring to his 'nervous obsession', 'nightmare' and 'stammering confusion'. Read concluded that 'the stammering confusion has grown worse with every successive batch of cantos, until in the latest cantos the incoherence is absolute'. Of all Pound's disciples and imitators he declared, 'they mirror a great confusion and call it the modern style'.

After such a cursory and despairing evaluation of these major literary innovators and innovations, Read, the high modernist and pioneer of cultural revolution, turned to the visual arts: 'I must now turn all too late in this lecture to the visual arts, for the process of disintegration is even more evident in painting and sculpture than in literature'. He praised the early work of the first modernists: Picasso, Miró, Kandinsky, Henry Moore, but argued that the majority of those who had come to maturity after the Second World War in their struggle to be original were 'compelled to deviate arbitrarily from the prototypes'. Earlier in the lecture Herbert Read had characterized the movements of action painting, pop art and op art as 'pseudo-movements . . . the creation of journalists . . . anxious to create an order where only confusion seems to exist.'

Read's extraordinary lecture finally ended with a plea that we reject 'contemporary nihilism in art' and 'withhold our approval from all those manifestations of permissiveness characterized by incoherence, insensibility, brutality and ironic detachment'. So much, then, for the artist having the acutest sense and for his audience following him to the final edge! The 'Limits of Permissiveness' is a moving, confused and disturbing document. It is permeated with a deep moral gloom and cultural apprehension. The despairing words *paranoia, confusion, incoherence, nihilism* litter the text. A despairing visionary, it would seem, speaks out against an autistic and disintegrating culture he had partly made possible. Had the prevailing expressions of 'cultural nihilism' engendered in him a sense of deep cultural conservation? Certainly the references to 'prototypes' and to 'the great literature of the past' imply both an enduring order greater than the modern and an aesthetic field of execution which, necessarily, transcended it. Aware of the paradox of his own position as the pioneer of modernism in art and of progressivism in arts education, Herbert Read must have felt deeply uneasy. He saw the crisis. He sensed the nihilism and the symbolic depletion. Yet, locked in his own progressive and modernist categories, he was unable to fully grasp the reasons for the collapse.

In the teaching of the arts we are still responding to the extreme condition of social confusion half diagnosed by Herbert Read in his last lecture. We are also responding to the negative consequences of much progressive arts education, which for the best part of the century eclipsed any sense of a common culture and that Herbert Read did much to father. In the story of arts education and in the light of the new arts paradigm he is destined to remain, therefore, an influential, but deeply ambivalent figure.

Notes

1 ERNST GOMBRICH (1984) *Tributes: Interpretations of our Cultural History*, Oxford, Phaidon, p. 89.
2 MARGARET DRABBLE (1985) *The Oxford Companion to English Literature*, Oxford, Oxford University Press.
3 JURGEN HABERMAS (1983) 'Modernity: an Incomplete Project', in HAL FOSTER (ed.) *Post-Modern Culture*, London, Pluto Press, p. 4.
4 HAYDEN WHITE. I am unable to trace this quotation.
5 JEAN JACQUES ROUSSEAU (1911) *Émile*, (translated by Barbara Foxley) London, Everyman Edition, pp. 10–1 (my italics).
6 HERBERT READ (1956) *Education through Art*, 3rd ed., London, Faber and Faber, p. 209.
7 *Ibid.*
8 HERBERT READ (1962) 'What is There Left to Say?', in *The Cult of Sincerity*, London, Faber and Faber, p. 57.
9 HERBERT READ (1960) *Art Now*, (rev. ed.) London, Faber and Faber, p. 11.
10 'The Limits of Permissiveness' is published in PETER ABBS (ed.) (1975) *The Black Rainbow: Essays on the Present Breakdown of Culture*, London, Heinemann Educational Books.

Chapter 11

Peter Fuller as Art Critic and Educator

He died at a time when his ideas were reaching full maturity. These ideas, if they were implemented, could bring great benefits to art education and the place of the visual arts in our society.

Leslie Cunliffe

Consciousness and aesthetics are the great untouched questions . . . And don't forget the sacred.

Gregory Bateson

Give us power in the Spirit and then art will come; but the taste for art will not arrest the decay of the Spirit.

P.T. Forsyth

Introduction

It is difficult to forget picking up *The Independent* on 11 May 1990 and stumbling upon the obituary to Peter Fuller. At first, not fully awake, glancing through the pages and seeing his name I thought I was about to read another one of his eloquent essays when the appalling news became gradually clear. Edward Lucie Smith began: 'Peter Fuller's death in a motorway accident removes a major figure from the contemporary art scene.'[1] It was impossible immediately to grasp the truth of this shocking statement or to begin to measure the loss. A major figure? Most certainly. He was the man, who more than anyone else in the world of the visual arts, had the insight and audacity to stand against the British avant-garde arts establishment, to propose alternative spiritual and aesthetic terms for the critical mediation of art and in so doing to contribute to the redrawing of the cultural map of our times.

For some reason when a person we care about dies we desire to know the circumstances of the death. The information I was able to extract from the obituaries was sparse. During the following days and weeks I compulsively asked anyone who I felt might know more whether they had further details. Slowly, the major pieces came together.

On Saturday 28 April Peter Fuller had been making his way from his home in Bath to the office of *Modern Painters* – his own brilliant journal – in London. He was with his family: his second wife Stephanie – who was expecting their second child – and their son Laurence Ruskin. They were being driven by a chauffeur in a Volvo limousine. The chauffeur had fallen asleep over the wheel and driven the car over the edge of the M4. The chauffeur had two broken ribs, the small boy a serious femur fracture; Stephanie lost the child she was expecting; Peter Fuller was killed. He was 42. These stark details entered my consciousness with such force that, at unexpected moments in the following days, I was overcome with an unsettling mixture of sadness, of unfocused anger and a sense of futility. It seemed so entirely the wrong death for the man with his emerging, if equivocal, commitment to the spiritual element in life. It was a death to justify the blind despair of a Samuel Beckett character, the shrill scream of a Francis Bacon anti-hero or many similar manifestations of nihilism that Peter Fuller had judged morally unacceptable and, seeking a broader affirmation, turned his back against.

If it was fitting that Peter Fuller was born in Damascus – where else could a man of such intense conversions be born? – it was, in the same manner, deeply disconcerting that he should die under the sign of the contingent and absurd, at the edge of a heartless motorway. It was the last death he deserved. Albert Camus, who also died in a road accident, believed in the absurd; Peter Fuller did not.

How, then, did the obituaries I read so carefully characterize his work and his personality? Most of them referred to his combative style, his occasional ferocity of critical judgment, his indignation at the culturally banal and pretentious. Andrew Graham Dixon called him the most talented critical batman of his time, while the anonymous writer for the *Daily Telegraph* noted how 'the word evil came naturally to his pen. Gilbert and George represented "the evil of banality", as for Francis Bacon, "his evil genius demands a moral refusal" '.[2]

At the same time some of the obituarists in the tactful manner demanded by the genre hinted that his criticism had a source in his own divided and obsessive identity. 'His intellectual progression', wrote Edward Lucie Smith, 'had also been a painful matter of exorcising certain personal demons'.[3] Somewhat more specifically Paul Barker, former editor of the *New Society*, pointed to Fuller's tendency to identify totally with spiritual father figures. 'In his early articles', he revealed, 'I suggested he cut out too frequent homage to John Berger. Later, I suggested the same restraint with Ruskin . . . Advice one might add, which judging from the manifestations, was never taken'.[4] Peter Fuller's early addictive gambling was also recorded.

But most of all, the obituaries stressed Fuller's vision of the visual arts as imaginative and transformative, his recognition of a distinctively English tradition of painting, his influence on the renewal of figurative and symbolic art in our time. Two further qualities were mentioned: his stylistic eloquence and his growing commitment to the spiritual. 'In recent years', wrote Lucie Smith, 'he wrote the clearest and most flexible prose of any British art critic';[5] while Paul Barker linked, with a certain felicity, his power with language to his growing emphasis on the sacred. 'He was a man of the Word', he wrote, 'Religion would, I suspect, have become increasingly important to him'.[6]

The Distortion of Peter Fuller's Thinking

There are, or should be, constraints on the writers of obituaries. They exist to honour the other, to pay homage, to affirm without rancour or perversity the distinctive qualities and actions of the dead person. I must now turn to an obituary that failed to do this; I do so not simply because it broke a tacit convention but because, I believe, it is symptomatic of a certain powerful segment of our culture and because it takes me into the first part of my theme, the insidious and unjust political assimilation of Peter Fuller to the revolutionary Right. The other major theme I am anxious to develop – the actual contribution of Peter Fuller to our common democratic culture – will return us, soon enough, to the just observations of the other obituaries.

It is necessary to quote at some length *The Guardian's* obituary published on 30 April 1990. It was written by Waldema Januszczak, the paper's art critic:

> Peter Fuller was the most important art-critic working in Britain in his time – or at least that is what I am quoted as saying on the back of several of his books. He kept putting it in the blurbs even when he knew that I had long since changed my mind about his youthful claim. Indeed, he kept putting it in precisely because he knew I had changed my mind. Oh my, how Peter liked to annoy people. He was that rarest of creature – an art historian with a sense of fun.

This may come as a surprise to the scores of cultural com-
mentators in various fields who have entered into very serious
wars of words with him. He was renowned – justly – as an
intellectual trouble-maker. And often gave the impression of
arguing for the sake of it. The truth of the matter is that he was
probably born a century too late: Peter Fuller was the nearest
thing the welfare state of art world has produced to an opinion-
ated nineteenth century man of letters.

The easy thing to say about Peter Fuller in the 1980s is that
he represented the reactionary right wing of British art criticism. He stood for old British values and appeared to hate
German, French and, above all, American ones. He liked old-
fashioned British artists such as John Piper and Henry Moore.
He had a week-end house in Suffolk in one of those impossibly
quaint Suffolk villages. He was a man of churchyards and book-
lined studies.

His great weakness was a kind of giggling vanity that made
him over-use his own name and adopt a rather camp tone in
most things he wrote, notably in the editorials he did for *Modern
Painters*. He was having fun with his readers, of course, but
they did not always catch the intended note of sarcasm, and he
was easily mistaken for a self-opinionated twit in the familiar
Young Fogey line.

But God, he will be missed. Peter Fuller was a doer . . .

The only thing that stopped his from being a history-
changing critic was the absence of a truly insightful eye to go
with his truly ambitious mind.[7]

The cheap mockery must not hold our attention too long. It is
contemptible stuff – the journalistic patter betrays a stunning crassness
of mind – even more contemptible for being couched as a major obituary in what should have been one of our major newspapers. But it
signifies something more than the writer's ego. It is characteristic of
the puzzling rejection and rank stereotyping of a radical and challenging thinker by the intellectual liberal-left consensus in our culture. In
Januszczak's obituary one is just waiting for the arrival of the standard-
ized left-wing vocabulary: *élitist, bourgeois, white, Euro-centred, outmoded*.
All the judgments and stereotypes relating to a class-based historicism,
fostered by such leaden language, are palpably there. I remember how
when Peter Fuller's autobiographical *Marches Past* came out in 1986, in
an ICA interview on 16 April with Peter Fuller all that the left-wing
interviewer, Raphael Samuel, could do was to babble on about social

class while categorizing psychotherapy, around which the book centres, as 'a bourgeois construction'. Samuel struck me as a colour-blind man staring at a late Rothko, and asking all the wrong questions. He possessed no way of entering the human suffering documented in the book or of perceiving the symbolism through which it was expressed. It was as if he could understand nothing until it had been fitted fully into the grid of historical determinism.

What I am trying to hint at is a tragedy in British cultural life, a tragedy that Peter Fuller's life illustrates with a dramatic clarity of line. The real critical movement of consciousness during the last two decades has had to find its way out of an ossified left-wing ideology and has thereby been easily and quite wrongly confounded with the revolution of the Right. This new emergent sensibility has not found a home; it has had to squat in odd places, to reside in unlikely and at times compromising houses and, even, palaces. It was in a position where it had either to go underground or forge the most unexpected alliances. It was prematurely labelled by the Left as 'reactionary' (that judgment runs through every sentence of Januszczak's obituary) while it was often claimed and assimilated by the triumphant Right. It is time to put the record straight before it is too late, before the contending ideologies have frozen Peter Fuller into the greatest left-wing turncoat and Tory art-critic of our over-ideological times.

It is true that Peter Fuller began his writing life scribbling articles and reviews for *Seven Days* and the *Black Dwarf* and ended it by writing for *The Salisbury Review* and becoming art editor of *The Sunday Telegraph*. It is true – and the strength of his writing stems partly from it – that he disowned Marxism and modernism and became critical of many of the figures we associate with those movements: Raymond Williams, Terry Eagleton, John Berger, Eric Hobsbaum, Victor Burgin and Co. It is false that he never stopped being a socialist or one of the fiercest critics of Thatcherism – indeed he often claimed (to antagonize both sides) that he detected a similar philistinism in both the extreme Right and Left in our divided culture. When Fuller rediscovered what he saw as the essential wisdom of Kenneth Clark's position and pitted it against John Berger he was pleased to register that Kenneth Clark had remained a socialist, though not of the revolutionary, materialist kind. In his growing appreciation of Roger Scruton's aesthetics Peter Fuller was always quick to disown the extreme politics of the author. In a public review of *The Aesthetic Understanding* he wrote:

> It may be there is little hope for the maintenance of conditions
> favourable to those aesthetic and ethical experiences, rooted in

> a common culture, in which Scruton and I believe. But if there
> is I believe it is more likely to be found in a revised socialism
> rather than the resurrected ravagings of a 'free market' capitalist
> economy.[8]

While in a private letter to me he expressed his own position somewhat more savagely: 'I cannot abide his politics either . . . But it is, I
know, so difficult to handle these situations, where one agrees with
one half of a man's belief and despises the other'.[9]

In the last pamphlet he wrote, *Left High and Dry*, Peter Fuller
expressed his own unease with the power of market economies by
quoting the economist E.J. Mishan who while accepting that free markets
should ensure a better material life for the ordinary citizen went on to
point out that a smoothly-working, competitive, market economy is
'evidently consistent also with declining into cultural barbarism'.[10] It
was *that* possibility that obsessed Peter Fuller and fired his writing with
an all but visionary intensity.

And it was here that the problems arose, for the pamphlet *Left High
and Dry* first commissioned by Chatto and Windus for their Counter-
Blast series was rejected on arrival and picked up by Roger Scruton as
the first of his Blast series which has gone on to include Anthony
O'Hear's *Against Education*, Roger Scruton's *Against Equality* and David
Marsland's *Against the Health Service*. It is as if in our culture as soon
as an author speaks of ethical values or visionary experience or a hierarchy of judgments he or she is immediately castigated by the Left
and cunningly incorporated into the Right, even without the author's
permission. (The decision to publish *Left High and Dry* as a Blast
pamphlet was made after his death.) Nor can it be an accident that the
small group set up to organize the 'Annual Peter Fuller Memorial
Lecture' includes Professor Scruton and Professor O'Hear. The support
from one side is not wholly disinterested; nor the silence from the
other. We detect a cultural collusion here of the most complex and
insidious kind and a crude collective delimiting of the adventure of
thought and speculation.

To return to the obituary in *The Guardian*. If we invert most of
the remarks made against Peter Fuller we will be nearer the truth of the
matter. He was *not* a critic with a sense of 'fun', but with a sense of
gravity; he *never* once gave the impression of arguing merely for itself;
and he *did* possess a truly insightful mind that was able to change our
sense of history in relationship to the visual arts. The tragedy is that
the obituarist, along with most of the liberal-left establishment, was
unable to see these things clearly. Or put it another way, and in a more

concrete form, it is a tragedy that Peter Fuller was not made the art-critic of *The Guardian* in 1986 when, with the publication of *The Images of God*, the importance of his subversive work had become ringingly clear. That book amply demonstrates how Peter Fuller had made his own intransigence of spirit into a moral virtue and how, even more effectively, he had turned his anger at our cultural mediocrity into an engaging and developing critique of modernism and Marxism. It showed, too, that he had evolved his own compelling simplicity of style with a purchase on recognizable experience in contrast to those fuliginous abstractions and theoretical mists of many fashionable continental thinkers. He was a very English writer and a very radical one, determined to get to the roots of things. Yet *The Guardian* at his death could only use a condescending irony, point to his personal ambition and rubbish the achievement.

The Evolution of Peter Fuller's Thinking

In one of his last essays which, not uncharacteristically, was rejected by those who had first commissioned it for the catalogue of the Lincoln Cathedral exhibition *The Journey* (summer 1990) Peter Fuller reflected on his own growth, on his own journey:

> I have written often enough before about how I grew up, in an intellectual sense at least, at a time when materialism of one kind or another was the orthodoxy in critical theory; in the late 1960s and throughout the 1970s, 'serious' critics invariably seemed to pride themselves on the thoroughness with which they renounced the idea of a transcendent in art. Words like 'soul', 'grace', 'spirit', and even, unbelievably as it now seems, 'imagination' were taboo.
>
> At that time, such an intellectual ambience was congenial to me – not least because I was reacting against the somewhat claustrophobic religious atmosphere I had inhabited as a child. Inevitably, I was drawn towards the intellectual ambience of Marxism, then a great deal more prevalent in Britain than it is today. Indeed, it was among Marxists that I acquired much of aesthetic education.
>
> John Berger was, in an unofficial sense at least, my teacher in criticism. In his book, *Ways of Seeing*, he associated aesthetic valuing with 'bogus religiosity'. As far as he was then concerned, the 'spiritual' dimension of art was an anachronism, a

sort of penumbra of the function of art as property and a market place commodity. Berger had, of course, nailed his colours to the mast of 'realism'. But almost all the rival theories of art also presented themselves as thorough-going materialisms; indeed, formalists, structuralists and poststructuralists alike all justified their respective viewpoints on the grounds that they were more materialist than those of the next man or, very occasionally, woman.[11]

Peter Fuller's critical work, without a doubt, begins in this milieu of materialist revolution. Yet to understand it one has to go further back to his father's severe Baptist faith, to his sacramental immersion as a young boy and to a sadistic beating he received at the English prep school Epsom College. The reaction against his father drove him into Marxism and the search for father figures, just as the trauma of the beating, added to his anxiety about the father, drove him into therapy. The analysis lasted from November 1972 to March 1977 in which for the first three years he went five times a week on the National Health Service. Many of the intellectual influences of his youth Peter Fuller was to disown, but at least two important writers were to provide him with the pillars from which he was to make his own bridge to escape the mind-set of the ideological Left. The first of these was the Psychoanalyst D.W. Winnicott who formulated the notion of 'transitional objects' in early infant play, a notion which suggested an innate biological urge towards transformative symbolism which could not be entirely explained by the culture. The second was the Marxist thinker Herbert Marcuse. In a book published after his death, *The Aesthetic Dimension*, Marcuse defended the transcendent nature of aesthetic engagement. He wrote:

Art has its own language and illuminates reality only through this other language. Moreover art had its own dimension of affirmation and negation, a dimension which cannot be co-ordinated with the social process of production.[12]

So much for historical materialism and the reduction of the symbols of consciousness to the economic base!

In the first partial step from the Marxist and modernist view (related through a common historicism) Peter Fuller began to develop his own brand of psychoanalytic art criticism. He was, surely, uniquely equipped to do so. *Art and Psychoanalysis* came out in 1980. The intentions are made explicit in the acknowledgments at the front of the book:

Kleinian aesthetics enable me to move towards a fuller account of . . . the aesthetic experience . . . I use the work of Winnicott and Bion to illuminate the nature of the spatial structures, chromatic effects and emotional meanings of certain . . . recent paintings. This book is exploratory and speculative rather than definitive.[13]

The next stage in Peter Fuller's development came with the critical questioning of the final adequacy of the psychoanalytical aesthetic. It seemed to him unable to provide the necessary means for discriminating between one work and the other or for defining the specific aesthetic qualities of artistic work. It was not able to reach the art, though it was able to interpret some of the processes through which it was made and received. What it failed to locate was the distinctive aesthetic element, the aesthetic element in its own right. Peter Fuller presented the problem to himself as follows:

was my own brand of materialistic criticism bringing me any closer to the palpable and yet mysterious presence of art itself? I could describe the 'psychodynamics' which informed a Rothko painting, but my critical vocabulary could not say much about the hair's breadth which divided one of Rothko's successes from his most abject failure. Was that vocabulary then worth having at all? I came to feel that all that I had written failed to give any explanation of the central question of evaluation in our response to art.[14]

In retrospect Peter Fuller judged the approach as not invalid, so much as 'imperfect' and 'partial'. It was, in fact, an understandable trap into which the earlier art critic Herbert Read had also fallen, with devastating cultural consequences in our schools. For four or five decades the tendency to 'psychologize art', deriving from Herbert Read's famous book *Education through Art*, had attenuated the aesthetic field and excluded the historic continuum of painting.

The clue to the problem had already been provided by Herbert Marcuse's insistence on the *autonomy of the aesthetic*. It was to take Peter Fuller next to the work of Clement Greenberg, 'the greatest critic of art that America has yet produced'. Here he found the recognition of the aesthetic dimension strongly confirmed and extended but failed to find the necessary grounds for aesthetic judgment. But in the end, Fuller wrote:

I found myself parting company with Greenberg too; if only because his approach seemed to me to be positivist, by which I mean that he assumed there was nothing more to aesthetic experience than that which is immediately given to the senses. And I realise that if this was true, then the sort of emotion to which a beautiful red scarf gave rise in me would be indistinguishable from that which I felt when, say, contemplating the ceiling of the Sistine Chapel.[15]

It was at this stage in his development as an art critic, at the very end of the 70s, that Peter Fuller moved with greater and greater conviction towards a commitment to the ethical and the aesthetic. In terms of a tradition it involved a recognition of what he saw as a distinctively English tradition of art making, running from the great Gothic cathedrals to the sublime works of Turner through to the essentially symbolic and figurative work of, for example, Graham Sutherland, David Bomberg, John Piper, Paul Nash, and Cecil Collins; Henry Moore, Elizabeth Frink and Glyn Williams. In terms of a critical language it meant a new identification with the art critic John Ruskin (Fuller's *Modern Painters* is named after Ruskin's *Modern Painters* just as his son was to be named after him: Laurence *Ruskin*). It meant also a reclamation of Ruskin's distinction between *theoria* and *aesthesis*. *Theoria* for Ruskin involved working through sensation to the apprehension of value, while *aesthesis* involved the blind submission to the elements of sensation. The creation of significant art demanded the working of an evolving judgment through the aesthetic, whereas corrupt art lost itself in the sensation and was thus able to represent nothing for the active contemplation of the mind. Not *in*, but *through* sensation was Ruskin's command. Yet, of course, in some cases, and particularly in the case of Francis Bacon, the painter was obviously working through theoria, only to provide a judgment that had to be ethically resisted. 'Bacon', declared Peter Fuller, 'is an artist of persuasive power and undeniable ability, but he has used his expressive skills to denigrate and degrade'.[16]

Under the influence of Ruskin Peter Fuller thought he could see more clearly the secondary and often irrelevant nature of much art criticism. He came to loathe the word 'discourse' as much as he loathed the word 'postmodernism'. He claimed that it smothered and obscured pictures and sculptures, as art. Discourse could, he felt, so easily become a defence against aesthetic exposure and spiritual discovery. *The supreme value of art was that it disclosed through aesthetic contemplation spiritual and ethical insights one could not reach in any other way.* The function of the art critic, then, was to bear witness to the best and, from time to time, to clear the conceptual rubbish generated in 'quality' newspapers (as well as polytechnics and universities) and the physical rubbish placed in so many museums, churches and art galleries. If, as Fuller (echoing Marcuse) claimed 'the aesthetic is a category which struggles to affirm human potentialities which the dominant version of society seems to suppress', then the function of the critic was, by writing with a brilliant clarity, to keep the avenues of aesthetic intelligence open.

This task led Peter Fuller more and more towards a commitment to the spiritual and the theological. From the materialist, to the psychoanalytical, to the aesthetic, to the spiritual. The titles of his last books indicate dramatically the nature of the directions: *Images of God* (1985) with the subtitle *The Consolation of Lost Illusions* and *Theoria* (1988) with the subtitle *Art and the Absence of Grace*. Tellingly, one of the last books quoted in one of the last essays was Rudolf Otto's *The Idea of the Holy*. The preoccupation is no longer with the dynamics of 'objective relations', but with the loss of spiritual belief in relationship to art; with, to put it biographically, the paradox of his own emerging religious needs coupled with the conviction of his own atheism. Where his pilgrimage would have taken him, had he lived, it is impossible to surmise. That paradox of religious apprehension and biological common sense was deeply rooted in his own nature. His individual odyssey was not complete. He was struck down in mid-journey. He had not written the great work of synthesis (joining the psychological, the aesthetic, the ethical and the religious into a coherent representation of the nature of art). Had he lived, he would most certainly have done so. Even so, he was able, in a matter of two decades, to alter radically our conception of the visual arts in our own time and it is to that great revisioning of the visual arts that I now wish to turn, before, finally, examining the spiritual element in his last writings.

The Revisioning of the Visual Arts

We live so intensively and, often so narrowly, inside our own cultures it is difficult to register moments of change or to delineate the deep structural shifts that underlie them. Yet one can now say, without social anxiety, what could *not* have been said easily in the late 80s, namely, that modernism is over. Recently the *Independent* drew its readers' attention to a new research centre for modernism in the lines of a baby Bauhaus. It was called, without any self-consciousness, *a revivalist project*. Modernism – the movement committed only to a present and future tense of time – a *revivalist* project? There you have it, modernism, relinquishing finally to the contemporary imperative for museums! The remembering of modernism, though, marks its end. And with its ending, it becomes easy to forget how absolute and tyrannical it was, at least in its last phase.

It is necessary to go back to the early 80s to understand what modernism in the visual arts was like in its last years. It will help to illuminate the position of Peter Fuller and allow us to see his courage and influence. It is true, of course, that much of the old nonsense continues – I remember watching recently on the avant-garde show *Late Night Late* (where else?) the artistic brother of Andy Warhol (who else?) painting the feet of a helpless chicken and then persuading the poor bird to strut across his white canvas – but no one takes such pranks with the brittle seriousness of the 70s and most people now are quick to suspect both the motives and the performance, except in New York where apparently nothing has changed – and where Andy Warhol's brother now no doubt sells his chicken's paintings for countless bucks. As Prince Charles has pointed out, modernism served faithfully 'the spirit of the age' but the fundamental problem was that the age had no spirit. Thus most of the 'art' produced was not symbolic, but merely symptomatic of something that had gone badly wrong.

To show how things stood in the 70s, the decade of late modernism, one has only to glance at Norbert Lynton's guide *The Story of Modern Art*. It does *not* offer a critique but it does provide an accurate account of the state of the visual arts during that period. In a chapter entitled *Beyond Painting and Sculpture* Norbert Lynton lists some of the movements that reached their climax, or, rather, nadir in the 70s. They include 'political performance art' ('Artists make polemical statements not through performance but through relevant data. Statistics, photographs, statements, videotapes, press cuttings, and many other sorts of information are brought together in an exhibition likely to have an archival and journalistic character'[17]); 'eccentric action' ('A man walks along a plotted line in a remote part of the world, back and forth, until he has worn a path over previously untrodden earth. He brings back a photograph and a map'[18]); 'word art' ('Individually or in teams they produce elaborate texts that smack of semantics and philology'), 'concept art' (Remember John Cage's 4'33'? According to Norbert Lynton 'performance is wilfully withheld: instead we become conscious of the unreality of the music we have come for, of its importance to us as a shield against reality'[19]); and, of course, 'autodestruct art' (*Homage to New York* 'shook and burnt itself to pieces: made of rubbish it lived, cavorted briefly as a work of art in one of the great modern art museums of the world and turned itself back into rubbish'[20]). Finally, there was a movement that we might name 'self-destruct' which even the urbane professor has certain qualms about: 'it is more than a little troubling that . . . a kind of Performance Art "includes" the artist mutilating his own body. In one instance, at least, this culminated in the artist's willed death'.[21] It is difficult to remember quite how widespread, how powerful, how mindlessly tyrannical these and many other such vacuous movements were.

The poverty of the art and the poverty of the critical discourse interlock. There is a lack of aesthetic power in the practice and an unwillingness to make any judgments in the theory. Reflecting in this period Peter Fuller wrote:

> I could not evade the fact that there was always a qualitative aspect to the encounter with art. Without evaluation, there can be no appreciation, let alone criticism: every aesthetic response is an act of discrimination which implies a hierarchy of taste. The attempts of the academic critics to evade this – to anaesthetise seemed quite futile.[22]

The question was: how could late modernism and what Peter Fuller called 'the mega-technic tradition' be shifted? Rather like the critic F.R. Leavis, who was so effective partly because he was hated so much, Fuller used a mixture of bitter polemic against carefully selected individuals and a broad critical reconstruction that provided an alternative. More than anything else, the polemic generated conflict and, through conflict, consciousness. 'Without contraries is no progression',[23] wrote William Blake. He had no more ardent disciple than Peter Fuller.

The attacks are vicious and remorseless. Even reading them years later one experiences an uncomfortable sensation down the spine. The CIA have a brutal phrase for killing the enemy; they talk about 'exterminating with extreme prejudice'. That is exactly what Peter Fuller did. Listen, for one moment, to the tone and substance of the denunciation of three pop artists who became famous in the 60s:

> In 1961, a second wave of British pop artists erupted at the 'Young Contemporaries' exhibition. These included Peter Blake, who mingled nostalgia, banality, and commercialism into an image of England as eternal Lymeswold; Allen Jones, who mistook art for pornography; and Peter Phillips, who is now justly forgotten.[24]

The dramatic turning on John Berger, his original father figure, was even more disturbing because it is less just. In 1988 Peter Fuller recast his previous book *Seeing Berger* and with a similar display of savagery renamed it *Seeing through Berger*. The exchanges relating to Berger generated more hate than illumination and left one feeling morally embarrassed. There was, one has to admit, a propensity for self-display in Peter Fuller that has to be questioned. This is the one truth registered in Waldema Januszczak's obituary. This was not the way to advance any cause or insight, yet it was effective in that it dramatized the debate, compelling the reader to become aware of the issues, and to make some kind of decision. It challenged the smug consensus of those self-protecting cosmopolitan centres of British intellectual life. To that degree, it was good. It moved the debate on.

But occasional guerilla warfare and a fairly steady habit of sniping did not make Peter Fuller the significant critic he was. The artists praised in *Images of God* far outnumber those who are castigated. His evaluation of the work of Glyn Williams is exemplary and displays well all the positive values Fuller brought to the act of aesthetic appreciation. Furthermore, the chosen artists are envisaged as working within a common, if broad, tradition. It was this recognition of great talent and his power to place the recognition in an encompassing circle of philosophical and historical understanding that made his criticism so important. Artists, isolated by the standardizing power of modernism, were brought together, their connections made visible, and the continuities snapped by historical thinking boldly re-established. This was the work of reclamation and its positive import can be seen at work in his brilliant long essay on 'The Visual Arts' in *The Cambridge Guide to Arts in Britain* (1988) and in *Theoria* published in the same year. This is how the former study closed:

> None the less, today there is a growing recognition that if the achievements of British art in the nineteenth century were greater than the early modernist commentators allowed, those of the best British artists of the twentieth century – e.g. Moore, Hepworth, Nicholson, Sutherland and Bomberg – are second to none. Certainly, there is nothing in the mid-century French, German, or American traditions which can confidently be placed above them. More generally, it might be argued that now that modernist preoccupations are greeted with somewhat less enthusiasm than they once were, that quality which was once dismissed as British 'pastoralism', or British ruralism, is acquiring a universality, the significance of which extends far

beyond these shores. For if our native tradition involves something less than unqualified enthusiasm for ever-increasing production, it also affirms the necessity of developing a new,
imaginative response to the natural world, what Bomberg de-
signated as a quest for 'spirit in the mass'. Indeed, the best British
art appears to possess the capacity to speak more eloquently to
the ecological and environmental concerns of a 'post-modern',
'post-industrial' age than ever it could be to the mechanical
utopianism of 'progressive' modernity. As ethical philosophers,
naturalists, and poets alike, speak of the necessity of some kind
of renewed imaginative affiliation with the natural world, if we
are to survive as a species, there is likely to be a more positive
assessment of the highest achievements, past and present, of
the British tradition. And so, despite the cultural vandalism of
those who presently control the institutions of contemporary
art, some of us have begun to dare to hope that all might not
be lost.[25]

Thus the great tradition in English painting is celebrated and seen
to run through the century of modernism; individual painters and
sculptors are placed in the long continuum; a new mapping of movements is offered and those expressive and largely figurative movements are given a yet further importance in the light of our ecological
crisis and our current imaginative needs. It is what I have named elsewhere a *conservationist aesthetic*,[26] an aesthetic that places works of art in
a vital continuum, in an amazingly rich and subtle symbolic network
of energy, of association, of reference, of allusion, of visible and invisible
connection. Such a notion is, of course, the very opposite of high
modernism with its reference only to the contemporary, the outra-
geous, or the simply functional and mechanistic. It is a testimony to
Peter Fuller's art criticism that the reorganization of the Tate Gallery,
beginning at the end of the 80s, reflects much of this interpretation of
art in the twentieth century. The daring to hope was, also, a daring to
embrace spiritual values.

Art and the Spiritual

Peter Fuller was after what Nietzsche called 'a common culture' that
would 'answer to real necessities'. This brought him, eventually, to
confront the need for the spiritual and transcendental. This was no easy
matter for it reactivated traumas relating back to childhood experience

and to the severe Baptist theology of his father. It could be said that his religious impulses were buggered up from the outset by evangelical religion. His thinking was, perhaps, never finally free from the internalized and prohibiting shadow of the Father. He had freed himself from the formal content of Christian belief, of course; but he could not so easily free himself from its web of assumptions or from the compelling power of its aesthetic expression in Gothic art. This emotional servitude expresses itself in his late writing in the form of nostalgia, as if all that we were entitled to spiritually in the twentieth century was a kind of post-Christian whimper, a powerless melancholy attendant upon the long withdrawing roar of faith.

Influenced by George Steiner's *Real Presences*, these are some of the last words Peter Fuller wrote:

> For myself, I remain an incorrigible atheist; that is my proclamation of faith. Yet there is something about the experience of art, itself, which compels me to re-introduce the category of the 'spiritual'. More than that, I believe that, given the ever-present absence of God, art, and the gamut of aesthetic experience, provides the sole remaining glimmer of transcendence. The best we can hope for is that aesthetic surrogate for salvation: redemption through form.
>
> 'What I affirm', writes Steiner, 'is the intuition that where God's presence is no longer a tenable supposition and where His absence is no longer a felt, indeed, overwhelming weight, certain dimensions of thought and creativity are no longer attainable.' Quite so. And under these circumstances, all that we can fall back on are, perhaps, the consolations of lost illusions.[27]

This conception of the religious domain is less than convincing. At a psychological level it keeps the son inside the shadow cast by the Father; at an emotional level, it feeds a limiting and even sentimental nostalgia; while at a metaphysical level, it just will not do. 'All we can fall back on are, perhaps, the consolations of lost illusion'. But why? And anyway how can consolation and lost illusion nurture for long the imaginative creation of art? It is the most quirky and negative definition of religious aspiration ever formulated.

At the root of the formulation one can sense that old psychoanalytical deposit: all religious experience is a substitute for the absent 'good breast' of the Mother with the oceanic illusions it invited and gratified. So in the one formulation we have tacit commitment to *one* historic world-religion and to its psychological interpretation in infant experience. Both commitments strike me as superfluous to the under-standing of the religious impulse. The first ties it, far too specifically, to one dogmatic faith; the other merely psychologizes the phenomenon: *The consolations of lost illusions!* After the adroit and impassioned subversion of modernism, it is a curious emotional and intellectual cul-de-sac to find ourselves in.

I will conclude, in the iconoclastic spirit of Peter Fuller by, mak-ing a different move. The move involves, in the first place, no more than a different definition of the religious impulse and, therefore, a different orientation. The religious impulse might be better envisaged as a kind of universal instinct for developing the psyche within an encompassing sense of a whole universe. As such it has *no* content. It is not Buddhist, not Muslim, not Christian, not Marxist. In our own times it is that inchoate impulse that seeks connections with the great historic continuum as well as with the vast order or chaos of nature.[28] It seeks to contemplate and to create those life-giving symbols, through aesthetic creation, which will return in sharper form the lineaments of our own suppressed longings. It has to work now within cultures, now across cultures, and, sometimes, dangerously outside any known forms, for the religious impulse is an active process of becoming, a prospective movement of the imagination working through the arts, prefiguring an integration in advance of human behaviour.

This is what Peter Fuller's argument against modernism might lead us to, not a desperate nostalgia, but more an inner aspiration without doctrinal content, universal, and free from the shadow cast by the Father. It is a conception that bypasses the village of nostalgia, keeps the human spirit in quest and on the open road, and that confers upon artists one of the greatest functions, the illumination of being through the power of symbolic expression. Art, with its power of *theoria*, is uniquely equipped to render the religious impulse and to develop its nature as can be seen in the work of the Welsh sculptor, John Merion Morris (see Plate 10) and the English painter Keith Grant (see Plate 11). The great poet Rainer Maria Rilke claimed that the arts had to *instate* what was seen and touched within the widest orbit, that the work required the conversion of the visible and tangible into the invisible vibrations and agitations of our own nature. At the moment this instating can be heard most clearly in the life of contemporary music: in the religious compositions of John Tavener, Jonathan Harvey and Henryk Gorecki. In this matter, of course, Mozart remains not only our greatest religious composer but also our finest theologian.

'Whereof one cannot speak, thereof one must be silent.'[29] That is true of any conceptual elaboration of the spiritual. It is here in the silence after propositions that the arts, however, *can* speak, in a variety of tongues, for and against their civilization, both within and beyond, symbolizing that new and ancient ground, which all but simultaneously invites and defies us. As the great artist Edvard Munch said of his own painting: 'People will understand the sacredness and greatness of it all, and will take off their hats as though they were in church'.[30] This points the way beyond the postmodernist cult of appearances and insubstantial surfaces, the present world of perpetual production unredeemed by inner needs and the claims of the religious instinct. And, this analysis in turn, points us, once again, back to the critical achievement of Peter Fuller.

Notes

1 EDWARD LUCIE SMITH (1990) 'Obituary: Peter Fuller', *The Independent*, 11 May.

2 *Daily Telegraph* (1990) 'Obituary: Peter Fuller', 30 April.

3 SMITH (1990).

4 PAUL BARKER (1990) 'Obituary: Peter Fuller', *The Independent*, 1 May.

5 SMITH (1990).

6 BARKER (1990).

7 WALDEMA JANUSZCZAK (1990) 'Obituary: Peter Fuller', *The Guardian*, 30 April.

8 PETER FULLER (1984) 'Review: The Aesthetic Understanding', *New Society*, 19 January, p. 95.

9 PETER FULLER (1986) Letter to the author dated 17 July.

10 PETER FULLER (1990) *Left High and Dry*, London, The Claridge Press, p. 43.

11 PETER FULLER (1990) 'Peter Fuller's Journey', *Modern Painters*, **3** (3), autumn, p. 45.

12 HERBERT MARCUSE (1979) *The Aesthetic Dimension*, London, Macmillan, p. 22.

13 PETER FULLER (1980) 'Introduction', in *Art and Psychoanalysis*, London, Writers and Readers.

14 PETER FULLER (1990) 'Peter Fuller's Journey'.

15 *Ibid.*

16 PETER FULLER (1988) 'The Visual Arts', in BORIS FORD (ed.) *The Cambridge Guide to the Arts in Britain Volume 7: Since the Second World War*, Cambridge, Cambridge University Press, p. 130. See also Peter Fuller (1985) *Images of God: the Consolations of Lost Illusions*, Chatto and Windus. See particularly the essay 'Raw Bacon', pp. 63–70.

17 NORBERT LYNTON (1980) *The Story of Modern Art*, Oxford, Phaidon, pp. 320–8. The whole chapter 'Beyond Painting and Sculpture' merits close

critical attention for all the examples given demonstrate, at another level, the excesses of late modernism.

18 *Ibid.*
19 *Ibid.*
20 *Ibid.*
21 *Ibid.*
22 PETER FULLER (1990) 'Peter Fuller's Journey'.
23 This is, of course, one of Blake's 'Proverbs of Hell' in *The Marriage of Heaven and Hell* first etched about 1793.
24 PETER FULLER (1988) p. 111.
25 PETER FULLER (1988) p. 145.
26 See PETER ABBS (1989) 'Towards a Conservationist Aesthetic in Education', in *A is for Aesthetic: Essays on Creative and Aesthetic Education*, London, Falmer Press, 1988. In that essay I concluded; 'Significantly, the word "ecology" derives form the Greek word for *house*. The arts can often intensify and enhance that sense of belonging, of feeling that, for all the suffering and anguish, this planet is our home. More than any other symbols, the symbols of art have the power to release and root that life-enhancing sense that: *in this vast structure I too belong and have my being.*'
27 PETER FULLER (1990) 'Peter Fuller's Journey', p. 49.
28 As I write this I realize that Peter Fuller in parts of his book (1988) *Theoria*, London, Chatto and Windus *was* calling for a natural theology, a theology without God, and linking it to the ecological movement. He wrote there, for example: 'Ruskin's dream of a natural theology without God is becoming a reality'. This is the most positive side of his work, but I still think much of his argument was couched in a kind of nostalgic sense of loss; and that the affirmations were *not* often free of the shadow cast by the Father and by his own former Christian doctrinal belief.
29 Ludwig Wittgenstein's famous aphorism which concludes *Tractatus Logico-Philosophicus* (first German edition published in *Annalen der Naturphilosophie*, 1921). One of the key aims of *The Educational Imperative* is to suggest that the arts *can* formulate meanings that defy the logic and order of propositions; that the arts can continue, as the stories do in Plato's dialogues, when the philosophy, at a propositional level, has had to stop, or, to put it another way, the arts can express the meaning of philosophical silence. After philosophy, aesthetic contemplation.
30 Quoted in VERNER TIMM (1969) *The Graphic Arts of Edvard Munch*, London, Vista, p. 48.

Chapter 12

David Holbrook, the Tradition of Poetic Humanism and the Teaching of the Arts

It is a terrific problem that faces the poet today – a world that is so in transition from a decayed culture towards a reorganization of human values that there are few common terms and general denominators of speech that are solid enough or that ring with any vibration or spiritual conviction.

Hart Crane

Knowledge taken in excess, without hunger, even contrary to desire, has no more the effect of transforming the external life, and remains hidden in a chaotic inner world that the modern man has a curious pride in calling his personality.

Nietzsche

The Tradition of Poetic Humanism

David Holbrook's various and once influential writings on education from *English for Maturity* (1964) to *English for Meaning* (1979) belong to an English tradition of educational thinking. The more time passes, the easier it is to see this tradition clearly; it has a moral vision of education and a vision of the English teacher as a cultural transmitter, an agent of the articulate life of consciousness in an age in which civilization itself is in question. This tradition can be seen to run from Blake and Coleridge to Matthew Arnold, from Matthew Arnold to George Sampson, from Sampson to F.R. Leavis and Denys Thompson and from Leavis and Thompson to David Holbrook, Raymond Williams and Richard Hoggart to a small group of writers (both educationists and critics) still working and extending, in the most hostile circumstances, the tradition today. It has never been called the tradition of English poetic humanism but, all in all, I think that would be a fitting title.

It is certainly true that the tradition has much in common with classical humanism (Matthew Arnold's 'disinterested play of consciousness' sounds very classical) yet it has qualities that both distinguish it and make it distinctive, for example, its emphasis on the exploratory rather than the mimetic nature of literature, its commitment to intuition and imagination with its concomitant scepticism, if not hostility, to the power of reason and abstract thinking. Along with these unclassical virtues there is a further unclassical commitment, namely to the English language, as shaped by its speakers and, particularly, by the authorized version of the Bible, Shakespeare and the truly significant writers through the centuries, who have made English a subtle language of resonance and sustaining echo. As Leavis put it: English is 'a product of an immemorial *sui generis* collaboration on the part of its speakers and writers. It is alive with promptings and potentialities, and the great creative writer shows his genius in the way he responds'.[1]

The titles of books are nearly always indicative of their central preoccupations. Thus if we glance at some of the titles of David Holbrook's educational work – *The Exploring Word, The Secret Places, English for Meaning, English for Maturity* – we can immediately sense something of the poetic humanism I am trying to define. In the classroom the English teacher, according to this vision, is there to release in his or her pupils the exploring word, which has power to enter the secret places of their lives to disclose their latent meaning and, in so doing, to induce a greater maturity of understanding, judgment or, another key word in much of the tradition of poetic humanism, discrimination. My use of the word poetic in this context is, of course, broad. Poetic first of all is best understood negatively as the antithesis to all that is prosaic, literal, mechanical, factual, all that remains untouched and unredeemed by the transformative powers of individual sensibility and transpersonal imagination. But, of course, it also has a positive charge of meaning and this involves a profound recognition of, to quote Wordsworth, 'a dim and undetermined sense of unknown modes of being'[2] together with the apprehension that we are implicated in a world which requires our recognition, our contemplation, our symbolic acts to complete it.

The Wordsworthian sense of dim apprehensions – of other forms of knowing, relating and being – is defended throughout David Holbrook's educational writing. What is involved here is a recognition of preconceptual, almost bodily, processes of rhythmic half articulation and absorbed reverie, which are often the foundations of creative work in the arts and which need to be understood and respected by the teacher. In *English for the Rejected*, Holbrook defended what he called 'the poetic function' and defined it as 'the capacity to explore and perceive by the exercise of the whole mind and all kinds of apprehensions, not only intellectual'.[3] This entails a more refined epistemology than we have at the grim moment in British schools and one that I will return to later. The second positive connotation of poetic (closely related to this notion of various apprehensions of meaning and value) is best illustrated – for it cannot be finally argued or fully conceptualized – by a quotation from Leavis's scathing polemic against C.P. Snow. Referring to that lack of depth that marks civilizations when creative questioning has atrophied, Leavis went on to defend what he saw as the crucial value of literature:

> In coming to terms with great literature we discover what at bottom we really believe. What for – what ultimately for? What do men live by – the questions work and tell at what I can only call a religious depth of thought and feeling. Perhaps, with my eye on the adjective, I may just recall for you Tom Brangwen, in *The Rainbow*, watching by the fold in lambing-time under the night-sky: 'He knew he did not belong to himself'.[4]

Religious here clearly does not denote any doctrinal belief but rather the apprehension of *being engaged beyond oneself*, being bound into something larger than the ego. The connection established, with a Tolstoyan intensity, is the connection between art and living, between aesthetics (not a word used in the tradition I am defining) and ethics, between book and belief – a connection which during the last decade has become deeply unfashionable. One other characteristic of the tradition of poetic humanism must be mentioned. It is *oppositional* in nature. It is the anxious and, at times, febrile voice of critical dissent.

In this tradition both teacher and artist have little choice but to act as the alert critics of their own society, of a society driven predominantly by material and mechanical imperatives: produce – consume; consume – produce. In *English for the English*, a seminal book in the tradition of poetic humanism, a book that is consciously repeated and rephrased throughout Holbrook's early volumes, George Sampson is emphatic about the need to prepare pupils not for their jobs but *against* their jobs, not for earning a living but for living itself.[5] Once again, these have become deeply unfashionable commitments in our own conformist and consumer age. This resistance to the dominant society and its standard iconography (to advertising, to art as entertainment packaged in terms of extrinsic marketing rather than intrinsic meanings) permeates poetic humanism. It gave birth to the first critical classroom reader on mass culture. (*Culture and Environment* by F.R. Leavis and Denys Thompson was published in 1933). The general nature of the cultural challenge and the implications for the teacher of English are brought out in the following characteristic passage from *English for Maturity*:

> What is missing from the music of our young people, from their entertainment, and from their social life together is the germ of positive vitality. They have few cultural sources of succour to develop positive attitudes to life, and develop human sympathy. The home is afflicted by the influence of the mass-media, by the pressure of advertising and by the new illiteracy. As Richard Hoggart points out, such traditions as standing by one another, or of passing on traditional wisdom, have declined in working people's lives under these influences. Thus it remains to the school – and mainly the secondary modern school – to supply new positives.[6]

Ironically, as the whole of the media in Britain has become more and more subject to mindless market forces and the ideology of profits, in the last decade this voice of critical opposition inside the life of schools and universities has become more and more a hesitant whisper, a half suppressed stammer expressing an almost taboo notion of the student as active critic and creative agent, rather than satisfied client and well adapted consumer.

The poetic tradition of humanism is a tradition of dissident thinking, of moral and prophetic formulation, against established values and the general drift of collective life in our times. It is a tradition which, like any other, has its own canonical texts: its key manifesto was Matthew Arnold's *Culture and Anarchy*, its selected work of polemical fiction was Charles Dickens's *Hard Times* and its favoured conversion narrative was that given in Chapter 5 of John Stuart Mill's *Autobiography* where, under the title of 'A Crisis in My Mental History One Stage Onward', the author described his discovery of Wordsworth's poetry and outlined its transformative effects upon his own excessively regimented and over-analytical consciousness.

These quickly etched and somewhat unsubtle descriptions are intended merely to indicate some of the basic features of the tradition to which David Holbrook's work substantially belongs. A number of sharp and telling criticisms can be brought against it. It often held – particularly in its Leavisite version – an all but whimsical view of a lost organic society and of a dignified oral culture that was envisaged as existing before the social alienation engendered by the Industrial Revolution. It was, for the most part, peculiarly insular in reference and disposition, failing to encounter the whole mental and imaginative life of Europe, especially with regard to literature before Chaucer (virtually nothing on Homer, Virgil, Dante, Petrarch) and any literature after D.H. Lawrence. It had a number of blind spots (for example, it missed the distinctive genius of Virginia Woolf) and it was poor at seeing the other arts disciplines as the essential, interacting and equal partners of literature – thus critical and celebratory work on drama, dance, music, art and architecture is minimal. Something of the *verbal* bias of the tradition comes out well in Matthew Arnold's much quoted phrase 'the best that has been thought and known', where the emphasis falls on the intellectual and cognitive and not on what has been (like architecture) constructed or apprehended through the non-verbal, non-conceptual symbolism of dance, mime, music, paint and sculpture. Even within literature the range was often narrow and puritanical in tone. The tradition of poetic humanism was also, at least in the case of Leavis, absurdly negative about the value of philosophy and the place of creative work within the programme of English studies. In spite of all the rhetoric about creative engagement, Leavis seemed to rely all but exclusively on the well worn academic essay for the evaluation of his students.

In a number of important respects the work of David Holbrook served to correct some of these severe limitations (as did the work of Raymond Williams and Richard Hoggart, especially with regard to the political and historical). As a serious poet and an amateur painter, Holbrook knew intuitively from his own practice the value of imaginative work and the way in which it immediately connects the maker with a tradition of achieved work and tested technique. He was, thus, with an inner authority able to insist on the importance of seeing pupils and students as artists and explorers in their own right. He was able to broaden the programme of activity so that it included creative activity – poetry, drawing, art, drama – and a broader recognition of the multiform ways in which feeling and impulse can find expressive configuration. In this, as we shall see, he was aided by the work of psychoanalysis and philosophical anthropology. And here, again, we can detect in Holbrook's writing a dramatic expansion of the Arnold–Leavis tradition, a courageous moving out into new ground, an opening up to other humanist traditions of enquiry and speculation.

After *English for Maturity* Holbrook sought for a more comprehensive understanding of the origins of symbolism and the creative act that makes it possible. In *Human Hope and the Death Instinct* (1971) (another key title neatly encapsulating the dialectical preoccupations of nearly all his discursive work on symbol and culture) Holbrook evaluated the post-Freudian psychoanalytical theories of Melanie Klein, W.R.D. Fairbairn, Harry Guntrip, D.W. Winnicot (whose influence on Holbrook as with Peter Fuller was to be as great, if not greater, than that of Leavis) and many others.

He argues in that volume that their work demonstrated that Freud's underlying assumption that humans were animals creating culture symptomatically out of sublimation was misconceived. What was more true, and amply demonstrated by the work of the post-Freudians, was that humans have *a primary need to create culture and to seek relationship and meaning in a community of being, first established in the profound matrix of the mother–child relationship.* Here, then, in object-relations psychoanalysis there seemed to exist another tradition that offered a biological and psychological justification of many of the values and practices of the poetic humanist tradition. The discoveries of the psychoanalysts, particularly the formulations of D.W. Winnicot, grounded it and at the same time gave it a broader base. It took the debates of embattled literary coteries out of privileged enclaves and placed them in the daily dynamics of ordinary life and the general human struggle to secure a cultural shape for an inherently precarious existence. In *English for the Rejected* Holbrook talked about the: 'nourishing of imaginative power, and psychic vitality by sympathy and creative work in all children, not excepting those who are least endowed with intellectual capacities'.[7]

The conceptions of psychoanalysis offered – or so it must have seemed to Holbrook – a number of principles on which the Arnoldian tradition could more firmly stand and more easily move out into the democratic life of culture, unencumbered by academic exclusiveness or any kind of literary preciousness. Later he was to join to his evolving argument various notions taken from phenomenology, existentialism and philosophical anthropology. It has to be said, at once and unambiguously, that in creating this broader orientation within the tradition of poetic humanism, David Holbrook was often less than convincing. Too often the style of writing deteriorates and forfeits the lucidity of the earlier work. Many sentences become clotted with jargon or, if not with jargon, with regimental lists of approved names. Too much of the argument is not made through logic or example but simply through quotation: 'as Winnicot says'; 'as Marjorie Grene says'; 'as Buytendijk says'. Too often the interpretation of symbols and expressive images, inherently polymorphic, are too simple or too reductive. Indeed, it would seem a characteristic difficulty of a psychoanalytical approach to art that it tends to narrow the radically plural life of metaphor in the interests of its own more limited and more focused view, whereas metaphor in art frequently means more than what can ever be said discursively.

One can only surmise that a sense of messianic urgency overruled the prudent interior voices of the author which call for revision, for selection, for that individual shaping of language which makes an argument (whatever its content) at first reading compelling to the receptive mind. The result was a torrent of work – much of it diffuse and repetitive – that alienated many of those who, if the work had been more accomplished, would have been the first to welcome and support it. Yet it is important to recognize that within the work there *are* fine moments of analysis (the analysis of Edward Thomas's *Old Man*[8] and *Tall Nettles* in terms of philosophical anthropology in *English for Meaning* is, for example, both moving and entirely convincing), and that further-more the ambition to embrace these broad philosophical and psycho-logical movements *was*, potentially, productive and illuminating. Holbrook's attempt was, perhaps, not altogether dissimilar from that of Coleridge to relate the poetic insights of English Romanticism to the architectonic philosophy of Kant at the beginning of the nineteenth century. It can also be no accident that one of the best art critics of the last two decades, Peter Fuller, sought to connect aesthetic experience to psychoanalysis using, once again, the seminal work of D.W. Winnicot. It must surely be the case that any criticism that becomes highly specialized, that no longer refers art to the life of relationship, reflection and encounter is not only bound towards intellectual scler-osis but, more importantly, misses what art is most essentially about: the intimate elaboration of consciousness and understanding. To ex-plore the dynamics that inform the creative act can only remind us, again and again, of this urgent existential element. In this respect, in spite of its blemishes and bludgeonings, Holbrook's work of ground-ing poetic humanism by connecting it with other forms of enquiry has been more than challenging. It has forged an essential key for further work across the arts and, even more broadly, across the philosophy of education.

On the Primacy of Culture

David Holbrook has insisted that all those committed to the creative teaching of English and the arts should attend to the work of Marjorie Grene who claimed that: 'the whole structure of the embryo, the whole rhythm of growth, is directed, from first to last, to the emergence of a culture-dwelling animal'.[9] Certainly it would seem that a propensity to symbolize, a propensity to create image, narrative and expressive configuration, is innate. Our involuntary acts of dreaming (for we do not learn to dream) demonstrate as much; and in the dream one can identify many of the elements later given expression in the collective art forms of humankind: narrative, character and image, for example. It is as if at birth we already possess a number of genres for shaping and telling 'reality'. Anthony Stevens, in his study of archetypes, has spoken of the infant's ability to find its mother's face as depending 'on the capacity to rediscover in reality the object which corresponds to what is present in the imagination'.[10] Such thinking, while deeply alien to the fashionable theories propounded by deconstructionists and postmodernists, parallels that of both a number of philosophical biologists – one thinks not only of Marjorie Grene but also of Mary Midgley[11] – and many ethologists (particularly Konrad Lorenz[12]) who sought to provide a biological origin for the a priori categories of Kantian philosophy. Culture, from this perspective, is a wholly natural phenomenon and the analogical imagination a biological gift that can only be released and developed, in all its potential variety, within a particular society, within a specific culture and span of historical time.

As David Holbrook has persuasively argued this conception of life has many implications for education and the teaching of the arts. To begin with: if we are *born* cultural beings we do not have to be *made* cultural members of society; nor are we ever mere vessels or *tabulae rasae*, blank sheets for professionals to write on. It cannot be the unambiguous function of education to socialize the child or to transfer 'communication skills' (as the current jargon would have it), simply because the child already possesses innate social aptitudes as he or she also possesses the ability to create images, narratives and the rhythmic patterns of speech. These are not new insights – for as Leavis pointed out, one finds in William Blake an affirmation of 'the essential creativeness of life' running from 'a continuity from the creativeness of perception to the creativeness of the artist'[13] – but they remain axiomatic and now gain a further weight by the recent evidence, tabulation and explication of biologists and philosophers.

Furthermore, during the current takeover of education in England by a handful of politicians and a leaden medley of managers and bureaucrats, they have a further and somewhat daunting urgency. If this view of the child as cultural agent born with the schemas and aptitudes necessary for cultural creation is true, then the concepts of education as 'delivery' and 'socialization' are seriously mistaken and can only dangerously repress the deep inner sources of creativity. That is the negative side; that is the indictment of the educational status quo in England. The positive side is an affirmation of teaching as the social art that culturally connects, releases, amplifies, develops. Good teaching becomes the task of relating; of bringing together the natural form-seeking energies of the individual pupil *and* the inherited cultural forms of creation and enquiry; real teaching seeks an encounter between the two and their constant refinement and expansion. Educational experience thus lies neither exclusively with the individual (it is not 'self-expression') nor with the culture (it is not indoctrination) but in that vast, conscious and unconscious, web of categories, metaphors, narratives, arguments, icons, interpretations that draw them indivisibly together creating ever new possibilities of thinking, imagining, speculating, apprehending and judging. This view might be usefully called, in contrast to the progressive and the traditional view, the symbolist conception of education and it lies at the heart of the new arts paradigm. But the symbolist view of education not only recognizes education as encounter, it also seeks to broaden our understanding of the nature and range of symbolic activity. David Holbrook has urged us to consider the arguments of Ernst Cassirer and Susanne Langer for it is their work particularly that has created the necessary terms for this broader recognition.

Art as a Form of Cognition

It was one of the major contributions of philosophical anthropology to demonstrate analytically that there are many forms of coherent understanding and that conceptual thinking is but one way of coming to knowledge or, rather, one *kind* of (provisional) knowing. Yet the idea that knowledge is essentially a matter of concepts has held such sway in western civilization that other forms of intellection, through, for example, analogy, through dance, through the sequencing of sound and through narrative have become widely misconstrued. As we have seen, for the most part, the arts in education have been conceived during the last hundred years as activities that are therapeutic and cathartic, to do with private release and personal discharge of emotion, as now they are becoming the means of leisure, entertainment and relaxation (linked to tourism), rather than acts of attention concerned with the great task of understanding human existence. Yet, as Holbrook claimed twenty-five years ago: 'Metaphor is not, as we were taught at school, a figure of speech. In language it is the means by which we extend our awareness of experience into new realms'.[14] And the same is true, one must quickly add, of the metaphor created by the non-verbal arts.

Susanne Langer's work has been particularly eloquent in establishing the pluralistic nature of knowledge. In all symbolism, she argued, there is an act of intellection, an import of meaning. 'Wherever a symbol operates there is meaning' she claimed and went on to declare that she was after 'a theory of mind whose key note is the symbolic function . . . whose problem is the morphology of significance'.[15] The symbolism of the artist is not merely about the expression of an emotion but about *its conception*. In *Feeling and Form*, her seminal book on the arts, Langer put her position as follows:

> How can we capture, hold and handle feelings so that their content may be made conceivable and presented to our consciousness in universal form, without being understood in the strict sense, i.e. by means of concepts. The answer is: we can do it by creating objects wherein the feelings we seek to hold are so definitely embodied that any subject confronted with those objects and emphatically disposed towards them cannot but experience a non-sensuous apperception of the feelings in question. Such objects are called works of art and by art we designate the activity that produces them.[16]

One might want to take issue with a number of specific words in this passage – why, for example, allow the 'strict sense' of understanding to be determined by 'concepts' and why not a *sensuous* 'apperception' of feeling? – but even so the central hypothesis is loud and clear. Art embodies the invisible logic of the life of feeling and sentience and, in so doing, brings it to conception and consciousness. Once this is clearly recognized the common educational distinctions between cognition and affect, between meaning and expression, between objective and subjective, between public and private break down and give way to what would seem a more valid differentiation between kinds of knowledge, between kinds of intelligence, between kinds of symbolic forms, between kinds of public language.

It is on this understanding that it is now possible to build a more coherent philosophy of arts education, and some of the elements of its good practice can still be derived from the best of David Holbrook's writing on education. In *English for Maturity*, in defending his approach to creative work in the classroom, Holbrook offered the following three principles:

First, I wanted to encourage the expression of feelings, in an atmosphere in which such expression was regarded as seriously as the expression of facts. I wanted to make the child explore his own feelings, whether he realised he was doing so or not, and to have between him and me – in a public world, outside ourselves – a statement of them . . .

Secondly, and complementary to the first point, I felt the only way to achieve this expression was by using as stimulants poems, passages, and themes which the child already recognised as means to the depersonalising of his individual emotion – a way to that 'third ground' which is a meeting-place between the 'mind' of a community and his own.

Thirdly, I was concerned to maintain attention on the poem or tale as poem or tale: it was assumed between us that the content, the emotions and thought expressed, were to be respected. And if they are to be respected, they must not be taken outside the pattern whereby the child has realised them. This is the reason for the need for emotional sparseness in the poetry lesson – and in the teaching of imaginative composition: to be 'emotional' is to betray the child into having to consider explicitly something he could only grasp implicitly.[17]

Thirty years later, they remain good principles and serve to extend Langer's philosophy of art into a classroom practice. What is more, with a few changes, they could be adapted to fit the teaching of the other great art forms. The notion of entering 'the third ground', that place where the creative energies of the individual and the creative energies of the culture meet, is quite crucial. It is precisely this that characterizes the new model of arts education.

Some of the agitated disputes that Holbrook's prolific and uneven writing stirred up – the question as to whether the teacher should or could act as therapist, the question as to whether original work by children should be corrected – did much to eclipse the essential sanity and balance of the approach. It is pertinent to note *now* that Holbrook explicitly attacked the notion of 'self-expression' and Herbert Read's notion of 'pure expression'.

Creation cannot, I think, be as spontaneous as Sir Herbert suggests: the creation can only be made through technical conventions which because they are involved in a tradition 'outside' the individual, provide a kind of control. This 'control' is not 'suppression'; it may be a means to creation that seems 'spontaneous'.[18]

Creative fullness of being, he went on to claim, could only be achieved by the obtaining of a tradition. It is precisely this insistence on the paradox of creativity that stands in need of reclamation. No doubt it was this commitment to the collaborative nature of creative symbolism that first drew David Holbrook to the writing of D.W. Winnicot. For it was Winnicot who, examining the origins of culture in the interaction between the child and the mother, wrote:

> In any cultural field it is not possible to be original except on a basis of tradition . . . the interplay with originality and the acceptance of tradition as a basis for inventiveness seem to me to be just one more example, and a very exciting one, of the interplay between separateness and union.[19]

We find our own voices in and through the voices of others; we find ourselves in and through the reflections of other selves; we become creative individuals the more we become members of a cultural community infinitely larger than the self. In educational activity in the arts we have to recognize the self with all its potentiality (its innate creativity) and the broad inherited culture (that evolving procession of styles, techniques, living works, exemplars). The task is to bring the two into vivid and perpetual conjunction.

It would seem virtually uncontentious to say that the politicians who are now actively shaping the curriculum of British schools are blind to both elements. They neither cherish the creative individual, nor the inherited culture. That is the scandal of the age and it is our predicament. At such a time to lose contact with the work of David Holbrook and the various intellectual schools it brings together, to lose touch with the long tradition of poetic humanism, would be tantamount to losing contact with education itself. We need a return to the Socratic principle, to the notion of innate creativity and the value of authentic culture. Nothing less will do.

Notes

1   F.R. LEAVIS (1975) *The Living Principle*, London, Chatto and Windus.
2   WILLIAM WORDSWORTH (1850) *The Prelude*, Book 1, 1850 Version, ll. 392–3.
3   DAVID HOLBROOK (1964) *English for the Rejected*, Cambridge, Cambridge University Press, p. 10.
4   F.R. LEAVIS (1962) *Two Cultures? The Significance of C.P. Snow*, London, Chatto and Windus, p. 23.

5 GEORGE SAMPSON (1975) *English for the English*, Cambridge, Cambridge University Press.

6 DAVID HOLBROOK (1967) *English for Maturity*, Cambridge, Cambridge University Press, p. 17.

7 DAVID HOLBROOK (1964) p. 10.

8 See Chapters 4 and 7 of HOLBROOK (1979) *English for Meaning*, London, NFER Publishing Company.

9 MARJORIE GRENE (1968) *Approaches to a Philosophical Biology*, New York, Basic Books.

10 ANTHONY STEVENS (1982) *Archetype: A Natural History of the Self*, London, Routledge and Kegan Paul, p. 57.

11 See, for example, MARY MIDGLEY (1979) *Beast and Man: The Roots of Human Nature*, Brighton, Harvester Press.

12 See, for example, KONRAD LORENZ (1977) *Behind the Mirror: A Search for a Natural History of Human Knowledge*, London, Methuen.

13 F.R. LEAVIS quoted in PETER ABBS (1974) *Autobiography in Education*, London, Heinemann Educational Books, p. 5.

14 DAVID HOLBROOK (1967) p. 69.

15 SUSANNE LANGER (1960) *Philosophy in a New Key*, Cambridge, MA, Harvard University Press. See particularly Chapter 2 'Symbolic Transformation'.

16 SUSANNE LANGER (1953) *Feeling and Form*, London, Routledge and Kegan Paul. See Chapter 3.

17 DAVID HOLBROOK (1967) pp. 114–5.

18 pp. 113–4.

19 D.W. WINNICOT quoted in HOLBROOK (1964) p. 104.

Coda

In spite of all the promises, manifestos, utopian and progressive rhetoric, it has not been a benign century. On the contrary, some of the worst excesses have been committed systematically against millions of the human race and, morally and spiritually, we seem more lost than ever. Rationalism has led, too often, to a frightening reductionism and positivism to a poverty of spirit where all the problems have been relegated to the ragged edges of consciousness, while progressivism in education often unwittingly created a powerless narcissism of the self.

As for the consumer society, it has trivialized on an unprecedented scale. It has tarnished whatever it has touched; it has manipulated and degraded all our most distinctively human longings: erotic, communal, ecological, spiritual. Advertising, entertainment and hype are the dominant counterfeit arts of our time and they have, without doubt, seriously corrupted the poetic and prophetic languages we need to make some substance of our personal and collective lives.

It is, of course, unreasonable, even fraudulent, to ask Socratic and arts educators to resolve the inner vacuity and outer violence of our late consumer societies. We have expected education to do too much for too long. What education can do, with good practice and compelling philosophy, is to secure a disinterested and protected space in which some of the essential critical and symbolic material is released for further analysis and artistic development, for education is essentially a transformative activity.

We need, as never before, to adopt and apply the Socratic conception of education and to extend its spirit into the teaching of the arts. It lies at the source of a long, if erratic, tradition of philosophy and teaching. If we are to secure a future worthy of the restless spirit of life it will depend upon the questing nature of our consciousness and all those educational contexts and cultural invitations that direct and animate it. This is the educational imperative that I have defended in these pages.

It is axiomatic to Socratic thinking that one cannot know the outcome in advance; in a fundamental sense, the informing spirit and the commitment to journeying (in a culture where others have gone before leaving innumerable log books, sketches and maps) is all that we have to go on and, with the next millennium nearly upon us, all that most of us can finally invest our faith in. Such an education, on a democratic scale, has never, so far, been given a real chance. Perhaps that is the task of the next millennium?

Chapters

Chapter 1: Earlier versions of this chapter have appeared in *The Guardian* as 'Monday Agenda Page' February 1986 and in *Sapere* Vol. 1, No. 2, February 1993. **Chapter 3:** Part of this chapter has been previously published as 'Signs on the Way to Understanding' in *Times Higher Education Supplement* 18 November 1989. **Chapter 4:** A small section of this chapter has previously been published as 'Making the Art beat Faster' in *Times Higher Education Supplement* 18 September 1992. **Chapter 5:** Most of this chapter has been previously published in *The Journal of Art and Design Education* Vol. 11, No. 3. **Chapter 6:** The section on Virginia Woof's *The Waves* has been previously published as 'From Babble to Rhapsody: Understanding the Dynamic of the Creative Act' in *The British Journal of Aesthetic Education*, Vol. 31, No. 4, October 1991. **Chapter 7:** Parts of this chapter have been previously published as 'Drama and the Renewal of Aesthetic Education' in *London Drama*, Vol. 7, No. 4, Summer 1987 and as *Open Letter to Gavin Bolton* in *National Drama*, Summer 1992. **Chapter 8:** A small section of this chapter has previously been published as 'The Dynamic Centre of English' in *The Use of English*, October 1987. **Chapter 9:** This chapter has previously appeared as 'The Place of Creative Writing in the Development of Teachers' in *Teaching Creative Writing: Theory and Practice* edited by Robert Miles and Moira Monteith (Open University Press, 1992). **Chapter 11:** A small section of this chapter has previously been published as 'High Art, Lofty Spirits' in *Times Higher Education Supplement*, 10 May 1991. **Chapter 12:** A version of this chapter has previously appeared in *Festschrift to David Holbrook* edited by Edwin Webb (Associated Universities Press, 1994).

Illustrations

Plate 1: The bust of Socrates: from the National Museum at
Frontispiece: Naples.

Plate 2: *Rembrandt* van Rijn: *Self-Portrait* by kind permission of the National Gallery.

Plate 3: Van Gogh: *Self-Portrait*, 1889 by kind permission of the Musée d'Orsay.

Plate 4: Martha Graham in *Strike*, 1927 by permission of Hulton Deutch Collection.

Plate 5: Jane Lapotaire: MA Language Arts and Education master class at the University of Sussex in 1992. Photograph by Lynne Gibson.

Plate 6: Painting by Katrina Schwab, aged 6 years, Daubeney Primary School, Hackney with kind permission from her art teacher Madeleine Paterson and Katrina Schwab.

Plate 7: David Powell: *Unicorn*, Creative Project for *MA, Language, Arts and Education*, Summer 1993. With kind permission of David Powell. Photograph by Wivi-Ann Wells, Brighton.

Plate 8: Eugene Delacroix: *Tiger Attacking a Wild Horse*. With kind permission of the Louvre.

Plate 9: Close up of *Unicorn, op cit.*

Plate 10: John Meirion Morris: *Modron*. With kind permission of the sculptor.

Plate 11: Keith Grant: *Aurora Borealis, Mountain and Stars* 1992. With kind permission of the artist.

Plate 12: Herbert Read, by kind permission of Benedict Read and the Estate of Herbert Read.

Plate 13: Peter Fuller, by kind permission of Stephanie McDonald.

Bibliography

The bibliography is divided into three sections; the first section relates to work on Socrates and Socratic thinking, the second to aesthetics and arts education, the third to the six major arts disciplines in education. The author is indebted to Edwin Webb, Marian Metcalfe, Robert Watson, Anna Carlyle, Christopher Havell and Robin Morris for the bibliographies on English, Music, Film, Dance, Drama and Art.

On Socrates and Socratic Thinking

Abbs, P. (ed.) (1993) *Socratic Education, Aspects of Education*, **49**, Winter, Hull, The Institute of Education, The University of Hull.

Cornford, F. (1932) *Before and After Socrates*, Cambridge, Cambridge University Press.

Ferguson, J. (1970) *Socrates: A Source Book*, Milton Keynes, Open University Books.

Fisher, R. (1990) *Teaching Children to Think*, Oxford, Oxford University Press.

Havelock, E. (1963) *Preface to Plato*, Oxford, Basil Blackwell.

Jaeger, W. (1941) *Paideia: The Ideals of Greek Culture*, Vol. 2, Oxford, Oxford University Press.

Lipman, M. (1988) *Philosophy Goes to School*, Philadelphia, Temple University Press.

Lipman, M. (1993) *Thinking, Children and Education*, Iowa Kendall/ Hunt.

Matthews, G. (1980) *Philosophy and the Young Child*, Cambridge, MA, Harvard University Press.

Murdoch, I. (1986) *Acastos: Two Platonic Dialogues*, London, Chatto and Windus.

Nelson, L. (1940) *Socratic Method and Critical Philosophy*, New Haven, Yale University Press.

Oakeshott, M. (1991) *The True Voice of Liberal Learning*, New Haven, Yale University Press.

PATEMAN, T. (1987) *What is Philosophy?* London, Edward Arnold.

POPPER, K. (1962) *The Open Society and Its Enemies*, Princeton, Princeton University Press.

REED, R. (1983) *Talking with Children*, Denver, Colorado, Arden Press.

SPIEGELBERG, H. (1964) *The Socratic Enigma*, Illinois, Library of Liberal Arts.

TAYLOR, A. (1932) *Socrates*, London, Peter Davies.

VERSENYI, L. (1963) *Socratic Humanism*, New Haven, Yale University Press.

VLASTOS, G. (ed.) (1971) *The Philosophy of Socrates: A Collection of Critical Essays*, New York, Anchor Books.

VLASTOS, G. (1991) *Socrates: Ironist and Moral Philosopher*, Cambridge, Cambridge University Press.

On Aesthetics and Arts Education

ABBS, P. (ed.) (1987) *Living Powers: The Arts in Education*, London, Falmer Press.

ABBS, P. (1988) *A is for Aesthetic: Essays on Creative and Aesthetic Education*, London, Falmer Press.

ABBS, P. (ed.) (1989) *The Symbolic Order: A Contemporary Reader on the Arts Debate*, London, Falmer Press.

ANDREWS, G. and TAYLOR, R. (1991) *The Arts in the Primary School*, London, Falmer Press.

BANTOCK, G.H. (1976) *Education, Culture and the Emotions*, London, Faber & Faber.

BANTOCK, G.H. (1981) *The Parochialism of the Present*, London, Routledge & Kegan Paul.

BERLEANT, A. (1970) *The Aesthetic Field*, Charles C. Thomas.

BEST, D. (1990) *The Rationality of Feeling: The Arts in Education*, London, Falmer Press.

BLOOMFIELD, A. (ed.) *Creative and Aesthetic Education in the Journal Aspects* 34, University of Hull.

BROOK, P. (1987) *The Shifting Point*, London, Harper & Row.

BROUDY, H. (1972) *Enlightened Cherishing: An Essay in Aesthetic Education*, Chicago, University of Illinois Press.

BRUNER, J. (1962) *On Knowing: Essays for the Left Hand*, Cambridge, MA, Harvard University Press.

CASSIRER, E. (1944) *An Essay on Man*, New York, Bantam Books.

CASSIRER, E. (1955/8) *The Philosophy of Symbolic Forms* (three volumes) New Haven, Yale University Press.

COLLINGWOOD, R.G. (1985) *The Principles of Art*, Oxford, Oxford University Press.

DANTO, A. (1987) *The State of the Art*, New Jersey, Prentice Hall.

DEWEY, J. (1934) *Art as Experience*, Victoria, Minton Balch & Company.

DONOGHUE, D. (1985) *The Arts Without Mystery*, London, BBC.

EAGLETON, T. (1983) *Literary Theory*, Oxford, Basil Blackwell.

EAGLETON, T. (1990) *The Ideology of the Aesthetic*, Oxford, Basil Blackwell.

ELIOT, T.S. (1975) FRANK KERMODE (ed.) *Selected Prose of T.S. Eliot*, London, Faber & Faber.

FREUD, S. (1973) *Introductory Lectures on Psychoanalysis*, Harmondsworth, Penguin.

FREUD, S. (1973) *New Introductory Lectures on Psychoanalysis*, Harmondsworth, Penguin.

FRYE, N. (1957) *The Anatomy of Criticism*, Princeton, Princeton University Press.

FULLER, P. (1980) *Art and Psychoanalysis*, London, Writers & Readers.

FULLER, P. (1980) *Beyond the Crisis in Art*, London, Writers & Readers.

FULLER, P. (1982) *Aesthetics after Modernism*, London, Writers & Readers.

FULLER, P. (1985) *Images of God*, London, Chatto & Windus.

FULLER, P. (1988) *Theoria*, London, Chatto & Windus.

GIBSON, R. (1986) *Structuralism and Education*, Oxford, Pergamon.

GOMBRICH. E. (1960) *Art and Illusion*, Oxford, Phaidon.

GOMBRICH, E. (1966) *Norm and Form*, Oxford, Phaidon.

GOMBRICH, E. (1978) *The Story of Art*, Oxford, Phaidon.

GOMBRICH, E. (1979) *The Sense of Order*, Oxford, Phaidon.

GOMBRICH, E. (1984) *Tributes: Interpreters of our Cultural Tradition*, Oxford, Phaidon.

GREENE, M. (1988) *The Dialectic of Freedom*, New York, Teachers College Press.

GULBENKIAN FOUNDATION (1982) *The Arts in Schools*, London, Gulbenkian Foundation.

HARGREAVES, D. (1982) *The Challenge of the Comprehensive School*, London, Routledge & Kegan Paul.

HEGEL, W.F. (1993) MICHAEL INWOOD (ed.) *Introductory Lectures on Aesthetics*, Harmondsworth, Penguin.

HODGSON, J.T. (1988) *Batsford Dictionary of Drama*, London, Batsford.

HODGSON, J.T. (1992) *Drama from Ibsen to Fugard*, London, Batsford.

HOSPERS, J. (1969) *Introductory Readings in Aesthetics*, New York, Collier Macmillan.

JONES, D. (1973) *Epoch and Artist*, London, Faber & Faber.

JUNG, C. (1967) *The Spirit in Man, Art and Literature*, London, Routledge & Kegan Paul.

JUNG, C. *et al.* (1964) *Man and His Symbols*, London, Aldus Books.

KANT, I. (1952) *Critique of Pure Reason*, Oxford, Oxford University Press.

KANT, I. (1952) *Critique of Judgement*, Oxford, Oxford University Press.

KNIGHTS, L.C. (1960) *Selected Essays in Criticism*, London, Chatto & Windus.

KOESTLER, A. (1975) *The Act of Creation*, London, Picador.

LANGER, S. (1953) *Feeling and Form*, London, Routledge & Kegan Paul.

LANGER, S. (1957) *Philosophy in a New Key*, Cambridge, MA, Harvard University Press.

LANGER, S. (1957) *Problems of Art*, London, Routledge & Kegan Paul.

LANGER, S. (1974) *Mind: An Essay on Human Feeling*, Baltimore, Johns Hopkins University Press.

LIPMAN, M. (ed.) (1973) *Contemporary Aesthetics*, MA, Allyn & Bacon.

LODGE, D. (1981) *Working with Structuralism*, London, Routledge & Kegan Paul.

MARCUSE, H. (1978) *The Aesthetic Dimension*, London, Macmillan.

MORDAUNT CROOK, J. (1987) *The Dilemma of Style*, London, John Murray.

MUMFORD, L. (1971) *The Myth of the Machine*, London, Secker & Warburg.

MURDOCH, I. (1992) *Metaphysics as a Guide to Morals*, London, Chatto & Windus.

O'HEAR, A. (1988) *The Element of Fire: Science, Art and the Human World*, London, Routledge.

PATEMAN, T. (1991) *Key Concepts: A Guide to Aeshetics, Criticism and the Arts in Education*, London, Falmer Press.

PHENIX, P. (1964) *Realms of Meaning*, McGraw Hill.

POLANYI, M. (1973) *Personal Knowledge*, London, Routledge & Kegan Paul.

READ, H. (1943) *Education through Art*, London, Faber & Faber.

READ, H. (1955) *Ikon and Idea*, London, Faber & Faber.

REDFERN, H.B. (1986) *Questions in Aesthetic Education*, London, Allen & Unwin.

REID, L.A. (1961) *Ways of Knowledge and Experience*, London, Allen & Unwin.

REID, L.A. (1970) *Meaning in the Arts*, London, Allen & Unwin.

REID, L.A. (1986) *Ways of Understanding and Education*, London, Heinemann Educational Books.

ROBERTSON, S. (1982) *Rosegarden and Labyrinth: A Study in Art in Education*, Lewes, Gryphon Press.

Ross, M. (1975) *Arts and the Adolescent*, London, Schools Council, Evans.

Ross, M. (1978) *The Creative Arts*, London, Heinemann Educational Books.

Ross, M. (ed.) (1983) *The Arts in Education*, London, Falmer Press.

Ross, M. (1984) *The Aesthetic Impulse*, Oxford, Pergamon.

Schiller, (1974) *On the Aesthetic Education of Man*, Oxford, Clarendon Press.

Scruton, R. (1974) *Art and Imagination*, London, Methuen.

Scruton, R. (1979) *The Aesthetics of Architecture*, London, Methuen.

Scruton, R. (1983) *The Aesthetic Understanding*, London, Methuen.

Smith, R. and Simpson, A. (1991) *Aesthetics and Arts Education*, Chicago, University of Illinois Press.

Steiner, G. (1967) *Real Presences*, Harmondsworth, Penguin.

Steiner, G. (1975) *After Babel*, Cambridge, Cambridge University Press.

Stokes, A. (1965) *The Invitation in Art*, London, Tavistock.

Storr, A. (1972) *Dynamics of Creation*, Harmondsworth, Penguin.

Taylor, R. and Andrews, G. (1992) *The Arts in the Primary School*, London, Falmer Press.

Tippett, M. (1974) *Moving into Aquarius*, London, Picador.

Valery, P. (1964) *Aesthetics*, London, Routledge & Kegan Paul.

Warnock, M. (1980) *Imagination*, London, Faber & Faber.

Whalley, G. (1953) *Poetic Process*, Chicago, Greenwood Press.

Winnicot, D.W. (1971) *Playing and Reality*, London, Tavistock.

Witkin, R. (1974) *The Intelligence of Feeling*, London, Heinemann Educational Books.

Wittgenstein, L. (1966) *Lectures and Conversations on Aesthetics, Psychology and Religious Belief*, Oxford, Oxford University Press.

Wollheim, R. (1970) *Art and Its Objects: An Introduction to Aesthetics*, London, Harper & Row.

On the Six Major Arts Disciplines in Education

English

Abbs, P. (1982) *English within the Arts*, London, Hodder & Stoughton.

Abbs, P. (1985) *English as an Arts Discipline*, Take up No. 2, London, National Association for Education in the Arts.

Allen, D. (1980) *English Teaching Since 1965*, Heinemann Educational Books.

Barnes, D. (1969) *From Communication to Curriculum*, London, Penguin.

BARNES, D. and TODD, (1969) *Language, the Learner and the School*, Harmondsworth, Penguin.

BRITTON, J. (1972) *Language and Learning*, Harmondsworth, Penguin.

COOK, C. (1917) *The Play Way*, London, Heinemann.

CREBER, J. (1965) *Sense and Sensitivity*, London, University of London Press.

DIXON, J. (1975) *Growth through English*, Oxford, Oxford University Press.

HARRISON, B. (1982) *An Arts-based Approach to English*, London, Hodder & Stoughton.

HOLBROOK, D. (1967) *English for Maturity*, Cambridge, Cambridge University Press.

HOLBROOK, D. (1979) *English for Meaning*, National Federation Educational Research Slough.

HOURD, M. (1949) *The Education of the Poetic Spirit*, London, Heinemann Educational Books.

ROSENBLATT, L. (1970) *Literature as Exploration*, London, Heinemann Educational Books.

SAMPSON, G. (1975) *English for the English*, Cambridge, Cambridge University Press.

SCHAYER, D. (1972) *The Teaching of English in Schools 1900–1970*, London, Routledge & Kegan Paul.

WEBB, E. (1991) *Literature & Education: Encounter & Experience*, London, Falmer Press.

WHITEHEAD, F. (1971) *The Disappearing Dais*, London, Chatto & Windus.

WILKINSON, A. (1971) *The Foundations of Language*, Oxford, Oxford University Press.

Music

BROCKLEHURST, B. (1971) *Response to Music: Principles of Music Education*, London, Routledge & Kegan Paul.

FLETCHER, R.D. (1985) 'New forms of examination in music: The assessment of listening: A discussion paper', unpublished paper generally available from the Secondary Examinations Council, Newcombe House, 45 Notting Hill Gate, London, W11 3JB, or from the author at 8 Olivers Battery Gardens, Winchester, Hants, SO22 4HF.

DES (1985) *General Certificate of Secondary Education: The National Criteria: Music*, London, HMSO.

DES (1985) *Music from 5–16*, Curriculum Matters 4, an HMI Series, London, HMSO.

HALE, N.V. (1974) *Education for Music: A Skeleton Plan of Research into the Development of the Study of Music as Part of the Organized Plan of General Education*, Oxford, Oxford University Press.

LONG, N. (1959) *Music in English Education*, London, Faber & Faber.

NETTEL, R. (1952) *The Englishman Makes Music*, London, Dennis Dobson.

PAYNTER, J. (1972) *Hear and Now: An Introduction to Modern Music in Schools*, London, Universal Edition.

PAYNTER, J. (1982) *Music in the Secondary School Curriculum: Trends and Developments in Class Music Teaching*, Cambridge, Cambridge University Press.

PAYNTER, J. and ASTON, P. (1970) *Sound and Silence: Classroom Projects in Creative Music*, Cambridge, Cambridge University Press.

PLUMMERIDGE, C. et al. (1981) *Issues in Music Education*, University of London Institute of Education, Bedford Way Papers 3.

PLUMMERIDGE, C. (1991) *Music Education in Theory and Practice*, London, Falmer Press.

PRESTON, G.H.H. (1986) 'A new approach to music examinations', *International Journal of Music Education*, May.

REIMER, B. (1970) *A Philosophy of Music Education*, New Jersey, Prentice-Hall.

SMALL, C. (1977) *Music, Society, Education*, 2nd ed., London, John Calder.

SWANWICK, K. (1979) *A Basis for Music Education*, NFER, London, Nelson Publishing.

SWANWICK, K. and TAYLOR, D. (1982) *Discovering Music: Developing the Music Curriculum in Secondary Schools*, London, Batsford Academic & Educational.

TAYLOR, D. (1979) *Music Now: A Guide to Recent Developments and Current Opportunities in Music Education*, Milton Keynes, Open University Press.

Film

Almost every aspect of film has its own immense bibliography. The following suggestions are simply introductions to a few relevant areas.

Courses Combining Theory and Practice
HERBERT, F.M. (1947) 'The American scene and the problems of film education', *The Penguin Film Review*, January.

WATSON, R. (1990) *Film and Television in Education: An Aesthetic Approach to the Moving Image*, London, Falmer Press.

WILLIAMS, C. (1981) *Film-making and Film Theory*. This paper gives a detailed outline of a degree course and is the most persuasive short account of film teaching I have found, especially taken in context.

See also:

ALVARADO, M. 'Practical work in television studies', London, BFI pamphlet.

BOBKER, L.R. (1969) *Elements of Film*, Sea Diego, Harcourt Brace.

DICKINSON, T. (1921) *A Discovery of Cinema*, Oxford, Oxford University Press.

HORNSBY, J. 'The case for practical studies in media education', London, BFI pamphlet.

LINDGREN, E. (1948) *The Art of the Film*, London, Allen & Unwin.

Practical Teaching Ideas

LOWNDES, D. (1968) *Film Making in Schools*, London, Batsford – highly recommended.

WALL, I. and KRUGER, S. (1986) *Reading a Film*. This pack of materials is available free, as part of British Film Year, from Film Education, 12 St. George's Avenue, London W5.

Literary Adaptations, Screenplays, etc.

BLUESTONE, G. (1957) *Novels into Film*, Baltimore, John Hopkins University Press – American cinema.

CORLISS, R. (1975) *Talking Pictures*, Newton Abbot, David & Charles.

COULOURIS and HERRMANN (1972) 'The Citizen Kane Book', *Sight & Sound*, Spring.

KAEL, P. (1971) *The Citizen Kane Book*, London, Secker & Warburg.

MCFARLANE, B. (1984) *Words and Images*, London, Secker & Warburg – Australian cinema.

Auteurism, Structuralism, etc.

BRITTON, A. (1978/9) 'The Ideology of Screen', *Movies*, **26**, Winter – fairly impenetrable but effective critique of theories derived from Althusser, Lacan and Barthes.

CAUGHIE, J. (ed.) (1981) *Theories of Authorship*, London, Routledge & Kegan Paul. – recommended.

COOK, P. (ed.) (1985) *The Cinema Book*, BFI – thorough summaries, but written in the deadly style of the new academicism.

NICHOLS, B. (ed.) (1976) *Movies and Methods*, California, University of California Press – highly recommended.

WOLLEN, P. (1969) *Signs and Meaning in the Cinema*, London, Secker & Warburg.

Critical Studies of Directors

ANDERSON, L. (1981) *About John Ford*, London Plexus – this is the most intelligent study of anybody at work in films. Anyone more interested in theory than film should perhaps consult the sections on Ford in *Theories of Authorship and Movies and Methods*.

ARANDA, F. (1975) *Luis Bunuel: A Critical Biography*, London, Secker & Warburg – interviews.

BAZIN, A. (1974) *Jean Renoir*, London, W.H. Allen.

BJORKMAN, MANNS, SIMA (1973) *Bergman on Bergman*, London, Secker & Warburg – interviews.

BOGDANOVITCH, P. (1978) *John Ford*, California, University of California Press – interviews.

DURGNAT, R. (1973) *Jean Renoir*, California, University of California Press.

MCBRIDE, W. (1974) *John Ford*, London, Secker & Warburg.

PLACE, J.A. (1974) *The Western Films of John Ford*, Victoria, Citadel Press.

PLACE, J.A. (1979) *The Non-Western Films of John Ford*, Victoria, Citadel Press.

RENOIR, J. (1974) *My Life and My Films*, London, Collins.

ROUD, R. (ed.) (1980) *Cinema, A Critical Dictionary*, London, Secker & Warburg.

SALLES GOMES, P.E. (1972) *Jean Vigo*, London, Secker & Warburg – recommended.

SARRIS, A. (1976) *The John Ford Movie Mystery*, London, Secker & Warburg.

SESONSKE, A. (1980) *Jean Renoir, the French Films, 1924–1939*, Cambridge, MA, Harvard University Press – highly recommended.

SIMON, J. (1973) *Ingmar Bergman Directs*, New York, Davis-Poynter.

TRUFFAUT, F. (1968) *Hitchcock*, London, Secker & Warburg – interviews.

WOOD, R. (1965) *Hitchcock's Films*, London, Zwemmer – highly recommended.

WOOD, R. (1968) *Howard Hawks*, London, Secker & Warburg – recommended.

Historical Development of Film

BROWNLOW, K. (1968) *The Parade's Gone By*, London, Secker & Warburg.

CERAM, C.W. (1965) *Archaeology of the Cinema*, London, Thames & Hudson.

COE, B. (1981) *The History of Movie Photography*, London, Ash & Grant.

DICKINSON, T. (1971) *A Discovery of Cinema*, Oxford, Oxford University Press.

MONTAGUE, I. (1964) *Film World*, Harmondsworth, Penguin.

SALT, B. (1983) *Film Style and Technology: History and Analysis* – highly recommended.

WENDEN, D.J. (1975) *The Birth of the Movies*, Macdonald & Jane's.

Dance

ADSHEAD, J. (1981) *The Study of Dance*, London, Dance Books Ltd.

ADSHEAD, J. & LAYSON, J. (eds) (1984) *Dance History*, London, Dance Books Ltd.

BANES, S. (1980) *Terpischore in Sneakers: Post Modern Dance*, Massachusetts, Houghton Mifflin.

BEST, D. (1974) *Expression in Movement and the Arts*, London, Lepus Books.

BEST, D. (1978) *Philosophy and Human Movement*, London, Unwin Educational Books.

BRINSON, P. (1991) *Dance as Education: Towards a National Dance Culture*, London, Falmer Press.

GULBENKIAN FOUNDATION (1980) *Dance Education and Training in Britain*, London, Oyez Press.

HUMPHREY, D. (1959) *The Art of Making Dances*, London, Dance Books Ltd.

KRAUS, R. (1969) *History of the Dance*, Prentice Hall.

LABAN, R. (1960) *The Mastery of Movement*, London, MacDonald & Evans.

LANGER, S.K. (1953) *Feeling and Form*, chapters 11 and 12, London, Routledge & Kegan Paul.

MYERS, G. and FANCHER, G. (eds) (1981) *Philosophical Essays on Dance*, New York, Dance Horizons.

PRESTON-DUNLOP, V. (1980) *A Handbook for Dance in Education*, London, MacDonald & Evans.

REDFERN, B. (1982) *Concepts in Modern Educational Dance*, London, Dance Books Ltd.

REDFERN, B. (1983) *Dance, Art and Aesthetics*, London, Dance Books Ltd.

SMITH, J.M. (1976) *Dance Composition*, London, Lepus Books.

SORELL, W. (1981) *Dance in Its Time: The Emergence of an Art Form*, New York, Anchor Press.

ULLMANN, L. (1984) *A Vision of Dynamic Space*, London, Falmer Press.

Drama

ALLEN, J. (1979) *Drama in Schools: Its Theory and Practice*, London, Heinemann.

BOLTON, G. (1979) *Towards a Theory of Drama in Education*, London, Longman.

BOLTON, G. (1983) *Bolton at the Barbican*, National Association for Teachers of Drama.

BOLTON, G. (1984) *Drama as Education*, London, Longman.

DAY, C. (1975) *Drama for Middle and Upper Schools*, London, Batsford.

HEATHCOTE, D. (1980) *Drama as Context*, NATE.

HEATHCOTE, D. (1982) 'Signs and Portents?', *SCYPT Journal*, 9 April.

HORNBROOK, D. (1989) *Education and Dramatic Art*, Oxford, Basil Blackwell.

HORNBROOK, D. (1991) *Education in Drama: Casting the Dramatic Curriculum*, London, Falmer Press.

JOHNSON, L. and O'NEILL, C. (eds) (1983) *Selected Writings of Dorothy Heathcote*, London, Hutchinson.

LINNELL, R. (1982) *Approaching Classroom Drama*, London, Edward Arnold.

McGREGOR, L., TATE, M. and ROBINSON, K. (1977) *Learning through Drama*, Schools Council Drama Teaching. *Project (10–16)*, London, Heinemann.

O'NEILL, C. and LAMBERT, A. (1982) *Drama Structures*, London, Hutchinson.

ROBINSON, K. (1980) *Exploring Theatre and Education*, London, Heinemann.

SLADE, P. (1954) *Child Drama*, London, University of London Press.

WAGNER, B.J. (1978) *Dorothy Heathcote: Drama as a Learning Medium*, London, Hutchinson.

WATKINS, B. (1981) *Drama and Education*, London, Batsford Academic & Educational.

WAY, B. (1967) *Development through Drama*, London, Longman.

Visual Arts

ADAMS, E. (1982) *Art and the Built Environment*, Schools Council, London, Longman.

ART ADVISERS ASSOCIATION (1978) *Learning through Drawing*, Art Advisers Association, North East Region.

BARRATT, M. (1979) *Art Education: A Strategy for Course Design*, London, Heinemann Educational Books.

BAYNES, K. (1976) *About Design*, London, Heinemann Educational Books.

BERGER, J. (1972) *Ways of Seeing*, Harmondsworth, Penguin.

EISNER, E. (1972) *Educating Artistic Vision*, London, Macmillan.

FRY, R. (1920) *Vision and Design*, London, Chatto & Windus.

GENTLE, K. (1985) *Children and Art Teaching*, London, Croom Helm.

GREEN, P. (1974) *Design Education: Problem Solving and Visual Experience*, London, Batsford.

LOWENFIELD, V. (1947) *Creative and Mental Growth*, London, Collier Macmillan.

LYNTON, N. (1980) *The Story of Modern Art*, Oxford, Phaidon.

READ, H. (1943) *Education through Art*, London, Faber.

RICHARDSON, M. (1948) *Art and the Child*, London, University of London Press.

ROBERTSON, S. (1982) *Rosegarden and Labyrinth*, Lewes, Gryphon Press.

ROWLAND, K. (1968) *Learning to See*, London, Ginn & Co.

TAYLOR, R. (1986) *Educating for Art*, London, Longman.

TAYLOR, R. (1991) *The Visual Arts in Education*, London, Falmer Press.

TAYLOR, D. and TAYLOR, R. (1990) *Approaching Art and Design*, Longman.

VIOLA, W. (1936) *Child Art*, London, Simpkin Marshall.

Index